The Chinese Taste

Eighteenth-century consumers in England, living in an increasingly globalized world, were infatuated with exotic Chinese and Chinese-styled goods, art, and decorative objects. However, they were also often troubled by the alien aesthetic sensibility these goods embodied. This ambivalence figures centrally in the period's experience of China and of contact with foreign countries and cultures more generally. David Porter analyzes the processes by which Chinese aesthetic ideas were assimilated within English culture. Through case studies of individual figures, including William Hogarth and Horace Walpole, and broader reflections on cross-cultural interaction, Porter's readings develop new interpretations of eighteenth-century ideas of luxury, consumption, gender, taste, and aesthetic nationalism. Illustrated with many examples of Chinese and Chinese-inspired objects and art, this is a major contribution to eighteenth-century cultural history and to the history of contact and exchange between China and the West.

DAVID PORTER is Professor of English and Comparative Literature at the University of Michigan.

The Chinese Taste in Eighteenth-Century England

DAVID PORTER

CAMBRIDGE
UNIVERSITY PRESS

CAMBRIDGE
UNIVERSITY PRESS

University Printing House, Cambridge CB2 8BS, United Kingdom

Published in the United States of America by Cambridge University Press, New York

Cambridge University Press is part of the University of Cambridge.

It furthers the University's mission by disseminating knowledge in the pursuit of education, learning and research at the highest international levels of excellence.

www.cambridge.org
Information on this title: www.cambridge.org/9781107662377

First published 2010
First paperback edition 2013

A catalogue record for this publication is available from the British Library

Library of Congress cataloguing in publication data
Porter, David, 1965–
The Chinese taste in eighteenth-century England / David Porter.
p. cm.
Includes bibliographical references and index.
ISBN 978-0-521-19299-6 (hardback)
1. England – Relations – China. 2. China – Relations – England. 3. China – Foreign public opinion, English. 4. Aesthetics, Chinese – England – History – 18th century. 5. Popular culture – England – History – 18th century. 6. Consumption (Economics) – Social aspects – England – History – 18th century. 7. Intercultural communication – England – History – 18th century. 8. Ambivalence – Social aspects – England – History – 18th century. 9. England – Social life and customs – 18th century. 10. England – Intellectual life – 18th century. I. Title.
DA485.P674 2010
303.48′24205109033 – dc22 2010033028

ISBN 978-0-521-19299-6 Hardback
ISBN 978-1-107-66237-7 Paperback

Contents

Illustrations

Acknowledgments

Every writer of cultural history aspires to tell a good story, and like most storytellers, I am beholden to many a muse. A fair number are listed in the bibliography; to others to whom my debt exceeds what a footnote can acknowledge, I express my gratitude here.

I should like first to thank my friends and colleagues in the Departments of English and Comparative Literature and the Center for Chinese Studies at the University of Michigan for their advice, encouragement, and companionship over the many years this book has been in the making. Gregg Crane, Lincoln Faller, Marjorie Levinson, Yopie Prins, Tobin Siebers, and Valerie Traub offered close, careful readings of individual chapter drafts. Michael Schoenfeldt and George Bornstein provided professional guidance and support at many a critical juncture, keeping me on track as best they could. Vanessa Agnew, Jim Cogswell, Steve Darwall, Dena Goodman, Mark Koch, Tina Lupton, Scotti Parrish, Adela Pinch, Sean Silver, and Viv Soni, in wide-ranging conversations, gave me new perspectives from which to consider problems in eighteenth-century cultural history, while Miranda Brown, Ellen Laing, Erik Mueggler, Christian de Pee, Marty Powers, and David Rolston contributed invaluable sinological expertise. To members of the Eighteenth-Century Studies Group, the First Draft Club, and my graduate seminars I am grateful for rich and provocative discussions that have consistently demonstrated the best of what intellectual exchange can be.

Email and the proximity of the Detroit airport have made it easier than perhaps it should be to impose on colleagues further afield as well. I especially appreciate the inspiration and guidance I have received at various stages from John Bender, Theresa Braunschneider, Timothy Brook, Rod Campbell, Terry Castle, Craig Clunas, Joseph Dennis, Benjamin Elman, Chris Gabbard, Robert Gordon, George Haggerty, Jing Jiang, Suvir Kaul, Michael Keevak, Dorothy Ko, Susan Lanser, Edward Larkin, Lydia Liu, Tina Lupton, Robert Markley, Paula McDowell, Felicity Nussbaum, Kenneth Pomeranz, John Richetti, Erik Ringmar, Haun Saussy, Patricia Spacks, Bin Wong, and Zhang Longxi. For special thanks, I would like to single out James Cahill, who has been a wonderfully generous correspondent on matters of Chinese art history.

I have been fortunate to receive generous funding support for this project from the Institute for Advanced Study, the National Humanities Center, and the American Council for Learned Societies, and I remain deeply grateful for their endorsements of this project and for the opportunities for sustained research and writing their grants made possible. The faculty of the School of Historical Studies at the Institute for Advanced Study were especially generous with their time and counsel; I would like particularly to thank Heinrich von Staden, Irving Lavin, and Giles Constable for their mentorship and encouragement. Among my colleagues at the National Humanities Center, I benefited from particularly helpful conversations with Sherman Cochran, Paul Griffiths, and James Knowlson.

Travel grants from the University of Michigan made possible a number of productive research trips, and the extraordinary expertise of the museum curators and research staff I met on several of these expeditions has proven invaluable in coming to terms with the richly evocative material worlds of Chinese and Chinese-styled objects in their collections. In particular, I would like to thank William Sargent and Karina Corrigan of the Peabody Essex Museum, Hao Sheng of the Boston Museum of Fine Arts, Jan Stuart of the Smithsonian's Freer/Sackler Gallery, Sarah Fayen and Jonathan Prown of the Chipstone Foundation, Hilary Young, Helen Clifford, and Clare Browne of the Victoria and Albert Museum, Katie Scott of the Courtauld Institute of Art, Linda Eaton at the Winterthur, and Oliver Impey of the Ashmolean Museum. Knowledgeable librarians have, as always, been indispensable; I am especially grateful for the assistance I received navigating various collections at Michigan, Princeton, Yale, Duke, the University of North Carolina, Beijing University, and the British Library.

The manuscript was improved considerably thanks to the thoughtful comments of two anonymous readers at Cambridge University Press. Karen McConnell, Geremy Carnes, and Angela Heetderks provided invaluable assistance with citations, references, illustrations, proofreading, and indexing. They and many of those named above have helped me catch errors and infelicities; those that no doubt remain are my own. Earlier versions of several chapters appeared in the journals *Eighteenth-Century Studies*, *Studies in Eighteenth-Century Culture*, *Eighteenth-Century Life*, and *Mosaic*, and in Jennie Batchelor and Cora Kaplan, eds., *Women and Material Culture: 1660–1830* (Palgrave, 2007). I am grateful to the publishers for permission to use this material.

Finally, I must thank my family for having been so wonderfully supportive of this all-too protracted enterprise. My parents showed me the way to my calling, and their own impassioned liveliness of mind has remained a model for me ever since. My wife Lani showed me the way to China, and has always encouraged my subsequent research pursuits with wisdom and good humor. Our boys Nathaniel and Nicholas, with their buoyant spirits and contagious *joie de vivre*, have provided constant reminders that curiosity and playfulness are among the most reliable paths to learning. I dedicate this book to the memory of my grandfather, the late Thomas E. Hill, whose gusto for good storytelling will remain an inspiration always.

Introduction: monstrous beauty

Take a stroll in any modern Chinese city with even a modest tourist trade and you will soon stumble upon street-side stalls offering for sale a cornucopia of antiquarian bric-a-brac. Corroded old coins, dusty ceramics, multi-limbed Buddhist figurines, and tattered scroll paintings jostle for space among vintage Mao Zedong alarm clocks, jade bracelets, sepia postcards, and foot-long opium pipes. Linger for more than a moment over this motley assortment and you will likely be offered a shoe. Not a leather shoe with which to prolong your stroll, but a delicately embroidered silk slipper to stroke, to admire, to cup in the palm of your hand as you struggle to imagine how it could ever have encompassed the foot of a full-grown woman. For you will, by now, have been assured, with a somber nod and a sigh, that this dazzling green or yellow or red piece of handiwork had once belonged to an elegant lady of the late Qing dynasty.

The price is negotiable, and once you have walked off with your prize, the quantity of equally ancient and equally immaculate silk slippers you will find offered for sale at markets, temples, and historical sites throughout the city will remind you that the supply of venerable "antiques" for the tourist trade is, in fact, inexhaustible, and that there are handsome profits to be made in the manufacture of historical relics. But their questionable pedigree notwithstanding, the ubiquitous silk slippers stand out among the jades, porcelains, coppers, and lacquerwares of the antique-dealer's stall. They are, by far, the most colorful and visually engaging objects in what is often otherwise a rather drab collection. They appeal to the touch as well, offering in their smooth surfaces and sensuous softness an alluring contrast to the cold metallic clamor of the copper coins in the neighboring bin. And inevitably, they conjure up a dim memory of a curiously cathected eroticism, dating from those dark pre-revolutionary days when the delights offered by her lotus-blossom feet topped every blazon of a beauty's charms.

Such a memory will prove an ambivalent one at best. With any scrutiny, after all, the scene of sensual pleasure quickly unravels into unspeakable childhood torments, aching legacies of blistered flesh and deformed bone. The gentlemanly relish of podial beauty appears, in retrospect, a perverse aesthetic irrevocably compromised by the inhumanity of the sacrifice it required. The shudder of disgust it evokes in the modern viewer opens a chasm across which identification is impossible. At the same time, it transposes the physical monstrosity of the individual misshapen foot onto the spectacle of footbinding as cultural practice, so that the entire social system in which it was embedded is tainted with the stench of barbarism. It is precisely this stench, I would suggest, this perversely poignant evocation of cultural monstrosity, that ultimately accounts for why the antique merchants of Beijing and Shanghai sell so many delicately embroidered slippers. Every shudder of disgust, after all, is accompanied by the thrill of self-righteousness. To recognize the barbarism of Qing patriarchal norms is simultaneously to revel in the humanity and progressivism of our own values and practices. Both the modern Chinese and the Western tourist require the commonly received history of footbinding as a crucial point of orientation for affirming and demarcating their own enlightened modernity.[1] Just as the erotic beauty of a bound foot at once veiled and derived much of its power from the signs of physical suffering that lay beneath the wraps, so the market-tested appeal of mass-produced four-inch slippers at once conceals and re-appropriates the monstrosity of an underlying historical reality.

As far as we know, embroidered silk slippers did not appear among the luxuriously extravagant displays of Chinese wares that filled the hundreds of china shops in seventeenth- and eighteenth-century London. The exotic imported goods these shops did offer, however, proved every bit as captivating to contemporary consumers. Chinese silks made up a large part of the trade, as did dozens of varieties of tea. The rapid emergence of tea drinking as a new national pastime required teawares, and these in turn demanded, in the well-appointed home, a fashionable complement of painted porcelain jars and vases and molded figurines. Fire screens, wallpapers, and lacquerware chests rounded out the inventory of better-stocked shops, offering the enchanting and often realized possibility of fitting out an entire room in the Chinese taste, especially once skilled European craftsmen began imitating and adapting Chinese motifs in the ceramics and furnishings that marked the advent of the chinoiserie style.

Chinese and Chinese-styled goods were so familiar, so thoroughly naturalized within the eighteenth-century English interior, that an aging Charles Lamb, speaking through his narrator Elia as he reflected dreamily in 1823 on the origins of a lifelong passion for old china, could not recall a time when porcelains had not been daily before his eye. Though the London shops where Elia would have acquired it surely provided a more luxurious setting than their modern Beijing counterparts, his infatuation with musty Chinese bric-a-brac suggests more than a glancing resemblance to that of the modern tourist. At once quaint and exotic, redolent of a storied history and unfailingly fashionable, Chinese objects then as now captivated the imagination with their novel forms and surface splendor. But a peculiar note of ambivalence that intrudes upon Elia's porcelain-induced reveries offers a more compelling parallel. "I had no repugnance then – why should I now have? – to those little, lawless, azure-tinctured grotesques, that under the notion of men and women, float about, uncircumscribed by any element, in that world before perspective – a china tea-cup."[2] While old china clearly owes much of its charm for Elia to such departures from familiar visual conventions, its grotesque figures and absurd deformations of the perspectival frame are also sufficiently unsettling to require a defensive denial of their repugnance.

The structure of this ambivalence in the aesthetic monstrosity underpinning the allure of Chinese wares functions for Elia, moreover, in much the same way as it does for his globe-trotting twenty-first-century successor. If Elia has difficulty in conjuring up an interior space before the appearance of old china, he has no trouble imagining a visual space prior to the invention of single-point perspective, for this is the lawless, uncircumscribed, visual world that old china makes available. This pre-perspectival lawlessness leads to absurdity: figures floating up in the air, a courtly mandarin handing tea to a lady who appears to be two miles away, another lady stepping into a boat "moored on the hither side of this calm garden river, with a dainty mincing foot, which in a right angle of incidence (as angles go in our world) must infallibly land her in the midst of a flowery mead – a furlong off on the other side of the same strange stream."

These "*speciosa miracula*" are delightful in themselves, in a playful, fairytale way, and Elia expresses his gratitude that the prosperity he and his cousin have recently enjoyed has made it possible for them "to please the eye sometimes with trifles of this sort."[3] But such goods are, finally, merely trifles, and the speaker surely finds pleasure also in the condescension that they invite. That the art of the Chinese reflects a world before perspective allows him to ask (if only rhetorically) "if far or near can be predicated of their world," and to posit for that world a non-Euclidean geometry in which angles shape space according to strange and unfamiliar rules, if they follow any rules at all. Accompanying such reflections, as lighthearted as they may be, is the comforting assurance that our own thoroughly rationalized, post-Renaissance visual world has advanced to the next level, and that we can recognize ourselves in this difference. The fantasies of monstrous beauty embodied by Elia's teacup and the modern tourist's embroidered slipper are cut of the same cloth. Quaint and charmingly lawless porcelain grotesques conjure for Elia a comfortingly pre-perspectival China in much the same way that equally quaint and enticingly barbaric silken artifacts evoke for his successors a reassuringly feudal Chinese past that both delimits and guarantees the privileged space of European modernity.

This book explores the role of the Chinese taste in the making of this modernity. Eighteenth-century consumers in England were, as Lamb suggests, infatuated with Chinese and Chinese-styled goods, even as they were amused, perplexed, or troubled by the alien aesthetic sensibility these goods embodied. This ambivalence, I will argue, figures centrally in the period's experience of Chinese exoticism and foregrounds the importance of the two questions, or sets of questions, I will set out to address in seeking to understand this experience. The first, quite simply, is how a foreign aesthetic that was so often depicted in negative terms – strange, monstrous, grotesque, repugnant, trifling – came to be so thoroughly and successfully assimilated within its host culture. What were the sources of an appeal that transformed curious emblems of otherness, in the space of little more than a century, into paradigmatic emblems of Englishness, and how did this transformation take place? The second set of questions concerns the significance of this appeal for the art, literature, and collective imagination of eighteenth-century England. How did the popularity of the Chinese taste inflect other important stylistic trends, such as classicism, Gothicism, and romanticism? What new meanings and values did Chinese objects make available to English consumers? What specific functions did these objects take on within the material and visual culture of the time? My working hypothesis here is that the thorough-going domestication of the alien Chinese aesthetic involved not merely a superficial shift in British taste or a passing fad, but rather a profound transformation of underlying constructs of gender, nation, and desire. It is well known that eighteenth-century consumers admired, collected, displayed, satirized, and roundly condemned Chinese wares; my purpose here is to ask how these seemingly trivial goods in turn acted upon the culture in which they were consumed.

In asking these questions, I hope to push back against three interpretive paradigms that habitually condition, in often unhelpful ways, our understandings of intercultural exchange in the early modern period. The most pervasive of these is the model of European diffusionism, which takes "modernity" in all of its guises to be a distinctly European phenomenon, and conceives the global history of the past several centuries as one in which major developments – capitalism, liberal democracy, the public sphere, Enlightenment rationality, industrialization, the novel, the modern subject – emerge initially in Western Europe and spread gradually outward across the globe. According to J. M. Blaut, diffusionism first emerged as a historical paradigm in the sixteenth and seventeenth centuries, became a fully formed scientific theory in the nineteenth, and experienced a resurgence in the work of post-World War II scholars and policy makers concerned with problems of modernization in the Third World.[4] While it has been subjected to increasing scrutiny in the past two decades, diffusionism underpins the implicit Eurocentrism that continues to condition much historical scholarship. As Dipesh Chakrabarty writes in *Provincializing Europe*, "Europe remains the sovereign theoretical subject of all histories" and the "silent referent in historical knowledge."[5]

Within the field of Chinese studies, the theory of diffusionism has guaranteed the dominance of a historical model that tends to regard developments in China from the seventeenth century onward, but most especially in the nineteenth and twentieth centuries, as mere responses to the Western impact in the realms of painting, politics, economics, mathematics, technology, education, literature, and the like. According to Paul Cohen, modern Western understandings of recent Chinese history have been based on the problematic assumptions that "the confrontation with the West was the most significant influence on events in China" and that "it was the West that played the truly *active* role in this period of Chinese history." One consequence of the persistence of such assumptions, I would suggest, is an anachronistic tendency to project this image of Western dominance back onto earlier periods. We are left to imagine, in the absence of compelling narratives to the contrary, that Western cultures were always already uniquely and self-sufficiently proto-modern, while China waited in a state of perpetual dormancy (Marx compared China to a "mummy carefully preserved in a hermetically sealed coffin") for the Western spark that would ignite the traumatic transformations of the past hundred years, leading to "the making over of Chinese culture in the Western image" that many a naïve China watcher still awaits, expectantly, today.[6]

While the present book has very little to say about Chinese history *per se*, part of my purpose in framing its central questions as I have is to complicate received narratives of early modernity in England by calling attention to the extraordinarily far-reaching cultural impact in the eighteenth century of the rising imperial power at the other end of the Eurasian land mass. If cultural diffusion was taking place between England and China, or more broadly between East Asia and Western Europe during this period, its dominant flows were clearly not in the direction we are accustomed to imagining. As Kenneth Pomeranz, Bin Wong, Andre Gunder Frank, and other revisionist historians have recently argued, England, when viewed from within a global macroeconomic perspective, occupied a rather peripheral position in what, until 1800 or so, was a largely Sinocentric world trade system.[7] To take seriously the question of the impact that Chinese aesthetics had on eighteenth-century England is then to extend this revisionist critique into the cultural sphere, and to open the door to exploring the material and imaginative ramifications of a less rigidly Eurocentric model of modernity.

A second barrier to fresh interpretations of the phenomenon of the Chinese taste in England is the tendency, especially pronounced within eighteenth-century studies, to read references to exotic luxuries in literary and artistic works as tropes reflecting and often celebrating Britain's rising imperial power. Students of the period take their cue from Addison, Lillo, Hogarth, and other contemporaries whose manifest pride in the expanding reach of Britain's trade networks is unmistakable, and there is no doubt that a consciousness of their nation's rising place in the world inflects their perception of the spoils of overseas trade that increasingly crowded London warehouses and fashionable shops. There is some danger, though, of reading too much of the Victorian era's imperial triumphalism back into the Stuart or early Georgian periods. As Gerald MacLean argues in his study of early modern English writing about the Ottoman empire, the emergence of British imperial pride was preceded by a considerably less swashbuckling era of imperial envy, a structure of feeling with respect to the material products and cultural achievements of an advanced and powerful Eastern civilization that was characterized by awe, admiration, and desire. While these responses were coupled with predictable anxiety and resentment, there was no question of the proto-colonialist condescension more familiar in later periods: "During the sixteenth and seventeenth centuries, English writers never forgot that they were dealing with an empire that controlled a great deal of Eastern Europe and a third of the known world, not a backward, vulnerable and somehow 'orientalized' space waiting to be conquered and controlled."[8]

Robert Markley finds a similar dynamic at work in English writing about China in the seventeenth and early eighteenth centuries. The frustrating awareness of the economic supremacy of the Far East and of Europe's marginalization in a Sinocentric global economy led to the emergence, according to Markley, of compensatory strategies for managing and concealing in narrative the profound anxieties generated by all-too-regular reminders of England's national abjection in the arenas of world trade. China's function as "the locus for dreams of attaining a golden age of prosperity and abundance," Markley suggests, posed for contemporary readers "a crucial set of challenges to Eurocentric conceptions of culture, personal and national identity" that we continue to grapple with even today.[9]

Prevailing attitudes in England towards China began to shift noticeably in the eighteenth century, as the generally admiring accounts of Jesuit missionaries and their followers gave way before considerably more hostile discourses of trade and diplomacy. Chinese imports and the imitations they spawned may have helped to catalyze this shift, by providing a material and visual context through which the vast, even overwhelming power and history of the Chinese empire could be re-imagined as fragile, superficial, and faintly absurd.[10] But at the same time, these objects and the storied civilization they evoked continued to remind their viewers, often uncomfortably, of England's cultural backwardness, material dependency, and relatively late arrival on the world stage. As in previous centuries, then, the East and its cherished luxuries evoked a complex range of responses best characterized, perhaps, as profound ambivalence. Only an awareness of this ambivalence, of the potential status of Chinese objects as a site of both imperial envy and imperial pride, can enable us to recognize the semiotic fluidity and transformative potency of these seemingly ephemeral objects in the English imagination.

This brings us to the third paradigm I hope to contest in the following pages. An air of ephemerality attaches itself all too readily to a Chinese teacup. Porcelain is a fragile material, and one whose decorative conventions in our period favor lightness and delicacy. Cobalt-blue figures float about in a shimmering glow of ethereal white, apparently beholden, as Lamb's Elia gleefully notes, to laws of neither gravity nor perspective. Regardless of the quality of its craftsmanship and artistry, the porcelain vessel (and its near cousins in lacquerware, textiles, printed wallpapers, and furniture) was consigned in the eighteenth century and remains consigned today to the domain of the merely decorative. Art was an evolving category in the eighteenth century, but however it was understood, Chinese imports did not qualify. Grand history paintings commanded the greatest respect in the art world, followed by portraiture, landscape painting, and still life; the decorative arts groveled down near the bottom of the ladder along with painted shop signs and rough woodblock prints.

While a lively culture of collecting and connoisseurship has sustained scholarship on decorative wares, modern museum curators and art historians readily confirm that we have inherited from the eighteenth century scales of artistic value that make it difficult to regard decorative objects seriously as agents and instruments of culture, if we can be troubled to regard them at all. As a result, few scholars ask the questions of, say, an imported

Chinese jar that they might ask of the painted portrait or volume of Dryden's poetry that once shared a room with it in an English country house. The decorative arts, like female-authored fiction for an earlier generation, serve as merely ornamental accoutrements to the true work of culture manifest in the heroic couplet or neoclassical pile. To consider such objects seriously as cultural artifacts requires not only an acknowledgment that, in the lingo of material culture studies, "things matter," but that merely decorative things may command special attention by virtue of that very "mereness," that potent combination of ubiquity, transparency, and utter irrelevance that enables them to perform the work of culture under the leisured, luxurious pretence that there is no work to be done.

So how, in particular, do Chinese things matter? Lamb's essay opens up a number of rich veins through which the question might be usefully explored and promising alternatives to outmoded paradigms pursued. The memorable confession that begins the essay – "I have an almost feminine partiality for old china" – reminds us that the meaning and appeal of Chinese-styled porcelains had long been understood in gendered terms.[11] How did this slightly embarrassing "partiality" first come to be coded as distinctly "feminine," and how did its meanings function and evolve over the course of a century noted for its obsessive concern with reshaping the unsettling contours of female desire? As static and clichéd as the association between eighteenth-century women and their tea-wares may seem to us today, I will argue that for the contemporary imagination it proved an endlessly dynamic, versatile, and productive one that not only reflected changes in the representation of gender positions but also contributed to shaping them. The "feminine" and the "Chinese," I hope to show, were reciprocally constituting categories throughout much of the century, collectively evoking otherness and extravagance while dialectically combining the tantalizing allure of superficial beauty with the troubling specter of transgressive monstrosity.

A partiality for old china on the part of a man requires an apology not only for the inversion of gender norms that it implies, but also for its defiance of established hierarchies among the arts. "When I go to see any great house," Lamb continues, "I inquire for the china-closet, and next for the picture gallery."[12] The narrator defends his indefensible preference on the grounds of idiosyncratic personal taste. But as the remainder of his narration amply demonstrates, he might have defended it more convincingly on the grounds that the insignificance of the ephemeral "trifles" he finds in the china-closet is itself a merely ephemeral signification, reproducing a scale of aesthetic value that serves particular purposes within a culture. Among these purposes is that of masking the role that mundane objects can play in constituting identities and other forms of meaning. In the following chapters, I will explore a number of ways in which the seemingly trifling objects of the china-closet can be seen to function alongside more privileged forms of expression (the Great Masters on the walls of the picture gallery, the canonical poets on the shelves) in both the formation and reformation of established structures of meaning and social practice. At the same time, I will suggest that the history of their trivialization casts light on the contemporary consolidation of hierarchies of gender, aesthetic value, and national identity.

A personal taste, Lamb's narrator goes on to explain, is often "of too ancient a date to admit of our remembering distinctly that it was an acquired one." The motif of memory and forgetting he introduces here will blossom into the extended reflection on the pleasing distortions of nostalgia and the ephemerality of dreams that occupies the bulk of the essay. Elia's comments on a set of blue and white tea-wares precipitate his companion's rhapsody on the simplicity of a youth yet unencumbered by wealth and unsullied by complacency. "I wish the good old times would come again," she begins, "when we were not so rich." After indulging her rambling laments, Elia gently reminds his cousin that those good old times are but dreams now, and calls her attention back to the image on his teacup: "And now do just look at that merry little Chinese waiter holding an umbrella, big enough for a bed-tester, over the head of that pretty, insipid, half Madonna-ish chit of a lady in that very blue summerhouse."[13]

There is a delightful irony in the circular structure of the essay, as Elia's effort to bring his cousin back from a fanciful, ungrounded reverie evoked by fanciful, ungrounded scenes painted on a piece of china requires engaging her with yet another, equally fanciful scene. At the same time, this structure begins to suggest an answer to the central question I raised earlier concerning the taming of the exotic, the process by which the visually alien is transformed into the familiar and quotidian. The process begins, Lamb's essay suggests, with a notable "partiality," an abiding fascination with the strangeness of the other that borders on infatuation. There follows an equal and opposite reaction of repudiation, of reaching wistfully back for the innocence of a taste yet unsullied by foreign luxury. The final moment of equilibrium achieves a synthesis of these two responses in the image of the domesticated other, the "merry little Chinese waiter" that marks the naturalization of the alien within a familiar framework and the re-ordering of strangeness under the sign of imperial ambition and cultural nationalism. The process captured so eloquently by Lamb reflects, as we will see, a pattern that repeats itself with striking regularity throughout the eighteenth century in the work of prominent writers and artists who shared with Elia a partiality for things Chinese that proved every bit as unsettling and potentially transformative as Europe's broader encounter with China in the early modern period. The understanding of "Englishness" that emerged through this encounter is neither pure nor hybrid in any straightforward sense, but rather is constituted paradoxically through a simultaneous appropriation and denial of "Chineseness" and an instrumental amnesia with respect to some of the decidedly non-English origins of British aesthetic culture.

The paradoxical structure of this process of assimilation is one of several discordant pairings suggested by Lamb's essay and evoked as well, I hope, by the "monstrous beauty" of this introduction's title. Chinese objects and aesthetic ideas are, for Lamb – as for many of his eighteenth-century predecessors – at once alluring and repulsive, charming and grotesque, strange and strangely familiar. Depending on the circumstances, they evoke delight or contempt, and stand as emblems of either highly cultivated taste or the nadir of tastelessness. By turns utterly foreign and paradigmatically English, they live a double life in the imagination of the period, leaving a tangle of tracks and traces abundant in interpretive possibilities.

The structure of the rest of the book reflects this doubleness. The eight chapters explore the problems and thematics briefly outlined above from two distinct methodological vantage points. Four of the chapters offer detailed case studies of prominent eighteenth-century figures whose intense and yet deeply ambivalent relationships with China and the chinoiserie style suggest both the range of responses they provoked and the potential of an alien aesthetic to transform the expressive outlook of its host culture. As I have suggested, I am less interested here in the obvious ways in which the Chinese taste "influenced" those arts in England that self-consciously adopted the characteristic techniques or visual hallmarks of the style than in the more subtle means by which the very gesture of accommodation or repudiation may in itself have generated unexpected literary insights and repositionings.

The first of these case studies, on Sir William Chambers, argues that the architect's firsthand exposure to Chinese design as a young man both complicated his relationship to the neoclassical tradition he famously promulgated and infused his rather fantastical writings on Chinese gardening with an emancipatory aesthetic vision modeled on the psychological response to cultural alienation. The second offers a feminist reading of William Hogarth and his seemingly vexed response to Chinese exoticism, suggesting that Hogarth's outward repudiation of the Chinese taste as an emblem of aesthetic and moral depravity, in both his writings and his art, masks an awareness of its congruities with his own aesthetic theory and an anxiety over the threatening forms of female agency it seems to imply. The third case study, on Horace Walpole, likewise traces a major cultural figure's initial embrace and subsequent rejection of the Chinese taste to suggest the ways in which the effects of a youthful infatuation might nonetheless have later returned to haunt the restless imagination that spawned the genre of Gothic fiction. Finally, I take up the case of Thomas Percy, the British prelate whose early fascination with Chinese literature and culture, I argue, prompted a nativist reaction that led, paradoxically, to an influential re-mapping of English literary history deeply informed by his sinological researches.

Although these four chapters are historically rooted in the eighteenth century, it is worth noting that they have a decidedly modern resonance. In August 2008, the world witnessed in the Beijing Olympics the spectacular coming-out party of a country poised to take an increasingly prominent – if not predominant – role in global political, economic, and cultural affairs in the twenty-first century. The rise – or more accurately re-emergence – of China as a world power has already begun to occasion, in the West, complex and dramatically ambivalent responses that resonate unmistakably with those evoked by the emergence of China, and Chinese aesthetic culture, in particular, in English consciousness in the eighteenth century. As China now reclaims a cultural status and prestige that it last enjoyed in the age of Hogarth, Percy, and Chambers, the time is surely ripe for a reconsideration of the historical dynamics of this encounter.

The remaining four chapters address the problem of aesthetic accommodation as a more general historical phenomenon, exploring from a variety of perspectives the peculiar fascination with "the Chinese taste" and attempting to reconstruct both the new sensibility that sustained it and the new, often gendered cultural meanings that it brought forth. As I have suggested, I am satisfied neither with the standard account of the period's China craze as a merely whimsical fashion prompted by the quest for novelty or exoticism, nor by the only slightly more promising reading of the collector's frenzy as a metonymic displacement of the lust for empire. I think that the array of meanings engendered by and affixed to the style were of considerably more richness, complexity, and historical importance than is commonly supposed; my aim in each of these chapters is to expose and reflect on this complexity.

The first chapter of this group sets out to explain the extraordinary popularity of Chinese and Chinese-styled goods, especially among women, by offering a close reading of the aesthetics of the Chinese taste as a kind of monstrous beauty, or anti-aesthetics, representing both an arresting combination of fashionable novelty and storied antiquity and a compelling reaction against the dominant aesthetic of neoclassicism. The second reflects on the extraordinary resonance between a dominant decorative motif on late Ming and early Qing porcelains that were imported to England in large numbers in the late seventeenth century and a central literary preoccupation of the elite women who owned and admired them, and argues that Chinese visual culture may have played a role in catalyzing transgressive imaginings of utopian female space. A third chapter further develops the theme of aesthetic translation, asking to what degree and by what process the conceptual impetus behind a stylistic motif, in this case that of contorted Chinese scholar's stones, might be preserved and transformed in its transposition to an alien cultural context. The concluding chapter in this group traces the widespread association of porcelain goods with their female consumers through three historical stages spanning the seventeenth and eighteenth centuries, examining how, at each stage, Chinese objects engendered new formations of female identity in the popular imagination.

As their descriptions suggest, a number of these chapters are of an unconventional cast. They approach their subject in unorthodox ways, and yield observations that some will find surprising or perhaps overly conjectural. As thought experiments, they are motivated by a belief in the generative value of reading against the grain and of informed speculation; they are concerned less with pronouncing definitive conclusions than with generating productive new modes and directions of inquiry. I have arranged the eight chapters in accordance with this aim. Rather than attempting to impose either a chronological or schematically unilinear narrative on a vast and polyvalent body of material, I have adopted instead a constellatory structure, intermingling the two types of chapters in four loosely thematic pairs that I hope will open up the material to the exploration of unforeseen interpretive pathways on the part of readers. The Chinese taste and William Chambers chapters, paired together in Part I, both explore in distinct yet complementary ways the problem of theorizing the aesthetics of exoticism. The gendered space and Hogarth chapters in Part II both focus on questions of female desire and explore the boundaries between the sociological and the aesthetic. In Part III, the chapters on the scholar's stone and Horace Walpole both situate the Chinese visual style within the context of English aesthetic nationalism in order to consider its role in the formation of new literary and social practice. Finally, the chapters on porcelain iconography and Thomas Percy in Part IV both claim a central role for Chinese ideas in the eighteenth-century construction of quintessentially English institutions.

The history of the phenomena of material encounters and cultural transformations that concerns me here does not end with the eighteenth century. The Chinese taste remains alive and well in Britain and throughout the world, where it continues powerfully to shape consumption patterns and inflect, typically in complex and polyvalent ways, local practices in cinematography, cuisine, electronics, gardening, fashion, interior design, and body art. We still speak of the globalization of consumer culture as if it were a recent development, and express astonishment and alarm that China's export industries have come to exert such a powerful role in the world economy. A longer view might suggest that after an interlude of two hundred years beginning with the first Opium War, China is now simply returning to an accustomed position of prominence in the world of international trade and aesthetic culture that it had enjoyed for many centuries before.

PART I

China and the aesthetics of exoticism

1 Eighteenth-century fashion and the aesthetics of the Chinese taste

How can we understand the aesthetics of exoticism? What are the origins and cultural significance of that seductive allure that we identify with stylized emblems of otherness? How can their uncontested appeal in the modern world be understood from the complementary vantage points of consumer culture and the philosophy of art? There are few richer contexts within which to explore such questions than early eighteenth-century England. The period once known best for the stately couplets of Augustan poetry has received attention more recently as the site of the origins of modern aesthetic theory, the birth of the consumer society, and the consolidation of nationalist pride in the cornucopia of exotic commodities procured through a rapidly expanding overseas trade.[1] The pervasive cultural motifs reflected in morally fraught debates over standards of taste, changing patterns of consumption, and the social effects of luxury coalesce in the period's pronounced and deeply ambivalent fascination with that style in the decorative arts known as chinoiserie.[2]

Chinoiserie, of course, was a pan-European phenomenon, and most existing studies have considered it as such. I focus on the English context in this chapter and throughout the book in order to attend to the specific meanings Chinese-styled objects took on within a more closely delimited cultural milieu. From this perspective, chinoiserie is a more intrinsically interesting phenomenon in England in this period than elsewhere as a result of its close association with the expansion of commercial activity, its dissemination across class boundaries, and the attendant debates on luxury, consumption, politeness, and taste that it produced. In this chapter I am particularly interested in the ways in which the experience of Chinese exoticism may have informed or interacted with the emergence of discourses of taste and aesthetics in eighteenth-century England. The philosophical tradition demarcated by Addison, Shaftesbury, Hutcheson, Hogarth, Reynolds, Hume, and others is the historically contingent product of a particular time and place, and a phenomenon that intersects in interesting and previously unexamined ways with the emergence of the "China craze" in precisely the same period.

Beginning as a trickle of exquisite luxury goods in the seventeenth century, imports of Chinese porcelain, silks, wallpaper, and lacquerware furniture surged in the first decades of the eighteenth, responding to, among other things, the steady increase in market demand for fashionable novelties and the rapid emergence of ritualized tea-drinking as a national pastime at every level of society. As was the case with other newly introduced foreign commodities such as coffee, sugar, and chocolate, Chinese products and the imitations they spawned initially appeared as luxurious markers of class distinction in the drawing-rooms of the social elite but soon spread to a much broader market, driven by the forces of fashion and the new merchant classes' contagious ambitions. In the 1690s Queen Mary was renowned for her magnificent porcelain collection. By the 1730s a Chinese room, decorated with imported paper and screens, plump figures of the laughing Buddha, porcelain vases on the mantelpiece and blue and white plate lining the walls, was *de rigueur* in respectable country houses. By the 1750s, when the style seems to have reached its peak, even David Garrick's modest London quarters featured a Chinese bed and chest of drawers, perhaps inspiring his foolhardy attempt to stage a French production called *The Chinese Festival* in England at the height of the Seven Years War. In the meantime William Chambers had erected the famous Chinese pagoda at Kew Gardens near London, countless Confucian temples and Chinese bridges had sprung up in landscape gardens across the land, and the mania for furnishings and follies in the Chinese taste had reached a point where satirists were forecasting that before long even country churches and humble dairies would be sporting pagoda roofs, with bells and dragons adorning their upturned eaves.[3]

The considerable existing scholarship on chinoiserie has generally approached it from one of two perspectives. Historians of the decorative arts have traced the origins and evolution of various phases of the style, their relationship to contemporaneous baroque and rococo sensibilities, and the complex, hybridizing exchanges of models and influences between European and Asian workshops that make it so difficult to establish a precise genealogy of influence for any given artifact.[4] Economic historians, meanwhile, have situated the China craze of the eighteenth century within the context of long-standing patterns of trade between East and West, and pointed to a decisive role for Chinese imports in stimulating many of the innovations in domestic manufacturing and marketing techniques that led, in turn, to the Industrial Revolution.[5]

As culturally embedded objects, however, with intriguing stories of their own to tell about patterns of taste, fashion, and consumption, the laughing buddhas and glimmering vases that adorned the eighteenth-century domestic interior have received little attention at all. This neglect is owing in part to the paucity of direct evidence: it is notoriously difficult to trace even the provenance and ownership history, let alone the personal or cultural significance, of material artifacts that lack, by traditional measures, any redeeming historical or artistic significance. But the lack of interest stems also, I suspect, from a traditional resistance to the serious historical study of consumer culture on the grounds both of its seeming triviality and its awkward associations with bad taste, crass materialism, and other less-than-noble impulses of human nature. Whether or not such associations are justified on moral or aesthetic grounds, they invariably obscure the generative processes at work within the world of goods, the elaborate networks of social ritual and private fantasy through which material objects participate in the construction of cultural meanings.

There may be, admittedly, something foolhardy in an attempt to read such meanings into exotic commodities that even in their own time were often regarded as mere ephemeralities, the inconsequential relics of a passing fad. And yet I would propose that the many hundreds of tons of Chinese ephemerality that traveled on East India Company ships to London docks in the early decades of the eighteenth century finally amount to a cultural phenomenon of some consequence. I would propose, further, that a history of such ephemerality attuned to its sociological and even anthropological dimensions might provide a fruitful approach to more familiar questions in aesthetic theory and the history of ideas. In particular, I am intrigued by the possibility of reconstructing those illicit forms of aesthetic agency and sensibility that were elided or marginalized in the ongoing debates over taste and beauty of the early eighteenth century. What coherent alternatives were available to the dominant classicist aesthetics of universality, just proportion, and the disinterested contemplation of form articulated by Shaftesbury, Hume, Reynolds, and others? How might we theorize those forms of aesthetic, or perhaps anti-aesthetic pleasure experienced by those large groups of consumers excluded by accident of class or gender from the charmed circle of the leisured and well-traveled man of taste? To what extent might the embrace of Chinese exoticism in the decorative arts represent a structural antithesis not only to the strictures of classical taste *per se* but also to the narrowly conceived forms of privileged and predominantly masculine social identity associated with it?

The early eighteenth century clearly does see a gradual displacement of the patrician, neo-Platonic classicism championed by Shaftesbury by a new conception of aesthetic pleasure more amenable to the consumption patterns of the commercial classes. But while Addison and Hogarth, among others, acknowledge the aesthetic value of novelty, their emphasis on moderation and decorum – as we will see in later chapters – leaves them largely unsympathetic to the perceived excesses of chinoiserie. In spite of – or perhaps because of – the immense popularity of the Chinese taste, in other words, the sensibility that sustained it was articulated in largely negative terms, so that from the standpoint of the established canons of eighteenth-century discourses on taste, whether patrician or bourgeois, it remains, at worst, a deviant obsession or, at best, a rather disreputable affectation.[6]

When the eighteenth-century mania for chinoiserie is understood as anything more than yet another arbitrary and inexplicable turn in the river of fashion, it is typically attributed to a contemporary fascination with novelty and exoticism tinged, perhaps, with the romance of empire. This was the age, after all, of the commercial revolution in Britain, a period of economic expansion driven at once by ever-increasing demand among the newly prosperous for ever-more eclectic markers of status and distinction, and by the progressive consolidation of a vast overseas trade network intoxicating in its implications for Britain's wealth and power. But while no doubt accurate in a general sense, an account of the China craze based solely on its generic novelty and exoticism fails to address either the origins of the underlying taste for the exotic, its cultural significance, or the striking particularity of the Chinese case. The widespread consumption of chinoiserie, I argue, signals the consolidation in the first half of the eighteenth century of a distinctive new form of aesthetic subjectivity in those oppositional spaces defined and defiled by the reigning discourses of classical taste and polite bourgeois culture.

Any credible defense of such broad claims for the cultural significance of chinoiserie must begin by addressing two obvious objections to them. The first, methodological objection concerns the validity of isolating the Chinese style for special consideration among consumer fashions of the period. The shores of Augustan England and the halls of the Royal Exchange were awash, after all, with foreign luxuries from all over the world: sugar and exotic fruits from the Caribbean, spices and calicoes from the East, operas from Italy, and the latest in *haute couture* and *haute cuisine* from those hopelessly decadent but ever-so-dashing aristocrats across the channel. Those who warned of the dire consequences of indulging extravagant foreign tastes mentioned Chinese vases in the same breath as French fashion dolls, and indeed China and France were often lumped together in popular writings as the most culpable purveyors of effeminizing foreign luxury. From the art historian's point of view, moreover, much European chinoiserie appears as more of an exoticized variation on a decidedly Western vocabulary of decorative motifs, whether rococo, Gothic, or grotesque, than as a distinct stylistic movement in its own right.

What, then, sets chinoiserie apart? To begin with, the association of the style with the country of its putative origin itself carried with it a manifold assortment of meanings dizzying in their ambivalence and complexity. Although nineteenth-century prejudices have tended to obscure the fact, far more was known about China in early eighteenth-century Europe than about almost any other distant port of call, with the result that it occupied an unparalleled position in the geographical imagination of the period. The Jesuit missionaries who had been active first in Macao and Guangzhou and then in the imperial court at Beijing for over one hundred years had left voluminous accounts of their experiences and impressions, many of which had been widely translated and anthologized. Western readers were well aware of the peculiarities of the Chinese language and writing system, the rationalist moral philosophy of the great sage Confucius, the strict meritocracy of the examination-based civil service, and of course the famously naturalistic style in landscape gardening hailed by William Temple, Joseph Addison, and William Chambers, and adapted into what the French came to call *le jardin anglo-chinois.*[7] Nor were these renowned features of Chinese culture viewed as mere curiosities or freakish wonders from a sensational traveler's tale. They each served, at various stages during the seventeenth and eighteenth centuries, as both exemplary models and objects of impassioned speculation and controversy in polemics on language reform, natural religion, the philosophy of taste, economic policy, and the like. But, above all, the resulting dissemination of unusually detailed knowledge about a distant culture – and one that appeared neither in classical sources nor the Bible – stamped the European imagination with the indelible and, I think, deeply transformative awareness that there existed, on the far end of the globe, a highly advanced civilization with a rich and unbroken cultural heritage of over four thousand years.[8]

But if the sheer antiquity of China inspired Western observers with awe and admiration, it also complicates any interpretation of the cultural meanings that Western consumers attached to its exports or the imitations they inspired. Chinese vases and painted wallpapers, like hoop petticoats and three-foot hairdos, were initially prized for their novelty, but unlike the latest fashions in dress, the Chinese style offered the paradoxical distinction of novelty with a four-thousand-year-old lineage. Chinese goods were valued not only as a new fashion statement, but simultaneously as enchantingly unfamiliar tokens of a well-established cultural value.

Historians of consumer culture have pointed to a dramatic shift in the dominant modes of status display and legitimation in early modern England. Traditionally, social elites had valued durable possessions in proportion to the honor they conferred upon a family through their visible manifestations of venerable age, or patina. Elizabethan custom mandated a probationary period of five generations before an upwardly mobile family could be fully accepted within the ranks of the nobility. The accumulation of patina on the silver and other furnishings of a genteel household, then, provided a symbolic and outwardly visible record of the family's progress through its class apprenticeship. By the early eighteenth century, however, rapidly changing economic conditions had permitted luxurious novelty to displace hallowed antiquity as the pre-eminent marker of social status, and as the quality most highly prized in the possessions of the wealthy.[9]

The stunning ascendancy of chinoiserie just at the moment of this shift in the symbolism of class distinction raises the possibility that an imported Chinese vase, for example, might have represented for its admirers a reassuring synthesis of the old standard and the new, a bold statement of fashionable iconoclasm tempered by a virtual patina of cultural legitimacy accorded by the object's association with Chinese antiquity. This is not to suggest that every purchase of blue and white porcelain would have been consciously inflected by sinophilic antiquarianism but, rather, to point out that unlike the taste for other stylish commodities of the time, a taste for things Chinese potentially occupied a dialectically charged position as at once both ancient and modern, and justified a claim to status on the grounds of both their fashionable newness and unimpeachable pedigree.

The second distinctive feature of chinoiserie likewise results from its mediating position between two conflicting cultural poles. The emergence of aesthetics as a philosophical discourse in the eighteenth century was accompanied by the invention, in England, of a newly sanctified sphere of high culture inhabited by the self-proclaimed inheritors of the classical mantle that could be found in the Scriblerus Club, the Royal Academy, and the elegant Palladian villas that dotted the English countryside. The "correct" taste that was revered and codified by this cultural elite was defined in opposition, as Pope reminds us, to the vulgarity of Grub Street poets, but also to the mercenary creed of Covent Garden traders and the brave new world of commerce and fashion they represented. The consumer revolution of the eighteenth century made accessible to ever-growing numbers the outward trappings of wealth and status; the discourse of taste arose in no small measure as a reactionary new regime of social demarcation, enabling those of a certain social standing to continue to distinguish themselves in a commercialist age from the promiscuous hordes of parvenus at their heels.

And yet the chinoiserie style seems consistently to have troubled this boundary between cultivated and vulgar taste, fine art and the fripperies of fashion. On the one hand, period satirists regularly denounce Chinese and Chinese-inspired goods as at best foolish trifles worthy of no more serious regard than this season's favored hat or velvet glove, or at worst as emblems of aesthetic monstrosity or perversion tending only to vitiate the taste of their admirers.[10] And yet on the other hand, one finds that Chinese productions in the realms of painting, poetry, and architecture are regularly compared by other writers with distinguished counterpoints from the Western tradition. Even if Chinese paintings fall short, in their eyes, for their lack of perspective, or Buddhist temple architecture for its failure to recognize classical rules of proportion, these works do seem to occupy the same conceptual category as their Western counterparts and to represent a competing aesthetic standard worthy of comparison to classical and Renaissance norms.[11] This dual status of chinoiserie as both legitimate art and fashionable commodity sets it apart from other classes of luxury goods and constitutes a significant challenge, as we will see, to traditional conceptions of aesthetic value.

These dualities in the temporal and aesthetic registers of chinoiserie further complicate the analysis of its reception within the historical context of the East India trade and the imperialist regard towards emblems of otherness that this trade enabled. Our understanding of colonialist dynamics would predict – and the treatment of emblems of Chinese cultural authority in European chinoiserie largely confirms – that the purchase and possession of exotic commodities often partake of the pride of empire. Ownership confers mastery, and early eighteenth-century Britons reveled in the spectacle, enacted daily at their docks and warehouses, of distant lands eagerly offering up their riches at the beck and call of the London marketplace. Chinoiserie plays a part in this drama of colonial subservience in its trademark trivialization of the figures of Confucius, the Chinese emperor, and other recognized symbols of Chinese cultural authority. By its very nature as a celebration of surface splendor, the chinoiserie aesthetic tends to hollow out every allusion to the potential authenticity of otherness, to evacuate any suggestion of a viable foreign subjectivity.[12] Its very appeal as novelty seems inseparable, in this regard, from the intoxicating gaze of orientalist objectification.

And yet the familiar Saidian paradigm suggested by this account simply does not apply within the historical context in which the Chinese taste first took hold. China in the early eighteenth century was no British colony, nor was it in any plausible sense in the process of becoming one. The foreign trade in Canton was conducted entirely on Chinese terms, under conditions that the British found deeply humiliating but were in no position to change. Chinese merchants had no use for British woolens and tin, so the East India Company was forced, at considerable political peril, to finance its purchases of tea, silks, and porcelain with silver bullion, a situation that seemed to many observers to give China, not Britain, the upper hand in the exchange.[13] Whatever part of their appeal, then, Chinese goods owed to the vicarious thrills of imagined colonialist mastery derived from a self-flattering illusion that must have been difficult to sustain in the light of the unfavorable arrangements the Company was forced to accept in conducting the China trade. The blue and white plate that adorned the tables of Britain's elite through much of the eighteenth century issued from a scene not of its proud domination but of an uncharacteristically servile obeisance.[14]

It is dangerous, in other words, to slip too complacently into the familiar assumption that a taste for the exotic is always, simply, an aestheticized mask for the lust of empire. Chinoiserie clearly presents a more complicated case. In spite of its obvious delight in superfice and its seemingly structural antipathy to weighty or consequential meanings of any kind, the historical circumstances of the China trade and the wealth of positive, even reverential views of that distant civilization to which chinoiserie inevitably alluded, meant that Chinese and Chinese-styled goods potentially evoked a far more complex range of responses than did other contemporary fashions and commodities. The patina of Chinese antiquity suggested not only a site of ancient glory to rival the pre-eminence of imperial Rome in the historical imagination but an entire array of remarkable cultural achievements that an embattled island nation just emerging from the tumult of the seventeenth century was predisposed to admire. The Chinese writing system suggested to observers from Bacon to Swift a rational, philosophically grounded mode of representation impervious to the corrupting agents of historical change and ambiguous usage. As a system of government and ethical code, Confucianism likewise seemed to offer a rationalist antidote to the miseries of political and sectarian strife. To conjure up the idea of Chinese civilization in the early eighteenth century, whether in a treatise on childrearing or the temples and rock gardens of a wallpaper design, was to evoke an aura of cultural legitimacy constantly in tension with the aesthetic trivialization set in motion by the products of its export trade.[15]

I have argued up to this point for the unique status of Chinese and Chinese-styled objects as cultural signifiers in the eighteenth-century marketplace. A second potential objection to the interpretive approach I propose might concede their uniqueness but point to the risks of over-reading the capricious ebbs and flows of fashionable consumption of any kind. Modern theories of consumer behavior still give a prominent place to the Veblen effect, or the principle of emulative consumption, which reduces decisions to acquire luxury goods to an expression of social ambition and of the resulting desire to acquire for oneself those markers of distinction and privilege flaunted by one's social betters.[16] Within such an account, the particular nature of a fashionable commodity is largely irrelevant in understanding its appeal to a given class of consumers. The object has little independent cultural significance, little meaning as a locus of pleasure and desire apart from its passing pre-eminence within the constantly shifting economies of fashionable emulation. Wealthy aristocrats purchased porcelain, in other words, because they noticed it in the Queen's cabinet; the rising merchant classes acquired it in turn because they took it for an emblem of impeccable aristocratic taste. The particular nature of a Chinese vase as an aesthetic object or as a marker of cultural difference figures not at all in such an account. The choices of fashion are largely arbitrary: buyers consume to accrue the social dividends of consumption, not to express a personal affinity with the intrinsic nature or prior cultural significance of an object in itself.

My response to this objection is twofold. First, the model of emulative consumption does not adequately account for the historical specificity of fashion. How do successful fashions begin? Why do certain fashions emerge at the particular moment they do, while other potential fashions never emerge at all? Even Josiah Wedgwood, perhaps the eighteenth century's most successful marketer and manipulator of fashion, discovered that certain of his immensely popular porcelain creations caught on better than others for which he had entertained equally high hopes.[17] He learned, in other words, that a certain prior degree of collective desire is the precondition for the commercial exploitation of the Veblen effect. The unending quest for novelty and the prestige it confers, of course, plays a key role in catalyzing this collective desire, but it is secondary to the originary longing. As Herbert Blumer argues, "[it] is not the prestige of the elite which makes the design fashionable, but rather the suitability of the design which allows the prestige of the elite to be attached to it. The design must correspond to the direction of the incipient taste of the fashion-consuming public."[18] Pierre Bourdieu elaborates the idea of incipient taste further through his notion of aesthetic disposition. For any given type of cultural production – whether in music, clothing, or interior design – to appeal to a given class of consumers, Bourdieu argues, it must conform to a specific configuration of taste and lifestyle preferences corresponding to the social condition and self-perception of that group.[19] A fashion like chinoiserie, which tended to be associated with largely female consumers of the upper and upper-middle classes, would have embodied, then, a distinguishable matrix of aesthetic qualities that rendered it attractive to that segment of the population. For Bourdieu, one's class and social identity are unfailingly constituted through and revealed by the myriad judgments of taste that inform every aspect of one's daily life. Bourdieu based his conclusions on a study of 1200 French families in the 1960s. If we can take them to be more generally valid, however, then a close analysis of a stylistic trend at once as prominent and as controversial as eighteenth-century chinoiserie is bound to cast light not only on that aesthetic disposition to which it appealed but also on corresponding formations of eighteenth-century social identity.

What, then, was the distinctive aesthetic appeal of chinoiserie? One searches, alas, in vain for direct answers to this question among contemporary aficionados of the style. The occasional country house visitor may remark that a room done up in the Chinese style is "exceedingly pretty"; the avid collector may comment in passing on some porcelain "of the very best quality" acquired at a recent auction. But the overwhelming majority of written reflections on the fashion are in the dismissively satirical vein of the essayist in the mid-century periodical *The World* who described Chinese-inspired design as comprising only "monstrous offspring of wild imagination, undirected by nature and truth."[20] The vituperative backlash against chinoiserie suggests that it posed an implicit challenge to classicist norms. But one longs for an articulate champion of the porcelain sensibility, a contemporary theorist of the exotic sublime, who might help us to reconstruct the imaginative disposition that sustained the China craze. The public discourse of taste from Shaftesbury onward, as I suggested earlier, was weighted so heavily against chinoiserie that an explicit defense of the style – at least outside the realm of gardening – may well have been inconceivable at the time. In the absence of direct testimony accounting for its favorable reception, one can only extrapolate something of the nature of its perverse appeal from the unceasing tirades of its exasperated critics.

The foremost hallmark of the Chinese taste, in the eyes of those who condemned it, was an exaggerated concern with superficial prettiness. The very fragility of porcelain seemed emblematic of a transient visual appeal without depth or substance. A China vase, like the painted coquettes of eighteenth-century verse, presented a glittering, hollow shell of seductive charm, a resplendent mirage of visual delights that could only deceive and lead the viewer astray. The pleasures of gazing upon its fanciful designs were low, uncultivated pleasures, in that they consisted of an immediate, sensual, child-like delight in bright colors and intricate patterns rather than the studied, disinterested appreciation of formal properties that characterized refined taste. The consequences of indulging such a false taste were grievous indeed. Suppose, writes Lord Shaftesbury, that

> Effeminacy pleases me. The Indian figures, the Japan work, the enamel strikes my eye. The luscious colours and glossy paint gain upon my fancy . . . But what ensues? . . . Do I not for ever forfeit my good relish? How is it possible I should thus come to taste the beauties of an Italian master, or of a hand happily formed on nature and the ancients?[21]

True beauty, for Shaftesbury, is a cultivated taste. The subtle ironies, classical allusions, and elaborately structured meanings of a grand history painting or a couplet from Pope required – and require still – considerable erudition and experience to enjoy in the way they were meant to be enjoyed. To fancy the delights of chinoiserie, by contrast, demanded knowledge neither of Latin poetry nor of the architectural marvels of the Grand Tour.

The untutored sensuality encouraged by chinoiserie, then, offended polite taste in its supposed aesthetic vacuity, but it was also potentially disturbing on moral grounds. Shaftesbury and his followers, after all, regarded the correct judgment of truth and beauty as inseparable marks of a refined sensibility, a view that contributed to an early eighteenth-century discourse of politeness increasingly preoccupied, as John Brewer argues, with the depth and authenticity of the model bourgeois subject.[22] A Chinese bedroom, viewed in the light of this ideal, could only be classed with the theater and the urban pleasure garden as a site of renegade, licentious desires and delights, improper entertainments privileging spectacle and sensuality over moral integrity and substance.

This brings us to a second aesthetic feature of chinoiserie lampooned by contemporary critics and bound to exacerbate concerns about substance and authenticity, namely, its inescapable hybridity as a style. In its creation, marketing, and decorative role in the eighteenth-century interior, chinoiserie steadfastly resists any essentializing impulse, revealing an essence that is itself a pastiche, a guiding principle not of purity and integrity but of thorough-going mongrelization. Having insisted earlier that chinoiserie merits consideration as an aesthetic and cultural phenomenon apart from the stylistic trends that informed it, I want to now complicate that claim by arguing that one defining characteristic of chinoiserie considered as a distinct phenomenon is precisely its insistence on boundless adaptability, its repudiation of any fixed standard or accepted model. While the importance of designs by Watteau and Pillement gave French-inspired chinoiserie a distinctly rococo cast, the English contribution to the evolution of the style was its amalgamation with the Gothic. As we will see in Chapter 6, Thomas Chippendale was only the best known of a cadre of designers who casually interspersed designs for Chinese and Gothic furniture in their publications, or even mingled bells and dragons with Gothic arches in the same architectural façades.[23] The delight in stylistic eclecticism apparent in these design books corresponds to a generalized nonchalance regarding the "authenticity" of chinoiserie goods. The knowledgeable collector of quality Chinese porcelain did not emerge as a type until the early nineteenth century. The discriminating regard of the eighteenth-century connoisseur of classical artifacts seems not to have troubled itself with the differences between Chinese imports and European imitations, let alone with the distinctions between the characteristic porcelain coloration schemes of the Ming and Qing dynasties.

But even imported Chinese originals were as often hybrids as not. Much of the Chinese export trade consisted of wallpapers, furniture, and porcelain sets made to order according to European designs, or even in imitation of Western chinoiseries, so that Chinese craftsmen found themselves striving to outdo one another in their renderings of Western preconceptions of Chinese art, and a Chinese observer would have been hard pressed to recognize in the exaggerated motifs of a clichéd oriental exoticism anything remotely Chinese at all.[24] In its predictable conventions and its mass-market appeal, in fact, much eighteenth-century chinoiserie has more than a passing resemblance to twentieth-century kitsch. But whereas kitsch functions by virtue of its apparent semiotic transparency, its untroubled correspondence between immediately legible sign and predetermined emotional response, even the most conventional of chinoiserie resists sentimental reductionism in its underlying allusion to the unintelligibility of radical difference.[25]

But the fashionable toyshops of London offered baubles and bangles aplenty that were merely pretty or of questionable stylistic pedigree. The third essential component of chinoiserie's appeal lay, of course, in its unmistakable exoticism. For the eighteenth-century critic, the exotic, as an aesthetic feature, was understood within the broader rubric of the strange or novel. But as suggested above, the novelty of the Chinese fashion was imbued with a rich array of cultural associations that distinguished it from other fashions whose appeal lay solely in being new. Whether or not a viewer had actually read one of the many hundreds of available publications on China, the experience of unfamiliarity in gazing upon a Chinese teapot must invariably have been mediated through some recognition, however vague, of the curious disjunctures of cultural difference to which it alluded and hence of its potential saturation with largely unintelligible meanings.

Joseph Addison, writing in *The Spectator,* famously classed the experience of the new or the uncommon as among the three principal pleasures of the imagination. But within his model, novelty pleases only as a kind of refreshing surprise, a momentary diversion from the insipidity of the familiar and commonplace.[26] To this basic pleasure in variety, I would argue, the exotic, by virtue of its *unheimlich* contortions of familiar experience, adds a tincture of sublimity in the more sustained, self-reflexive awareness it proposes of vast, unfathomable bodies of meaning and experience beyond the realm of the everyday. The seventeenth-century virtuoso's passion for the marvelous and the monstrous, as embodied in an uncommonly large pearl, for example, or a cock with four legs, testifies to the appeal of sublime strangeness in the natural world.[27] But there is a distinct pleasure as well in cultural illegibility, in the contemplation of human artifacts one recognizes as resplendent with meanings that, as a result of cultural distance, one cannot begin to penetrate. The best corollary evidence for this phenomenon in early eighteenth-century England is perhaps the striking popularity of the Italian opera, an entertainment roundly condemned at the time for its alienation of sound from meaning.[28] Like enchanted English opera-goers, collectors of chinoiserie seemed to revel in a surface play of sensual impressions divorced from any legitimating cultural context, to take a perverse pleasure in their own estrangement from rational forms of understanding.

And yet it was precisely the cultural estrangement it embodied, I think, that enables us both to account for the wild success of chinoiserie and to begin to reconstruct the alternative forms of aesthetic response that it enabled. Within the philosophical tradition extending from Shaftesbury to Kant, the idea of aesthetic pleasure always emerges as an uneasy compromise between carnal sensuality and sterile, disembodied form. The taste for pure beauty rises above the vulgarities of sensual gratification to seek a more intellectual fulfillment in the recognition of structure, pattern, and proportion, a refined awareness of that seemingly unmotivated formal coherence that Kant famously calls "purposiveness without purpose."[29] And yet the very renunciation of the sensual implied by the injunction of disinterestedness with regard to the object of beauty risks disemboweling altogether that fundamentally corporeal basis of imaginative felicity from which any pleasure to be found in the sensible world of art and nature must ultimately derive.

Chinoiserie so often failed the test of "beauty" for the eighteenth-century man of taste because its pleasures seemed to offer no promise of transcending the merely sensual. He would have predicted that any such taste as was pleased with a Chinese object could never be pleased for long, as it was in the nature of vulgar appetites rapidly to be satiated by the objects of their momentary fancy. His own pleasure in classical statuary avoided the risk of satiety – not to mention questionable motives – only insofar as it transcended this realm of sensual appetite. But how, then, was he to explain the success of the Chinese style in pleasing so many for so long, for its ubiquity among the furnishings of aristocratic homes, for its *de facto* claims, in short, to the kind of durable appeal that was meant to be the exclusive province of Palladio and Pope? I would like to propose – and this is a theoretical crux of my argument – that chinoiserie sustained its charm by mediating its immediate sensual gratifications through the simultaneous distancing effect of cultural estrangement. Its pleasures escaped the risk of vulgar satiety, that is, not through the usual, prescribed process of intellectual transcendence but, rather, through the inescapable recognition of unintelligible difference. The desire for masterful possession evoked by its sensual allure was endlessly postponed and hence enlivened and prolonged by its very illegibility as a cultural artifact. To delight in Chinese export art or its imitations was not, perhaps, to enjoy the pure, transcendent beauty celebrated by Shaftesbury and Reynolds, but nor was it simply to wallow in vulgar sensual indulgence, as its critics claimed. Rather, it was to draw on an alternative sensibility in which unassimilable difference replaces abstracted form as the precondition of aesthetic pleasure in its endlessly enchanting counterpoint of gratification and deferral.

In making such a claim, it should be clear, my aim is not to contest the Kantian understanding of beauty but, rather, to explore the possibility and workings of alternative sources of "aesthetic" pleasure, to find ways of theorizing some of those enchanting forms of visual experience that Kant and his predecessors were inclined to dismiss as impure. My reading of the major aesthetic theorists of the eighteenth century suggests a thoroughgoing attempt to establish clear hierarchies of aesthetic experience. While there may well be grounds, both political and theoretical, for contesting these hierarchies, my purpose here is rather to excavate from their attendant refuse heaps forms of experience and pleasure – such as that found in chinoiserie – that were commonly regarded as degraded or illegitimate in order to examine them more closely and try to understand how they worked.

Recent critiques of the eighteenth-century conception of authentic aesthetic experience have underscored its unrepentant elitism and its role in naturalizing and legitimating social hierarchies. Not only is the cultivation of refined taste contingent, according to this critique, upon the accumulation of wealth and leisure, the very judgment of beauty is predicated upon a social position sufficiently privileged to make possible the systematic disregard for vulgar materiality and the contemplative disinterestedness that it requires. The aesthetic preferences of elite classes, then, became a way of reaffirming their distinguished status and their apparently "natural" superiority over those whose place in the world and life-long conditioning within that place precluded a true "taste" for the "better" things in life. Aesthetic sensibility, we now recognize, is an essential component of social and political identity.[30]

What, then, might be the social or political implications of the alternative chinoiserie aesthetic I have posited here? In its unrepentant embrace of the sensual, the particular, and the immediate, it shares something in common with the vision of a "popular" aesthetics outlined by both Brewer and Bourdieu. Yet both the consumption history and popular mythology of the chinoiserie style suggest that the social division it marks most clearly and persistently is that of gender rather than class. The best-known collectors of porcelain and other chinoiserie – Queen Mary, Queen Anne, Henrietta Howard, the Duchess of Queensbury – were all women. Within upper-class homes, the Chinese style was favored in those intimate, interior spaces typically relegated to female taste and sociability. Even as Chinese porcelain spread to middling households, its firm associations with the feminized rituals of the tea table suggest that it remained predominantly, though by no means exclusively, an object of female consumption, and one which women tended to invest with a greater degree of personal significance.[31]

Though the prevalence of misogynist satire in the period renders problematic any attempt to read literary depictions of women's leisure activities as a form of historical evidence, the ubiquity of literary scenes and metaphors pairing women with chinoiserie objects of various kinds suggests that they most likely had some degree of experiential resonance. As I have argued at length elsewhere, the best-known literary depictions of porcelain fetishism in the period – Wycherley's *Country Wife*, Pope's *Rape of the Lock*, and Goldsmith's *Citizen of the World* – all share with countless periodical essays and a certain strand of eighteenth-century pornography not only a pronounced gendering of Chinese commodities but also an association of the Chinese taste with the supposedly vain extravagance of female passion in the aesthetic, economic, and sexual spheres.[32] Visual corollaries to this theme

Figure 1 William Hogarth (British, 1697–1764). *Marriage à la Mode*, Plate II, 1745.

abound in Hogarth's work, where the lure of the East consistently conjures up the dangers posed by feminine excess to staid bourgeois morality.

In the second plate of *Marriage à la Mode*, for example, the tea service on the table, the porcelain idols lining the mantelpiece, and the Chinese fire screen behind the master's chair contribute, along with his wife's enticingly outstretched foot, to the aura of fashionable dissipation that pervades the scene and, most pointedly, to the failure of masculine respectability announced by the broken sword lying at the master's feet (Figure 1). The iconic juxtaposition in this print of a symbol of emasculation alongside emblems of the Chinese taste and female subjectivity captures not only the gender dynamics of contemporary debates on fashion, luxury, and commerce, but also the specific cultural positioning of an alien decorative motif. The eighteenth-century cult of chinoiserie, as I will argue in subsequent chapters, marks the consolidation of an oppositional aesthetic widely embraced by contemporary women and coded along specifically gendered lines in its resistance to cultural assumptions embedded within the classicist norm.

Before turning to the final portion of my argument and my answer to the "so what?" question I posed above, it may be helpful to review the three principal claims I have made up to this point. First, chinoiserie in early eighteenth-century England constitutes a unique and significant cultural phenomenon, the distinctive characteristics of which reflect certain features of the society in which it thrived. Second, the extraordinary appeal of chinoiserie as well as much of the disdain it attracted from classicist critics can be understood as a function of its sensuality, hybridity, and exoticism. And third, there seems to have been a strong association both in historical patterns of consumption and in widespread literary and visual motifs between chinoiserie productions and certain classes of largely female consumers. I invoked Bourdieu earlier on in order to establish the possibility of reading social identity formations through their structural correspondence with the distinctive aesthetic preferences of particular social groups. It remains now to consider how the significance I am ascribing to chinoiserie may have manifested itself in the collective self-imagining of its admirers.

I will offer here three speculative answers to this problem, corresponding to the three aesthetic principles that constitute the Chinese taste as it was experienced in this period. The principle of sensual particularity, in its rejection of the patrician, neo-Platonic doctrine of an aesthetic attitude consisting of the disinterested contemplation of pure form, potentially opens up a pair of alternative spaces for aesthetic self-positioning. To begin with, Chinese-styled goods, as an art form that in its contempt for familiar formal principles exerted a notorious fascination for the "untutored" female eye, dramatically disrupted the sexual politics of the gaze as imagined by contemporary aesthetic theorists, for many of whom – Hogarth and Burke among them – the emblematic experience of beauty was that of the learned man of taste looking upon a well-proportioned female form. Within the intimate, domestic spaces of eighteenth-century china rooms, by contrast, it seems largely to have been women who did the looking, judging, admiring, and possessing, thereby carving out the possibility of a differently structured aesthetic subjectivity. The displacement of disinterestedness in this new aesthetic attitude by the experience of cultural alienation would seem to imply, furthermore, a rejection of the patrician disdain for the mixing of art and commerce, and to suggest that chinoiserie may have been associated with the troubling realities of female agency in the commercial and economic spheres. A disproportionate number of both the merchants and consumers to be found in London china shops of the early eighteenth century, after all, were women. Their active participation in this trade, like the aesthetic redemption of sensual materiality that fueled it, represented a powerful assertion of a disturbingly public role for women not just as followers but also as active purveyors of fashion and taste.[33]

To claim that early eighteenth-century women expressed various forms of aesthetic and commercial agency through their engagement with Chinese and Chinese-styled objects is to extend to the domain of material culture recent claims concerning the significance of women's public roles in the marketplace of print. As Ros Ballaster argues in her study of Behn, Manley, and Haywood, "the early woman writer was very far from the modest and amateur lady of letters most historians would have her be. She was rather a prostitute of the pen, trafficking in desire for profit and, in this respect, no different from many of her male contemporaries." Likewise, Paula McDowell's research on the London literary marketplace demonstrates that changing social conditions in late seventeenth- and early eighteenth-century England led to "unprecedented female political involvement through print."[34] Women's simultaneous embrace of the distinctive and novel stylistic sensibility found in chinoiserie might be understood as a comparably bold and consequential form of expression in the material domain.

This analogy between women writers and women consumers, which I develop at length in Chapter 3, also helps to complicate the opposition I have framed here between highbrow aesthetics and the Chinese taste. Anthony Pollock's argument that these same women writers precipitated a significant backlash within Whig public discourse is a useful reminder that early proto-feminist writing can be read not only as a reaction against established patriarchal norms, but also as a stimulus for their further elaboration and refinement in polite bourgeois culture.[35] Similarly, a contrarian aesthetic sensibility such as the Chinese taste might most usefully be understood in this context dialectically as both a challenge to the prescriptive doctrines of "cultivated" taste and as a notable contributor to the visual cacophony in the early eighteenth-century interior which precipitated the development of such doctrines in the first place.

The second aesthetic principle of the Chinese style, its thoroughgoing hybridity, evokes a corresponding social process of experimental self-fashioning. Eighteenth-century classicism, in its abstraction of universal truths from local particulars, embodies an ideology of stasis, timeless essence, and the uniformity of experience. Chinoiserie, in its promiscuous melding of incongruities, its irreverent disregard for authenticity, suggests cultural permutation, plurality, an aesthetic subject cut loose from naturalized hierarchies of taste and status. The eighteenth century is the first in which one can speak of a multiplicity of decorative tastes and styles. Chinoiserie embodies the newly found freedom to create eclectic, individualized living spaces and to imagine the subjects who inhabit them as capable of a degree of self-determination beyond the bounds of rigidly prescribed roles. The bastard pedigree embraced by the Chinese taste, the monstrous, unnatural offspring that it produced, could exercise such extraordinary and seemingly subversive appeal only in a context where the destiny assigned by family pedigree was increasingly subject to the flux of social mobility, and the traditional role of elite women in the reproduction of the social order was being undermined within the increasingly contested and anxiety-ridden field of gender identity. The consumers of chinoiserie were the aesthetic bricoleurs of the new commercial society, assembling new objects of taste and social sensibilities from fragments that had been cast adrift from their original meaning and purpose in a rapidly changing social universe.

The exoticism of the style, finally, contributed to the transformative potential of this aesthetic bricolage inasmuch as its reference to an alien artistic tradition provided an Archimedean vantage point from which to imagine alternatives to hegemonic standards of taste and propriety. China's cultural distance from the European origins of the aesthetic mainstream cast chinoiserie as a marginal aesthetic, but it thereby created a subject position for its adherents that in its very marginality gave voice to their disaffection with established models of aesthetic response and encouraged their efforts to locate and legitimize forms of pleasure and social experience that looked beyond the pale of both patrician humanism and bourgeois politeness. The consequences of this newly relativizing framework were felt, I would argue, well beyond the circle of those who embraced it. Through its prodigious exports of porcelain, lacquerware, silk wall coverings, and the artistic models they embodied, China undermined the status of classical Western civilization as the sole original forebear of English aesthetic culture. Arthur Lovejoy famously suggested that certain aspects of chinoiserie contributed to the romantic revolt against classicism in England.[36] Equally important, however, is the way in which the popularity of this alien aesthetic may have frayed the very conception of that rigidly patriarchal line of descent by which Augustan England imagined itself to have inherited the mantle of imperial Rome. Since Livy's time, the decline of that empire had been associated with the influx of effeminizing Asiatic luxury, and eighteenth-century satirists warned of a similar fate lying in store for an Albion overly enamored of its porcelain teapots. The followers of the chinoiserie aesthetic, in this view, seemed treacherously to beckon the barbarians at the gates. Yet from another perspective, they forced upon their contemporaries a grudging recognition of the inevitable promiscuity of taste and style, a heightened awareness of alternatives to classicist models of aesthetic pleasure, and a healthy skepticism towards the oft-repeated claims to a pure and certified Western lineage for the triumphs of English art. The mid- and late eighteenth century saw a dramatic and often chauvinistic consolidation of the idea of a national aesthetic culture in England. What now seems clear is that this consolidation was both stimulated by and bound finally to accommodate the new ways of seeing that accompanied an influx of seemingly trivial wares from halfway around the globe.

2 Cross-cultural aesthetics in William Chambers' Chinese garden

The most abundant harvest, within eighteenth-century studies, of recent developments in literary and cultural theory has occurred at the margins of the literary and historical disciplines as they have been traditionally constituted. Feminist scholarship has restored long-neglected women writers to a prominent place in the literary canon and foregrounded a series of historical and theoretical concerns – regarding, for example, sexuality, consumerism, and medicine – that have become mainstays of early modern cultural studies. The development of postcolonial criticism since the appearance of Said's *Orientalism* and the more recent and very promising emergence of what Felicity Nussbaum calls "critical global studies" have, meanwhile, generated renewed interest in the history of exchanges, crossings, and encounters in the century preceding Napoleon's conquests.[1] The formation of national identities and other features of modernity in the eighteenth century appears increasingly to have occurred through a process mediated in profound and complex ways by contacts with the foreign and engagement with broader global systems and networks. Within British literary studies, for example, interest in travel writing from the Grand Tour and beyond – Lady Mary Wortley Montagu in Turkey, Johnson and Boswell in Scotland, Mary Wollstonecraft in Sweden – along with renewed assessments of colonialist dynamics in India, Africa, and the Caribbean have brought geographical peripheries into the center of the historical stage, and prompted investigations of the role of foreignness even in works that evince little explicit interest in the foreign.[2]

If both feminism and postcolonialism, as theoretical paradigms, have contributed to the range and vitality of scholarship on the "new" and "global" eighteenth centuries, there remains a crucial distinction in the applicability of their methodologies and paradigms for work in this period. The central questions raised by feminist scholarship – questions about the cultural constitution of sexual identities, for example, and the social mechanisms of gender hierarchies – although configured differently in different contexts, are broadly applicable across geographical and historical boundaries. The questions central to postcolonial studies, in contrast, such as those involving the emergence of cultural identities in and between once-colonized territories and European states, by definition presuppose a historical context subsequent both to colonial occupation and, often, to certain epistemological foundations in Enlightenment thought. In part because the colonialist project itself has been seen as so central to the history of modernity, the significance of historical encounters that do not fit the contours of the colonialist paradigm have largely been obscured by dominant teleological narratives. We are well positioned now to scrutinize the preconditions of British hegemony in India in the second half of the eighteenth century or the hybridization of cultural forms on early Caribbean sugar plantations, but recent work has equipped us less well, I would argue, to take an equally full and nuanced accounting of profoundly important early modern instances of contact and exchange that were mediated less predominantly, if at all, by an underlying ethos of violence and coercion.

Analyses of Europe's non-colonialist encounters with distant peoples – those that recent cultural criticism, in other words, has tended to overlook – typically define their significance in terms of one of several distinct modes of cultural translation. The first mode consists of the construction of imaginary geographies: the emergence of sensualized images of the East, for example, in the wake of Antoine Galland's translation of *The Thousand and One Nights* (1704–17), or of the wise Eastern sage embodied in Montesquieu's *Lettres persanes* (1721) or Oliver Goldsmith's *Citizen of the World* (1762). The second mode is more distinctly mimetic, involving the straightforward imitation or adaptation of alien practices in Europe, such as we find in garden structures modeled after mosques and pagodas or in the British adoption of the Turkish practice of smallpox inoculation promoted by Mary Wortley Montagu. The third, and perhaps most frequently invoked category of cross-cultural translation, is that of less direct forms of influence, which are, of course, notoriously tempting to posit and difficult to prove. We might cite here debates over the degree of Chinese influence on the development of the economic theories of Quesnay and the physiocrats in France, or indeed on the emergence of the natural style of landscape gardening, arguably one of the most important aesthetic innovations in eighteenth-century England.[3]

Images, imitations, influences: these are the most familiar terms in which we are accustomed to thinking about cross-cultural perception and response outside the colonialist framework, and yet as paradigms for grappling with the translative component of encounter, I would argue, they often prove inadequate. Our attention is directed in each case primarily towards the cultural products of encounter, the "translation" of foreignness, as it were, as it appears in the target context. This translation may be compared and contrasted, on occasion, with its source, and discrepancies duly noted and accounted for, but even so, the emphasis remains with the product, rather than the underlying cultural process of translation. The work of cultural intermediaries, however, is never entirely disinterested, or fully removed from the two worlds they are attempting to bridge. Their representations of the foreign must always arise, first of all, from distinct subject positions whose historical and social particularities lend themselves to certain limited and limiting ways of seeing the world. But beyond this widely acknowledged phenomenon of epistemological lens warping, we should also take account of the very real psychological impact of the moment of encounter and its effects on the process of conceiving and representing the culturally alien. The act of "translation," even in the metaphorical sense in which I am using it here, always produces a degree of that "split consciousness" that Haun Saussy associates with specifically textual translation and the jarring juxtaposition of disparate semiotic systems it entails.[4] This cognitive dissonance may be experienced at the moment of encounter as surprise, self-alienation, perplexity, or – as suggested in the previous chapter – aesthetic delight, but it seems safe to assume that its effects color enduring memories of this seminal moment and leave their traces upon its subsequent representation.

In the previous chapter, I asked how we might understand, in general terms, the aesthetic appeal of Chinese exoticism in eighteenth-century England. I suggested that one component of this appeal was the mutual amplification of the effects of sensual pleasure and conceptual obscurity. In this chapter I pursue this suggestion further by asking how the cognitive dislocation implicit in any confrontation with radical otherness might both mediate and imprint subsequent textual artifacts of encounter. How does the elemental experience of foreignness itself, in other words, figure in the naturalization of the foreign? In this, as in the second paired chapter of each section of this book, I will explore this broader question through a case study of a single influential figure whose engagement with the Chinese taste exemplifies the ambivalence and complexity of the responses it evoked over the course of the eighteenth century.

William Chambers, the architect of Somerset House in London and the Royal Gardens at Kew, stands out as one of the most prominent and influential practitioners of cross-cultural translation in eighteenth-century England. He spent his formative years studying the architectural marvels of Rome and Paris, and has always been best known for his role, as the first academy-trained British architect, in transmitting the foundational design principles of neoclassicism to England. He left his mark not only in his many prominent commissions, but also in the hugely influential *Treatise on Civil Architecture* (1759), the first systematic textbook on the subject in the English language. Chambers' pre-eminence as an architect, however, and identification with the style of Roman antiquity has never obscured a secondary affiliation with the aesthetic culture of the Chinese. Prior to settling on an architectural vocation and undertaking his studies on the Continent, Chambers had journeyed twice to the port city of Canton, in 1743–4 and 1748–9, as an agent of the Swedish East India Company, returning with copious notes, drawings, and first-hand impressions of a country that Englishmen would not visit in large numbers for another hundred years. Though little is known about the details of these trips, apart from the fact that he visited temples and gardens in and around the city, his youthful travels clearly left an indelible mark on his subsequent career. His first publication on his return to England in the mid-1750s brought together a series of designs of Chinese buildings, furnishings, and costumes along with an essay "On the Art of Laying Out Gardens among the Chinese" (1757) which was widely reprinted and commented upon. The next several years gave him the opportunity to bring the ideas in his book to life at Kew Gardens, where a House of Confucius and glittering ten-story pagoda soon bore witness to his facility as a transmitter of the exotic design motifs much in fashion during the heyday of chinoiserie. His final gesture of cross-cultural translation in this vein came in 1772 and 1773 with a pair of extended treatises on oriental gardening that expanded on the principles elaborated in his earlier essay in the service of a polemical attack on the natural landscaping style promulgated with exasperating success by Chambers' rival, Capability Brown.[5]

The Chinese thread running conspicuously through the life and work of this co-founder of the Royal Academy and patriarch of the late eighteenth-century architectural establishment has proven a source of considerable perplexity for Chambers' biographers and critics over the past two hundred and fifty years. Rome and Canton have always seemed unlikely bedfellows as sources of inspiration for an eighteenth-century Man of Taste, and Chambers' own reputation as a man as sober and conservative in his personal bearing as in the academic style he championed has never sat easily with a seemingly whimsical interest in fashionable exotica, let alone the outrageous Gothicisms and quasi-pornographic fantasies of his *Dissertation on Oriental Gardening*. Horace Walpole's contrasting assessment of the manifestos Chambers produced in support of each of the two styles provides some indication of the striking dissonance between them. Of the *Treatise on Civil Architecture*, Walpole wrote that it was "the most sensible book and the most exempt from prejudice that ever was written in that science;" on reading the Chinese gardening book when it appeared in the spring of 1772, however, he found it "more extravagant than the worst Chinese paper," and later complained that it "tended to bring back all manner of bad and whimsical taste."[6] Chambers himself, in a chapter of his *Treatise* devoted to Corinthian columns, warned aspiring architects against the dangers of novelty and excess in ornamentation that this most decadent of orders seemed to invite. In a harsh condemnation of "crude momentary effusions of a vitiated fancy," he cautions against "deviating from the origin or reason of things . . . as it opens a wide door to whim and extravagance, and leaves a latitude to the composer, which often betrays, and hurries him into ridiculous absurdities."[7] How are we to reconcile the seemingly conflicting credos of the *Treatise* and the *Dissertation*, and to interpret Chambers' wholesale capitulation in the latter to that very aesthetic exuberance that he had, in other contexts, warned so vehemently against?

Chambers continually wavered in his expressions of commitment to the Chinese style, a fact which suggests that he was acutely aware of the problems posed by his divided aesthetic loyalties, but which also makes it difficult to assess the true nature and depth of his interest in Chinese models. This ambivalence first appears in the introduction to his *Designs of Chinese Buildings*. On the one hand, he seems genuinely to admire Chinese architects for their originality and for the "singularity, justness, simplicity, and beauty" of their creations, going so far as to note certain resemblances to structures of classical antiquity. Yet on the other hand, he feels compelled, at least in part, by concerns for his reputation to disclaim any intent "to promote a taste so much inferior to the antique," and ultimately dismisses the Chinese buildings whose designs fill his volume as mere curiosities and "toys in architecture."[8] This equivocation reflects, in part, a contemporary ambivalence in Britain towards the much-vaunted achievements of Chinese civilization, as well as a common reluctance to grant too much credit to a potential rival on the world stage. When Chinese ideas were incorporated into contemporary thought, as Yu Liu suggests in a recent book, their Eastern origin was often denied, ignored, or nativized through an "assimilation . . . into an iconoclastic rereading of classical European antiquity."[9] The Chinese, celebrated in countless Jesuit-inspired accounts for the justice and efficiency of their civil administration and the wisdom of their rationalist moral code, were increasingly, by mid-century, coming under fire for their alleged dishonesty in business dealings and for the worthlessness, at least by classical standards, of many of their aesthetic productions.[10] Chambers was stepping out on a limb, in this climate, in his defense of Chinese design, and it is not at all surprising that he felt obliged to temper his praise.

Figure 2 William Marlow (1740–1813). *View of the Wilderness at Kew*, pagoda designed in 1757 by William Chambers, 1763.

A similar tension between admiration and disavowal appears in the collection of plans and panoramas from Kew Gardens that Chambers published on completing his design work there. The centerpiece of the volume is a fold-out depiction of the Great Pagoda that, now as in the eighteenth century, towers over the garden in incontrovertibly oriental splendor, as shown in a contemporary painting by William Marlow (Figure 2). His lavish description of this plan and its three accompanying illustrations of the pagoda in various sections and stages suggests considerable pride in the accomplishment, and the textual reminder that an engraving of the Chinese original had first appeared in the *Designs* volume six years before seems intended to reaffirm his own authority in the realm of Chinese architecture. Oddly, however, the one other important Chinese building in the garden, the House of Confucius, warrants only a single illustration and a summary description. John Harris has demonstrated persuasively that Chambers originally designed this two-story octagonal structure as well, and yet Chambers himself disowns the creation, vaguely asserting that it was "built a good many years ago, I believe from the designs of Mr Goupy," a contemporary craftsman in the rococo style.[11]

Signs of pronounced ambivalence regarding his own indebtedness to the Chinese influence accompany even Chambers' boldest contribution to eighteenth-century chinoiserie, the *Dissertation on Oriental Gardening*. He was sufficiently proud of his production to ship off copies soon after its publication to a host of European notables, including the king of Sweden and Voltaire, and to boast in at least one letter that it had "met with a very favorable reception" in England, though this seems not actually to have been the case. At the same time, other letters introducing the work to his correspondents describe it as so much "*coglionerie*," or foolishness, and "a piece of nonsense," gestures of dismissal considerably harsher than conventions of authorial humility would normally require.[12] In the "Explanatory Discourse" that accompanied the second edition of the *Dissertation* in 1773 as a response to the criticisms the first edition had provoked, Chambers initially repudiates any Chinese inspiration behind his ideas, describing their oriental setting in the earlier work as a mere ruse, a failed attempt to "[clothe] truth in the garb of fashion, to secure it a patient hearing."[13] And yet the main body of the "Discourse," which is presented as the words of a Chinese sculptor recently resident in London, both reaffirms the controversial claim to the superiority of the Chinese style of gardening over the English and prominently asserts its authentic Chineseness by providing the full transliteration and lengthy prose translation of a poem on tea-drinking by the current Chinese emperor in a footnote that extends over the first four pages of the text.

The paradoxical disjuncture between Chambers' aesthetic affinities together with his endless equivocations concerning his own allegiance to the Chinese style have rendered the interpretation of his Chinese writings, and the *Dissertation on Oriental Gardening* in particular, a bewildering task, and a critical consensus has remained elusive. Certain readers, on confronting his descriptions of the horrid and enchanted scenes found in Chinese gardens, with their imported tigers, elephants, implements of torture and bolts of artificial lightning, have been inclined to dismiss his more extravagant recommendations as nonsensical absurdities, playful diversions, or proto-romantic flights of fantasy, while others have confessed to ambivalence in ascertaining the seriousness with which they are intended. At least one garden historian has demonstrated that Chambers' central ideas about gardening derive from earlier English sources, while others have shown, equally persuasively, that they are firmly rooted in Chinese theories of gardening as transmitted through William Temple, Joseph Addison, and Jean Denis Attiret. Some critics have seen the jealous attack on Capability Brown as the chief *raison d'être* for the work, while others have stressed the prophetic importance of its original contribution to the theory of landscape design. One of the few points of agreement is that Chambers' presentation of the

Dissertation as a work of cross-cultural translation considerably complicates its reading, in that the substance of his ideas on gardening is distorted beneath the "fashionable garb" of chinoiserie.[14]

But what if this fashionable garb itself, in all its confounding ambiguity, is the substance we are looking for? What if we were to evaluate the act of translation not simply as a variously motivated and more or less accurate means of transmitting a set of ideas across cultural boundaries, but also as an intimate process of engagement with foreignness that itself conditions the emergence of these ideas within their new context? How might we read the traces of the primal drama of encounter, in other words, within the naturalized, domesticated spectacle of exoticism? Chambers himself, no doubt, would have objected to such an approach to his work. The Chinese setting of the *Dissertation* was a necessary artifice, he protests, a mere vehicle to be separated from the substance it contained, a mask that, for want of perspicuity in the writer, careless readers have tended to mistake for the reality.[15] But Sir William, I would maintain, doth protest too much. We have seen how his considerable Chinese *oeuvre* is rent through with a dizzying ambivalence towards the Chinese taste that it riffs upon, even to the point of prompting a disingenuous disavowal of his own artistic progeny. He deeply admired the Chinese model, but simultaneously despised it – or perhaps more accurately despised his own admiration for it. This ambivalence, while making it impossible to take as definitive any one of his pronouncements on the subject, may provide in itself a point of departure for more adequately addressing the various conundrums posed by his work.

Chambers' architectural career, it is worth remembering, was entirely devoted to the task of cultural translation. Quite apart from his instrumental role as the only eighteenth-century European architect of any note to have visited China, his extensive travels and systematic studies in France and Italy positioned him as a crucial conduit for the foreign ideas that sustained architectural innovation in neoclassical Britain. Architectural historians acclaim his contribution, in both his writings and his designs, as that of a master borrower and synthesizer, rather than as a creative genius in his own right. For all the success enjoyed by his *Treatise*, its author made no claim to originality in the work. The role he saw for himself, rather, was that of a compiler and an adjudicator of taste, as he set out "to collect from the works of writings of others, or from his own observations, in all parts of Europe, famed for taste; such particulars, as seemed most interesting; or properest to give a just idea of so very useful, and truly noble an art."[16] It is worth noting that Chambers' early volume of Chinese designs with its accompanying essay on gardening was premised on a similar methodology, grounded in the fastidious observation and unbiased evaluation of foreign aesthetic models. This systematic procedure might justly be considered, then, as a habitual *modus operandi*, and the cornerstone of his essentially mimetic approach to the work of cultural translation.

To the extent that the *Dissertation* recycles the basic account of Chinese gardening Chambers had presented in the earlier essay, it remains in keeping with this approach. But the text is more obviously characterized by the extravagant polemics and hyperbolic exoticisms that have perplexed and beguiled generations of subsequent readers. A more nuanced understanding of the latent workings and myriad possibilities of imaginative engagement with the foreign is called for by passages like the following:

> Their summer scenes compose the richest and most studied parts of their Gardens. They abound with lakes, rivers, and water-works of every contrivance; and with vessels of every construction . . .
>
> In the center of these summer plantations, there is generally a large tract of ground set aside for more secret and voluptuous enjoyments; which is laid out in a great number of close walks, colonnades and passages, turned with many intricate windings, so as to confuse and lead the passenger astray . . . The whole is a wilderness of sweets, adorned with all sorts of fragrant and gaudy productions: gold and silver pheasants, pea-fowls, partridges, bantam hens, quails, and game of every kind, swarm in the woods; doves, nightingales, and a thousand melodious birds, perch upon the branches; deer, antelopes, spotted buffaloes, sheep, and Tartarean horses, frisk upon the plains.[17]

Such a passage recalls the three familiar modes of processing the spectacle of otherness outlined above. Chambers draws on both the clichéd eighteenth-century image of a richly sensual and eroticized East and the early modern image of China as a land of unmeasurable wealth that had spurred Columbus, Cabot, and Cartier on their respective voyages. He imitates the Chinese more directly in his carefully assembled menagerie of exotic species. The prominence of water in his fantasy garden, and of "close walks" and "intricate windings," suggests meanwhile a more generalized influence of Chinese gardening principles through some combination of his experience in China and previously published works that had brought Chinese gardening principles to the attention of readers in England.[18] The distinct aura of a traveler's tale, however, the Marco Polo-like wonder that suffuses the account, points to a mode of engagement with the foreign that transcends the analytic categories of imaginary projection, imitation, and influence. The *Dissertation* frequently reads, in fact, like an allegorical narrative of voyage and discovery, with its visitor described repeatedly as a "traveller" or "passenger" as he makes his way among the garden's seemingly endless labyrinthine passages. The magnificence of the vistas he encounters fully justifies the use of such terms: these are not backyard arrangements of rock gardens and goldfish ponds, but seemingly full-scale depictions of natural wonders that transport the reader/visitor into a compellingly "real" virtual world.

This allegorical component of the *Dissertation* seems particularly significant in light of Chambers' extended remarks on the benefits of travel in another context. Reflecting, no doubt, on the importance of his own youthful travels to his later professional success, he urges the aspiring architect who reads his *Treatise* to spend time on the road before presuming to set up practice at home. "An architect cannot aspire to superiority in the profession without having travelled . . . Travelling to an artist, is as the university to a man of letters, the last stage of a regular education." Although the purpose of this education in the artist's case is in part to cultivate his taste, sharpen his critical faculties, and fill notebooks with sketches for later study and imitation, there is a distinct romantic component as well to Chambers' pedagogical prescription. Not only does travel "[set] the reasoning faculties in motion" and "[open] the mind to a more liberal and extensive train of thinking," it also, crucially, "rouses the imagination; the sight of great, new, or uncommon objects, elevates the mind to sublime conception; enriches the fancy with numerous ideas."[19]

Read alongside Chambers' paean to the Grand Tour, the allegory of travel in the descriptive passages of the *Dissertation* begins to appear less an incidental literary motif and more a vivid dramatization of a deeply held credo and its nostalgic underpinnings in his own youthful experience. Indeed, a close analysis of the argument of the latter work reveals three fundamental claims that each bear the mark of Chambers' lived confrontation with Chinese otherness. Briefly, these claims concern the importance of proper training and genius in the landscape gardener, the role of contrast and variety in structuring a pleasurable garden experience, and the place of extraordinary scenes and artifices in achieving the desired psychological effect in the mind and imagination of the viewer. Each of these concerns, I will argue, is inscribed with the imaginative dislocation of encounter, suggesting that the dissonance and ambiguity that characterize Chambers'

Chinese work might be fruitfully reinterpreted from within a model attuned to the affective dimension of the process of cultural translation.

Chambers' depiction of the genius of Chinese gardeners in the *Dissertation* is directed at two polemical aims. The author intends, most conspicuously, to paint an unflattering contrast between the exalted abilities of landscape artists in China and those of their English counterparts, and especially of his nemesis Capability Brown. But he also hopes, more constructively, to elevate the status of the gardener's art in England to that which architecture – owing largely to his own exertions – now enjoyed. In the final version of the *Treatise* he would quote approvingly the bold claim of French architect Marc-Antoine Laugier that "there is perhaps as much genius, good sense, and taste requisite, to constitute a great architect, as to form a painter or poet of the first class."[20] The *Dissertation*, from its chiding opening lines, seems calculated to promote the art of ornamental gardening in much the same way:

> Amongst the Chinese, Gardening is held in much higher esteem, than it is in Europe; they rank a perfect work in that Art, with the great productions of the human understanding… Their Gardeners are not only Botanists, but also Painters and Philosophers, having a thorough knowledge of the human mind, and of the arts by which its strongest feelings are excited.[21]

The *Treatise*, to extend the comparison, defines the requisite genius of the architect as "a strong inclination and bias of mind towards the pursuit in question," that enables the artist "to comprehend, and to perform certain things, with much ease" and fills his imagination with "ideas, combinations and improvements, equally new, striking and agreeable." A corresponding passage in the *Dissertation* indicates that Chinese gardeners, likewise, express their genius through new and striking improvements:

> Poets and painters soar above the pitch of nature, when they would give energy to their compositions. The same privilege, therefore, should be allowed to Gardeners… [who], like poets, should give a loose to their imagination, and even fly beyond the bounds of truth, whenever it is necessary to elevate, to embellish, to enliven, or to add novelty to their subject.[22]

One senses, however, a marked difference in emphasis between these two passages. While the great architect is noted for his facility in innovation and the performance of his craft, the Chinese gardener seems to achieve an altogether more liberating imaginative transcendence that resonates tellingly with Chambers' account of the salutary and indeed sublime effects of travel on the impressionable mind. To soar beyond nature and fly beyond truth would seem, indeed, precisely the prerogative of an imagination roused from quotidian slumbers by the intrinsic sublimity of the foreign.

Chambers' conception of Chinese genius as transcending the realm of familiar orthodoxies refracts, in other words, his own recollected experience of alienation and radical unfamiliarity in China as a young man. The impression of striking novelty that often accompanies an encounter with the truly foreign, after all, bears close comparison with the effects of artistic genius. In Chambers' case, I am suggesting, the overwhelming impression of strangeness he must have received wandering the streets and gardens of Canton was ultimately transformed into a programmatic projection of imaginative virtuosity onto a favored class of Chinese artists. The disjunctive experience of the foreign sublime anchors his boldly original conception of Chinese aesthetic sensibility. As a cross-cultural translation, then, the *Dissertation* should be read not just as a more or less accurate rendering of "authentic" Chinese practice but also, crucially, as a narrative mapping of the subjective experience of Chinese difference. One might object that the sagacious oriental visitors familiar in French and English fiction since Montesquieu would have provided a more obvious source for Chambers' supercilious Chinese gardener. But my argument could easily be extended to these characters as well: the eighteenth-century archetype of the visiting Eastern sage was itself a product of the period's rapt fascination with the novelty of the cultures that Jesuit accounts and Arabian tales were rapidly bringing into view.

The genius of Chinese gardening expressed itself, for Chambers, through an aesthetic of contrast, variety, and surprise. While the modern English landscape park numbed the viewer with its monotonous repetition of formulaic conventions – the serpentine walks, clumps of trees, and vast expanses of lawn that were the hallmarks of Brown's style – the Chinese garden spurred the imagination with a splendid panoply of riveting scenes, calculated to lead the viewer through a succession of intense emotional catharses. The psychological premise of the experience lay in its very unpredictability: suspense, confusion, bewilderment, and awe were the necessary catalysts of the "strong sensations" and "uncommon degree of pleasure" it set out to achieve. The basic components of the aesthetic vision Chambers ascribed to Chinese gardeners had more obvious precedents not only in Burke's conception of the sublime but also in the English gardening theory of the previous half century, which itself, as Yu Liu demonstrates, often suggests an unacknowledged engagement with Chinese ideas on gardening. Alexander Pope had famously advocated a topography of "pleasing intricacies" in his *Epistle to Burlington* (1731):

Let not each beauty everywhere be spied,
Where half the skill is decently to hide.
He gains all points who pleasingly confounds,
Surprises, varies and conceals the bounds.

Thomas Whately, whose more recent *Observations on Modern Gardening* (1770) Chambers had carefully read and annotated, had likewise emphasized the importance of variety and contrast, and of the effects of "surprise and astonishment" produced by the "singularity" of a landscape scene.[23] John Dixon Hunt has shown that the theatricality of the garden setting, with its changing scenes, spectacles, and illusions, was an established trope of both Italian garden art and the countless pleasure gardens it inspired in early eighteenth-century England.[24]

The difference in Chambers lies in the centrality of the experience of geographical alterity in his conception of an aesthetic of novelty and surprise. Not only does he include distinctly "Chinese" elements in many of his scenes, he repeatedly stresses the usefulness of "transplanting the peculiarities of one country to another" in achieving the requisite variety of sensory impressions in gardens anywhere. The well-traveled gardener has no need of the vain extravagancies of topiary to realize the desired effect: "if the planter be a traveller, and a man of observation, he can want no such helps to variety, as he will recollect a thousand beautiful effects along the common roads of the countries through which he has passed, that may be introduced with much better success."[25] Chambers reinforces this identification of the aesthetic of novelty with the experience of foreignness in his treatment of the lavish scenes that distinguish the Chinese garden. While certain of these scenes he depicts as staged spectacles to be admired from a distance, at other moments his voice shifts from the mode of dramaturgy to that of travel writing, transforming the passive spectator into an intrepid explorer thoroughly immersed in a fantastic, all-consuming narrative of rapturous exoticism:

Sometimes the traveller, after having wandered in the dusk of the forest, finds himself on the edge of precipices, in the glare of day-light, with cataracts falling from the mountains around, and torrents raging in the depths beneath him; or at the foot of impending rocks, in gloomy vallies, overhung with woods, on the banks of dull moving rivers, whose shores are covered with sepulchral monuments, under the shade of willows, laurels, and other plants, sacred to Manchew, the genius

> of sorrow . . . [S]ometimes, in this romantic excursion, the passenger finds himself in extensive recesses, surrounded with arbors of jessamine, vine and roses, where beauteous Tartarean damsels, in loose transparent robes, that flutter in the air, present him with rich wines, mangostans, ananas, and fruits of Quangsi; crown him with garlands of flowers, and invite him to taste the sweets of retirement, on Persian carpets, and beds of camusathkin down.[26]

Chambers' fantasy transcends the illusionistic theatricality of the European pleasure garden to recreate the essential experience of unadulterated wonder in the traveler's encounter with the unknown. I use the term "wonder" here in Stephen Greenblatt's sense of "the decisive emotional and intellectual experience in the presence of radical difference." Greenblatt positions "intense wonder" as a central component of early European responses to the New World. By the early eighteenth century, the capacity of the Americas to evoke such a reaction may well have faded, but the Far East remained distant enough for Canton easily to have evoked for Chambers something of the same "startle reflex" that Greenblatt identifies in European culture in the century following Columbus' voyage.[27] While its celebration of an aesthetic of variety and novelty is indebted in its conceptual foundations to Addison, Pope, and others, the *Dissertation* infuses these terms with an unfamiliar power by aligning them incontrovertibly with a Chinese visual universe that served the early eighteenth century as the paradigmatic occasion of aesthetic éclat. For as well-traveled a man as William Chambers, the abstractions of aesthetic theory could not be separated from their epistemological origins in the psychology of the voyage.

The passage above points to a final crucial facet of the *Dissertation*'s argument: the implicit claim that a successful garden requires not only genius and variety, but also a pronounced excess or extravagance in its scenery. The seeming outrageousness of many of Chambers' prescriptions – the wolves, tigers, African giants, monstrous birds, impetuous cataracts, artificial lightning bolts, and dancing concubines in magnificently furnished seraglios – undermined the credibility of his scheme among his readers and occasioned a blistering satire by William Mason whose great success rendered Chambers something of a laughing stock, especially among his Whiggish adversaries. A number of critics, as mentioned earlier, have been inclined to dismiss the less plausible aspects of Chambers' account either as romantic flights of fancy or as so much unaccountable nonsense. The author himself gives support to such a reading in a letter to an unidentified correspondent who had objected to the "whimsical productions" in his plan:

> These little sportive Episodes are introduced, & are only to be considered as Episodes in a poem or Interludes in a Drama, which serve to relieve the fatigued mind, and prepare it for something of Greater Consequence. They are chiefly contrived to amuse the curious, the vulgar, or the childish.[28]

The defensive attitude is one we have seen before, and the precedents, I have argued, justify a certain skepticism on the reader's part. If the author had genuinely intended his whimsical interludes as comic relief for the vulgar and childish among his readers, surely he would have had the foresight to anticipate the bewildered reaction of the mature readership he hoped to impress with the seriousness of his underlying design. Chambers admits in the "Explanatory Discourse" to a "want of perspicuity" in writing the *Dissertation*, and indeed it would seem, on the whole, a less calculated enterprise than his polemical aims required.

To dismiss his "little sportive episodes" as a folly, however, is to overlook the distinct representational function of "nonsense" in Chambers' vision. Capability Brown's landscape gardens were characterized by their unassuming simplicity: a typical vista took in expanses of gently rolling turf punctuated only by strategically placed clusters of trees. In its embrace of "unadorned" nature, the Brownian revolution inaugurated a thoroughgoing shift from an emblematic to an expressive mode of representation in the English garden. The statues, grottoes, engraved obelisks, and other visual exhibits arranged strategically about the grounds at Stowe and Pope's Twickenham estate had offered up intricately coded meanings to those viewers with the necessary wit and erudition to read the elaborate iconography of their literary and historical allusions. The seemingly artless panoramas of the naturalistic garden, in contrast, required no studied examination to grasp, but rather seemed to speak immediately to the emotions, with all "the force of a metaphor," in Whately's words, "free from the detail of an allegory."[29] The Chinese garden, in Chambers' account, incorporates elements of both these modes. In addition to scattering ancient inscriptions, verses, and *memento mori* about their grounds, the Chinese layer their gardens with emblematic meanings by

> introducing statues, busts, bas-reliefs, and every production of the chisel . . . observing, that they are not only ornamental, but that by commemorating past events, and celebrated personages, they awaken the mind to pleasing contemplation, hurrying our reflections up into the remotest ages of antiquity.

At the same time, Chinese gardeners are attentive to the expressive quality of their plantings, surrounding rustic garden structures with wild scenery, for example, and complementing gay buildings with luxuriant foliage.[30]

But there is a third, rather more quixotic mode of representation in Chambers' Chinese garden, and one that subverts the underlying premise of the first two. Emblematic statues and expressive scenes both operate on the presumption of a degree of legibility, the presence of a definable and ultimately communicable idea or emotion that the creator sets out to convey and the viewer to absorb. And yet we find features in Chambers' garden that steadfastly resist and even parody this familiar economy of meaning and interpretation. The colossal dragons that lurk in certain dark passages cut in the rock, for example, "hold in their monstrous talons, mysterious, cabalistical sentences, inscribed on tables of brass; with preparations that yield a constant flame; serving at once to guide and to astonish the passenger."[31] The steady illumination and bold lettering hold out the promise of moral or spiritual guidance, only to snuff it out in the mocking obscurity of a forgotten, esoteric language. Certain pathways are designed, as we have seen, "so as to confuse and lead the passenger astray," while any number of compositions tend to evoke incertitude, anxiety, and a perpetual sense of mystery. Chambers extends the traditional garden motif of the labyrinth, in other words, into a dizzying phantasmagoria of perplexity and doubt, a "magnificent confusion" of conflicting impressions that cannot, finally, be resolved in the certainty of a single interpretive response.[32]

If the cabalistic writing and the air of mystery in the Chinese garden signal its resistance to interpretation, the sheer extravagance of Chambers' descriptions evokes the traveler's response to the radical illegibility of the foreign. The excess implied in all that is monstrous or fantastical points to a realm of experience that cannot be schematized, ordered, or contained, to the unassimilability of an object of interpretation within familiar structures of meaning. As Greenblatt suggests, the elusiveness and ambiguity of the experience of wonder in the face of the ineluctably alien derives precisely from the conceptual rift that marks its origin in the "cracking apart of conceptual understanding."[33] All that is wondrous and magical in Chambers' account may well be, as he rather peremptorily called it, "nonsense," and yet it is an emblematic non-sense in that it points precisely to that residue of translation that is beyond the reach of sense and that emerges into consciousness in the likeness of a dream. As he nears the end of the *Dissertation*, Chambers cautions that "European artists must not hope to rival [the] Oriental splendour" he has portrayed. His depictions, it turns out, may be less well-suited as models for imitation than as sources of inspiration, a reminder of the infinite possibilities entailed in the imagination's encounter with the unknown:

> To the generality of Europeans many of the foregoing descriptions may seem improbable; and the execution of what has been described, in some measure impracticable: but those who are better acquainted with the East, know that nothing is too great for Eastern magnificence to attempt; and there can be few impossibilities, where treasures are inexhaustible, where power is unlimited, and where munificence has no bounds.[34]

By way of justifying the extraordinary flights of imagination his hazy reminiscences of China had induced, Chambers extends the boundless wonder he has ascribed to the Chinese garden to the topos of the East as a whole, reverting, without a doubt, to a clichéd orientalist fantasy, but reaffirming, in the process, the evocative potentiality of the unintelligible sign.

Ironically, the most extravagant of all Chambers' recommendations turned out to be the most prescient in the subsequent history of garden design. Not content to confine his wild schemes within the limits of the country estate, he envisaged the transformation of the entire surrounding landscape in accordance with the principles he had set forth. "Any tract of land," he writes in the "Explanatory Discourse," "whose characteristick expressions have been strengthened by art, and in which the spontaneous arrangements of nature have been corrected, improved and adorned by the hand of taste, ought to be considered as a Garden." The possibilities for such improvement are far more than meet the untrained eye. Fields covered with corn, turnips, and beans, he suggests, if tastefully interspersed with country churches and cottages, require little modification to be more picturesque than a Brownian expanse of lawn "curiously dotted with clumps." The dismal sight of collieries, brick kilns, and glass works might be artfully blended with "gloomy plantations" to create a poignant landscape of desolation. Stone quarries might be transformed into amphitheaters, chalk pits into rustic arcades, and mines into grottoes, which features, with the addition of some planting, "might be converted into the most romantic scenery imaginable," and eventually "by these means the whole kingdom might soon become one magnificent vast Garden, bounded only by the sea."[35] If the achievement of the eighteenth century, according to a modern garden historian, was to bring the landscape into garden planning, the task facing the twentieth was, very much in accordance with Chambers' vision, to "bring the garden into the landscape."[36]

Although in Chambers' work this extension of his theories is less obviously a chinoiserie production than some of his more detailed descriptions, his utopian contribution to the evolution of landscape theory bears the distinct imprint of his aesthetic engagement with the Far East. If the Chinese garden, for Chambers, embodies the essence of his impressions of China in its genius, variety, and wondrous indecipherability, the dream of transforming the whole of England into a garden represents the transposition of an enthralling imaginative response to foreignness back to his more immediate surroundings. The dream is Chinese not in its specific content, in other words, but rather in the derivation of its aesthetic vision from a subjective confrontation with Chinese difference.

A reading of Chambers' work that remains attentive to the complex and conflicted affective dimensions of cross-cultural translation begins to resolve certain of the perplexities that an exclusive attention to its products has tended to foreground. The apparent dissonance within his own aesthetic sensibility fades from significance once we recognize that his simultaneous attraction to both Roman and Chinese models stemmed not just from their particular merits, but also from the rich and unfamiliar stimulation each provided, as an instance of foreignness, to his own imagination and critical faculties. His lifelong ambivalence towards the Chinese style appears less maddeningly equivocal once we distinguish his public judgments of particular examplars of the style from the invigorating source of private aesthetic insight and imaginative inspiration he found there. And finally, the unaccountable indulgence of whimsical fancy that colors the horticultural ruminations of a conservative Tory architect may appear somewhat less bewildering once we grasp the significance of wonder as an inevitable component of an earnest eighteenth-century European's contemplation of a largely unintelligible East. But the most far-reaching conclusion suggested by such a reading is that the experience of encounter, in the end, cannot be understood solely in terms either of power and mastery or of reciprocal influence and projected fantasies. The processes by which one culture finds meaning in another, rather, always entail adaptive strategies that are themselves potentially transformative. To read the artifacts of a moment of contact is to confront testimony to variously motivated acts of translation and response, but it is also to bear witness to the imaginative epiphany engendered by the recognition of difference.

PART II

What do women want?

3 Gendered utopias in transcultural context

In Addison's *Spectator* essay of April 12, 1711, the narrator describes his visit to a wealthy widow's library. Prominent among Leonora's literary collections are slightly scandalous narratives by the well-known and contemporary women writers Madame de Scudéry and Delarivier Manley, along with a variety of other works written for a largely female readership, including popular French romances, a midwifery guide, and women's conduct manuals. While the satire on the owner's literary taste is relatively gentle, it clearly foreshadows the dramatic repudiation of early French and British feminocentric fiction that would accompany the rise of the more respectable domestic novel in subsequent decades.[1] At the same time, it pointedly situates her taste as both occupying and corresponding to a distinct material context, consisting largely, as it happens, of Chinese porcelains. Alongside a row of finely bound folio volumes, the Spectator admires the "great Jars of China placed one above another in a very noble Piece of Architecture." The octavos share a cabinet with "Tea Dishes of all Shapes Colours and Sizes," while the plays and pamphlets are enclosed by "a thousand . . . odd Figures in China Ware."[2]

The essay's explicit association of imported Chinese objects with a female literary space, while striking, is not altogether surprising as a satirical motif. Twenty years earlier, Queen Mary had first inaugurated the fashion in London of decorating interior spaces with Chinese wares, filling every room in her apartments at Hampton Court with imported porcelain and lacquerware, and adorning doorframes, chimney pieces, cabinets, and tables with 154 pieces of porcelain in one gallery alone.[3] Well-heeled collectors like Lady Betty Germaine (1680–1769) and the Duchess of Portland (1714–85) followed suit, and for most of the eighteenth century, the use and display of these exotic objects would be closely associated with women's quarters in the homes of the elite.[4] While both men and women admired and purchased china, surviving household inventories make clear that chinawares in eighteenth-century country houses were concentrated in women's rooms, a conclusion corroborated by indications in contemporary design books that the china cabinets built to display these precious goods were intended primarily for women's bedrooms, dressing rooms, and closets.[5]

Addison's juxtaposition of romances with Chinese imports in Leonora's library may also reflect a perception that they shared common stylistic features, characterized from a contemporary perspective by an aesthetic of strangeness and curiosity and a pointed lack of verisimilitude. The eighteenth-century literary historian Clara Reeve described romance, for example, as "a wild, extravagant, fabulous story," while the iconography of Chinese goods was typically described as being "fantastic," "curious," "monstrous," or "grotesque."[6] Both Chinese visual art and French romance, in other words, served emerging schools of naturalistic representation in England as a foil, highlighting the rationality of new literary and artistic norms by contrast with their foreign others. This alleged cultural contrast was deployed by satirists, in turn, to demarcate increasingly divided gender spheres, so that the consumption of both romance and Chinese goods came to be widely associated in the eighteenth century with female extravagance and the morally suspect indulgence of a debased foreign taste. As Ros Ballaster's reading of Addison's Leonora episode suggests, "female reading is revealed to be nothing more than a form of conspicuous consumption, form without matter."[7]

But recognizing the congruity of Addison's description with contemporary tropes of misogynist satire does not preclude our accepting the approximate historical truth of his description. Upper-class English women are known, after all, to have been avid collectors of Chinese wares and to have displayed them prominently in their homes, and we can readily imagine that these vases, jars, and tea-wares might have often wound up in close physical proximity to the treasured books we know these elite consumers also purchased in large numbers. To what extent might each class of goods have created a resonant space for the consumption of the other, leading the delights of reading and viewing to be reciprocally enhanced? John Richetti encourages us, in his study of early eighteenth-century fiction, "to discard the customary pious gestures that 'literature' exacts and to treat fiction as a cultural artifact, a set of emotional and ideological stimuli, machines for producing pleasurable fantasies."[8] Laurie Langbauer ascribes a similarly functionalist role to romance fiction, in particular, when she describes how the genre has been used "to try to imagine some realm of freedom for women outside the constraints of male power."[9] If literature functions as a cultural artifact, a tool for the imagination, in short a fantasy machine, might not certain material artifacts also function as imaginative literature, transporting their readers through richly evoked spaces and situations that can be perceived only dimly, if at all, in the contextual world of lived experience?

Literary critics often take it upon themselves to reconstruct the particular fantasies that texts made available to readers of a given time and place. Academic devotees of the written word have traditionally been less adept, however, at taking a larger anthropological view of how texts and their material contexts might function together in the production of cultural meanings. What if we allowed the possibility that the Chinese wares that graced the shelves of a woman's library in the late seventeenth or early eighteenth century might have functioned as material correlatives to the books arrayed beside them? Having perhaps spent too much time in the company of Augustan wits and wags, scholars of the eighteenth century have long been accustomed to dismissing the phenomenally popular Chinese taste in the decorative arts as a mere fashionable exoticism, perhaps tinged, in our postcolonial age, with the romance of empire. Examined more closely alongside the feminocentric fictions, poetry, and essays that provided the immediate literary context of their consumption in England, however, some of the scenes depicted on the illustrated porcelains of the early Qing dynasty evoke an alluring imaginative space that is likely to have resonated in profound and unexpected ways with Leonora and her peers.

If the two preceding chapters were concerned in general terms with the aesthetic components of exoticism, the two chapters in this section take up my earlier observation that the appreciation of Chinese visual exoticism, in particular, was a strongly gendered one in much eighteenth-century discourse, in order to explore some of the intersections of women's desires and the Chinese taste that may have lent credence to this contemporary cliché.

How, then, might an English consumer steeped in the European visual tradition have responded to the striking and unfamiliar visual spectacle presented on imported Chinese artifacts? Art historians and curators who have posed such questions warn that the scantiness of direct evidence of their reception makes their "original meanings . . . very difficult – if not impossible – to unravel and retrieve," as those who purchased and admired Chinese goods rarely recorded their specific reasons for doing so.[10] We do, however, know enough about the visual and iconographic world these consumers inhabited to recognize those elements of contemporary Chinese design which would have seemed most immediately new and foreign to them. On a purely sensual level, Chinese porcelains would certainly have struck the first-time English viewer, accustomed to vessels of wood, pewter, silver, or coarse earthenware, as astonishingly smooth, bright, colorful, and translucent. From a more practical standpoint, their visual appeal would have been considerably heightened by the additional virtues – rare and remarkable in the world of contemporary European ceramics – of being heat resistant and easy to clean. The exquisite designs decorating the blue and white porcelains that dominated the import trade from the fall of the Ming dynasty (1644) onward would have evoked yet another layer of responses to the exotic scenes they represented. A visitor to a London china shop in 1700 would have been immediately struck, for example, by the strangely shaped rocks, unfamiliar flora, and supernatural creatures that often grace Chinese imported wares from this period. Indeed, the many English critics of the Chinese taste who sprang up over the subsequent decades regularly seized upon its fondness for "unnatural" and "monstrous" forms in attempting to demonstrate its inferiority to the dominant modes of representation in the recent European tradition.[11]

The visual and tactile qualities of Chinese porcelains and the curious nature of the designs that adorned them would have been immediately obvious in their novelty to even the most casual English observer. Once she began attending more closely to the iconography of human figures in many of these designs, however, she might well have noticed another remarkable divergence from familiar visual norms. As any visitor to the medieval and early modern European galleries of a major art museum can attest, the roles accorded to women in the best-known paintings of these periods are generally rather limited. In a disturbing proportion of these images, when a woman appears in the scene, she is either being groped, gawked at, seduced, or raped by a lascivious male or suckled by the son of god. If she has any clothes on at all, she is very likely suffering from a wardrobe malfunction that seems to signal her complicity in the gendered gaze by which she is defined. While there are notable exceptions to this pattern, as Lynda Nead and others have argued, her sexualized presence is so ubiquitous within the painterly canon as to have become a recognizable emblem of the Western art tradition as a whole. "More than any other subject," Nead writes, "the female nude connotes 'Art.'"[12]

On stepping over into the Chinese wing of the same museum, the first difference one notices is the remarkable absence of blood and carnage. All those gruesomely graphic renderings of martyrdoms, beheadings, crucifixions, and shootings-through with arrows to which we have become so thoroughly habituated are replaced by stylized images of tranquil, cross-legged Buddhas, poised in a timeless state of peaceful equanimity. But on turning to the adjacent cases of splendid Ming and Qing porcelain vases and jars, one becomes vividly aware of an equally striking difference in the gendering of visual space. Nudes, artful or otherwise, are nowhere to be seen.[13] In their place, one finds clusters of elegantly attired women, lolling about in small

Figure 3 Vase. China, Qing dynasty, Kangxi period (1662–1722). Porcelain painted in overglaze famille verte enamels and gilding.

groups in garden-like settings (Figure 3). They might be depicted burning incense and making music, or, as in this example, admiring paintings and playing board games. Inevitably, they seem to be at leisure, and appear, like the Buddhas across the gallery, tranquil and content. Their gracefully flowing robes conceal their forms, often giving them, to the jaded Western eye, a curiously asexual or even androgynous appearance, and effectively warding off a habitual male gaze reared on Botticelli, Titian, and Boucher.

But even the visual space these Chinese women inhabit seems strangely free of the importunities of men. Many characteristic designs include no male figures at all; when males do appear, they are typically either young boys or wizened old sages. While one occasionally finds discrete courtship scenes, the visual world of late Ming and early Qing Chinese porcelains would seem to be almost entirely free of those familiar emblems of impetuous, phallic masculinity that so dominate the Western iconographic tradition from St. George to Leda, Susanna, and the Sabine women. When viewed against the backdrop of the dominant European tradition, these Chinese designs conjure up a protected utopian space of female dignity, autonomy, intimate community, and pleasure that is relatively inaccessible within the imaginative confines of Western visual iconography.[14]

Within the Chinese tradition, in contrast, such images have a long and varied history. As far back as the sixth century, guides to the classification of paintings draw upon an elaborate terminology for describing various groupings of elite women depicted in scenes from the households of high officials. By the late Tang dynasty (618–907), the expression *shinühua*, or "paintings of women," had come into use to denote what was by then a well-established genre, and one that characterized the figural arts of the period from handscrolls and screen paintings to murals and tomb figurines.[15] The genre continued to flourish in subsequent dynasties, with representative masterpieces bearing such titles as *Ladies Playing Double Sixes*, *Morning Toilette in the Women's Quarters*, *Beauties on an Outing*, *Women Embroidering*, and *Ladies Enjoying the Cool Air*. Such paintings generally depict one or more small clusters of elegantly dressed women enjoying each others' company in conversation or the pursuit of refined leisure activities: painting, boating, arranging flowers, playing chess, making music, dancing, eating, embroidering, reading, or admiring spring blossoms.

These engaging scenes of play and repose typically include no men at all, let alone male lovers or voyeurs. They seem to delight, rather, in depictions of affection and intimacy between women, as two companions lie together on the grass to read a book (Figure 4), or as a maid positions a peony blossom in her mistress's hair.[16] The deep resonance of these motifs in China is suggested by their persistence well into the modern era, even as many other trappings of the now despised "feudal" society went the way of emperors, bound feet, and the classical written language. In the first half of the twentieth century, the creators of popular calendar posters and advertising cards in the commercial centers of Shanghai and Hong Kong adapted the established painterly repertoire of groupings of attractive young women to sell everything from cigarettes and cosmetics to batteries and bug spray – and to sell them much more successfully, it might be noted, than foreign advertisers who offered portraits of American presidents and scenes of Berlin, Rome, and Windsor Castle (Figure 5).[17]

During the previous period of dynastic transition in the mid-seventeenth century, resourceful artists in China had similarly adapted the *shinühua* motif to a new medium and reaped considerable commercial advantage in doing so. With the fall of the Ming, the imperial potters at Jingdezhen suddenly found themselves without a patron. They began to look to foreign markets and to the south of China, where they found a vibrant economy

Figure 4 Qiu Ying, *Spring Morning in the Han Palace* (detail). Scroll painting, late Ming dynasty.

and lively cultural scene increasingly dominated by wealthy merchants who, while lacking the exquisitely refined taste of some of their literati peers, sought to fill their homes with objects of luxury and elegance that would announce their hard-earned status.[18] Where the connoisseurs of the Ming court had preferred delicately balanced geometric forms on their blue and white porcelains, the *nouveaux riches* preferred figural imagery, and showed a special affinity for scenes they recognized from myth, stage dramas, and the woodblock prints that filled the popular illustrated plays and novels of the time.[19] The creators of these prints had, not surprisingly, long drawn on motifs from paintings and other media, including those of the *shinühua* tradition.[20] When red-bearded foreign traders began appearing in southern port cities in the 1680s offering Mexican silver for Chinese clay, they purchased vast quantities of porcelain plates, jars, and vases decorated in the new "transitional ware" style that was then in vogue; on finding that designs featuring human figures pleased their customers at home, they eagerly came back for more.[21] Given that the volume of the export trade reached two million pieces annually by 1721 and that decorative schemes remained predominantly Chinese in origin up to about 1730, it is no great surprise to find motifs of women in gardens with a genealogy dating back

Figure 5 Kwong Sang Hong advertising poster, *c.* 1920.

over 1500 years amply represented among the porcelain collections of British museums and country houses today.[22]

Visual artists are not, of course, ethnographers, and I do not mean to suggest that Chinese women during the imperial period typically lived anything like the "utopian" existence depicted in so many of these images. When real elite women did loll about in Chinese gardens prior to the twentieth century, many of them would have done their lolling on feet painfully bound since childhood to the size of a closed fist, and in the knowledge that the public world beyond those garden walls was largely beyond their reach. Resentment and jealousy surely contributed as much to the emotional landscape among the wives, concubines, and maidservants in the women's quarters as did affection and intimacy. While upper-class women were often well educated and could develop extensive networks of female acquaintances beyond the household, they enjoyed few of the opportunities pursued by their husbands and brothers for work, travel, or public service. While recent historical scholarship has done much to debunk the myth of women in "traditional" Chinese society being utterly passive victims of an unremittingly brutal patriarchy, we should surely regard depictions of women on seventeenth-century porcelains as being as highly idealized as they typically are in any decorative medium.[23]

But the historical facts of the matter would scarcely have detracted from the suggestive power of the fantasy that such images could potentially have made available to the female consumer in England. We know that significant quantities of porcelains and lacquerwares bearing these motifs found their way to the London marketplace in the decades after 1680, and we know that Chinese goods in general were prized in particular by upper-class English women. While there is no way to prove a direct causal connection, it seems likely that part of the multi-faceted appeal of these goods would have derived from their suggestion of bracingly new and liberating imaginative spaces of female community, a suggestion that might have enabled the visual conceptualization of possibilities for intimacy between women that had long been accessible only obliquely, if at all, through other cultural media.

Such a conjecture begins to appear decidedly more credible once we consider, with Addison, what sorts of books these elite English women were reading in their porcelain-bedecked libraries and bedrooms, and what kinds of imaginative possibilities they made available. Of the thirty-three titles in Addison's catalogue of Leonora's library, it is intriguing to note that three (by Juvenal, Sidney, and Manley) are excerpted at length in Terry Castle's recent anthology of lesbian literature, while a fourth (a romance by Scudéry) is mentioned as one of the many homoerotically inflected works inspired by the early modern rediscovery of Sappho.[24] But in positing a connection between the imaginative worlds conjured up by the books elite English women read and the porcelains they admired, I want to point to a related but considerably broader theme in women's writings of this period. In the hundred years from about 1660 to 1760, women (and some men) in England produced a remarkable number and variety of poems, plays, fictions, and essays quite explicitly concerned with articulating in various ways the contours of a utopian female space.

Two recognized topoi of women's writing from these years can be usefully brought together in mapping this phenomenon. The first is the frequently recurring theme of the female academy or utopian community developed in several plays by Margaret Cavendish (1662–8), Mary Astell's *Serious Proposal to the Ladies* (1694), and Sarah Scott's *Millennium Hall* (1762), among many other works. Fueled by some combination of frustration at limited opportunities for women's education, skepticism among many women regarding the desirability of marriage, and nostalgia for the institution of the nunnery in post-Reformation England, the idea of a protected space for female friendship, learning, and charity won the approbation of clergymen and prominent writers including Daniel Defoe and Mary Wortley Montagu, and presumably contributed to the eventual establishment of the first women's colleges in the mid-nineteenth century. Not surprisingly, the proposals varied in their seriousness and their specifics. Cavendish's "female academy" offered young women an education in witty speech and virtuous living. Astell's "Religious Retirement" promised spiritual and intellectual sustenance to elite women in a space safe from both the predations of men and "the scoffs that are thrown on superannuated Virgins." Scott's rural retreat catered to widows and spinsters committed to education, charity, and the arts. But all of them offered the radical vision of a nurturing community set aside for women as an alternative to marriage or isolated spinsterhood.[25]

The second component of this broader trend of what we might term feminocentric utopianism is the substantial body of female friendship poetry that first flourished in the late seventeenth century and is most closely associated with Katherine Philips – described by one critic as the "founding mother of female love poetry" – and several of her followers, including Lady Mary Chudleigh, Jane Barker, and Anne Finch.[26] This poetry, aptly characterized as "a Sapphic reworking of the Petrarchan tradition," draws upon established conventions of courtly love to explore and to celebrate the experience of intimate and even passionate friendship between women.[27] While generally not explicitly sexual, it often has a veiled erotic subtext, playfully hinting at possibilities that chaste decorum cannot name.[28] As several critics have argued, the classical tradition celebrating friendships between men pointedly denied the possibility of comparably deep and durable bonds between women, leading Philips and her followers to channel the intensity of their affection through elaborate metaphysical conceits and parodic manipulations of the imagery of traditional love poetry.[29] Occasional works are more explicit: Aphra Behn's hermaphroditic fantasy "To the Fair Clarinda, Who Made Love to Me, Imagined More than Woman" (1688) is one of the few poems "in which a woman writer openly depicts female-female desire," but even here, as Elizabeth Wahl demonstrates, sensual pleasures are rendered through a euphemistic rhetoric of teasing ambiguity and erotic confusion.[30] What began in the seventeenth century as a somewhat rarified poetic genre dominated by upper-class women of leisure grew into an increasingly conventional and middle-class cult of romantic friendship in the eighteenth, providing a language both for working through the psychology of women's mutual attachments in fiction and for understanding the behavior of real women, like the famed Ladies of Llangollen, who chose to live together rather than in the company of men.[31]

The reasons for the flowering of these two closely related forms of feminocentric writing during this period are no doubt complex and overdetermined. The misogyny of so much Restoration print culture, from comedies celebrating intricate schemes of male predation to popular ballads delighting in fantasies of rape, no doubt contributed to an interest among women in actively critiquing and seeking alternatives to heteronormative arrangements.[32] Although homosocial friendship and marriage were not mutually exclusive options, rising interest in the literary ideal of female intimacy corresponded to an increasingly critical attitude towards the institution of marriage. That Mary Astell's deeply pessimistic writings on marriage were sufficiently popular to go through several editions during her lifetime suggests that her ideas resonated deeply among women. Astell herself, along with many of the other outstanding women writers of the period – Jane Barker, Celia Fiennes, Anne Killigrew – remained unmarried throughout her life, and indeed historians have noted a marked decline in the marriage rate among daughters of the landed gentry in the late seventeenth and early eighteenth centuries, along with a badly skewed sex ratio in late seventeenth-century London. Bridget Hill connects rising rates of spinsterhood, in turn, with growing interest in cloistered female communities, while Emma Donoghue points to strong contemporary associations between spinsterhood and ideals of female romantic friendship.[33] On the literary front, the rediscovery and translation of Ovid, Juvenal, and Sappho clearly encouraged the imaginative exploration of heterodox sexualities – Katherine Philips was known to her seventeenth-century contemporaries as "the New Sappho" – while a pronounced medical interest in tribadism provided a language for understanding sexual activity between women.[34] At the same time, the renewed embrace of conventions of courtly love and the pastoral among royalist poets after the civil wars provided a fresh source of inspiration and legitimacy for the celebration of female friendship in poetry.[35]

And yet in considering the striking confluence of feminocentric themes and motifs in England at this historical moment, I find the questions of historical causality that it naturally raises less compelling than the patterns of synchronic resonance or convergence it illuminates among contiguous cultural forms. I have no interest in arguing, in other words, that viewing Chinese depictions of utopian female spaces "caused" or even "inspired" English women to write on this theme, or, for that matter, that the feminocentric writings in the bookcase enhanced their appreciation of the Chinese wares on the mantelpiece, though there might well be some truth to both assertions. Rather, I prefer to think of these texts and these objects as resonating with each other, like the entwined lines of a heroic couplet, in a reciprocal relationship of mutual reinforcement and legitimation. The utopian ideals and social and sexual possibilities evoked by both sets of artifacts within the context of Restoration society were potentially subversive ones, teetering always on the edge of the unthinkable. Chinese painters' images and English women's words played off one another in this politically and sexually charged liminal space, amplifying imaginative visions across representational vectors as they catalyzed for their consumers new possibilities of self-awareness and fulfillment.

These seemingly disparate cultural forms resonated along three distinct axes of their respective mappings of utopian space: topography, gender, and imaginative displacement. Each of these vantage points reveals strong systematic analogies between Chinese designs and the categories of English women's writing I am concerned with here. These analogies can help to explain why these artifacts were commonly thought together – by Addison, for example – and how they might also have worked together in fostering new conceptions of intimacy and community. But they also raise the intriguing possibility of broader, transcultural convergences. From one perspective, whether the rather remarkable confluence of thematic concerns in China and England identified here is purely coincidental, or – as I think more likely – reflects loosely comparable social, economic, and literary developments in England and the more prosperous regions of China, is to a large degree irrelevant: whatever cultural work Chinese porcelains performed in early modern England was to a large degree independent of the original meanings and associations they bore in the context of their production. From another perspective, however, and one more sensitive to the uses of what Andre Gunder Frank terms "horizontally integrative macrohistory," the appearance of significant parallels and congruencies across disparate contexts opens up the possibility of resituating each particular context within a generalizable

Figure 6 Qiu Ying, *Early Spring in a Palace Garden* (detail). Scroll painting, late Ming dynasty.

scheme, and recalibrating the search for certain kinds of historical pattern and process from the local and contingent to the trans-regional and global.[36] In the case under consideration here, it invites the contemplation of an imagined community of women that transcends the merely national and generates meanings that exceed the limits of any single isolated context.

The first axis of analogy is topographical. Women who appear in the visual arts of late Ming and early Qing China are, with few exceptions, depicted outdoors in garden-like settings featuring open pavilions, decorative stones, tropical plants, gnarled pines, and blossoming trees. The relaxed bearing and leisurely deportment of the obviously privileged women in these scenes suggest that their gardens are enclosed, protected, and cultivated spaces, far removed from the perils of the wilderness or the toils of the farm. The characteristically strange and contorted shapes of the ubiquitous scholar's stones hint at the wildness of nature, but their modest scale and containment suggest a safely aestheticized and domesticated wildness (Figure 6). In fact, the gardens of wealthy families in late imperial China were typically enclosed within the walled compound of the household, serving their owners at once as productive asset, status symbol, aesthetic object, quiet sanctuary, and emblem of the traditional ideal of a rural retreat from the corruptions and disappointments of a political career.[37] Countless poems and paintings dating back to at least the Tang dynasty celebrate the joys of friendship, wine, painting, and quiet contemplation among the rugged peaks and twisted pines of such a scholar's paradise, providing a rich repertoire of potential allusions for the garden visitor.

The traditional Daoist ideal of the rural mountain retreat is considerably contracted in the private urban garden, and elite women replace hermit scholars in *shinühua* porcelain designs, but these depictions preserve the ambience of a protected sanctuary at a safe remove from the dissonance of daily life. While the Daoist philosophers Laozi and Zhuangzi claimed few followers in late seventeenth-century England, the hedonist philosopher Epicurus claimed scores, and striking visual images of such a sanctuary might have resonated strongly, in their imaginations, with the innumerable poems of rural retreat and retirement they produced. Epicurus had famously "scorned the world from within the confines of his garden"; in the tumultuous years following the civil wars and the inglorious execution of their king, legions of poets of a royalist cast found a great deal in the world to scorn.[38] Striking a pose of stoic withdrawal from the world, they sought happiness instead in an idealized vision of perfect friendship enjoyed among the bucolic scenes of a serene and peaceful country life, a vision which achieved extraordinary popularity as an imaginative haven from the revolutionary currents of political and religious enthusiasm of the times.[39]

China was strongly associated with political stability and religious moderation in Jesuit missionary accounts of this period, and readers of either sex on the losing side of England's civil wars might well have taken comfort, in gazing upon a porcelain jar, in the ideals of civility and continuity this ancient and august society was taken to represent. But for royalist women like Cavendish, Philips, Astell, and Behn and their female readers, the peaceful garden scenes depicted on so many Chinese objects might well have evoked the fantasy of a retreat not only from the violence of political society but also, more pointedly, from the "crosses and sorrows" associated with the society of men.[40] The utopian communities that were a staple of women's writing in the seventeenth and eighteenth centuries often feature enclosed gardens that provide a protected sanctuary for women from patriarchal impositions. The self-sufficient "convent of pleasure" imagined by Margaret Cavendish in her play by that name, for example, "has so much compass of ground within [its] walls, as there is . . . room and place enough for Gardens, Orchards, Walks, Groves, Bowers, Arbours, Ponds, Fountains, Springs and the like."[41] Astell describes the gardens of her "religious retirement" as "such a Paradise as your Mother Eve forefeited," a Miltonic allusion that serves, according to David Macey, both to "naturalize her same-sex community" and "to construct an alternative mythology to justify women's withdrawal from the world of heterosexual social relations."[42] A decade after leaving her disastrous marriage and retiring with a lady friend to a country estate near Bath, Sarah Scott penned a utopian fiction that brought to its fullest flowering this pastoral conceit. Significantly, it is the beauty of the grounds that captivates the narrator as she first approaches Millennium Hall: she delights in the "the profusion of flowers which ornamented every field," "the fragrance wafted from the woodbines" encircling an avenue of oaks, and "the remarkable verdure and neatness of the fields." Handsome cattle graze in some of these fields, but are prevented from feasting on the woodbines and jessamine by thorny barriers of roses and sweet-briars that pointedly evoke the protective walls of the cloistered community that lies just beyond.[43]

Female friendship poetry likewise appropriates the classical ideal of a rural retirement from the rigidly heteronormative spaces of the city, and is, if anything, even more thoroughly entwined with elaborate pastoral motifs. Anne Killigrew's fantasy of same-sex bonding in "On a Picture Painted by Herself" is set in "lofty woods . . . hills and dales," while "the soft and gentle motions of Eudora" are compared in the eponymous poem to "the calmer growth of flowers [and] the ascending or the falling dew."[44] Jane Barker's elegy to her "Dear Friend and Play-fellow, Mrs. E. D." recalls the shared bliss of a summer garden:

When weary, we our selves supinely laid
On Beds of Vi'lets under some cool shade,
Where th' *Sun* in vain strove to dart through his *Rays*;
Whilst *Birds* around us chanted forth their *Lays*.

The thick canopy of leaves sheltering the pair of friends serves the same metaphorically protective function as the thorny hedges in the gardens of Millennium Hall, marking off the garden topos as an inviolable sanctuary for women's affections for one another.[45] Aphra Behn plays with delicious ambiguity on this trope in "To the Fair Clorinda," in which the narrator toys with the hermaphroditic allure of a lover whom she addresses in turn as "Fair lovely maid" and "Lovely Charming Youth," and whom she thanks for offering the possibility of innocent, crime-free sensual love while recalling that the appearance of innocence in a garden may be deceptive:

For who, that gathers fairest Flowers believes
A Snake lies hid beneath the Fragrant leaves.[46]

The topos of the garden in these writings evokes at once the paradise of Eden and the temporary suspension of the social order associated with nature in Ovid.[47] At the same time, it might have also resonated, in the imaginations of English women who gazed daily at their Chinese porcelains, with a vivid image of a strangely alluring garden retreat on the far side of the globe.

The second aspect of these idyllic enclaves I wish to consider is their explicit gendering in both Chinese visual and English textual media as exclusively female spaces. As we have already seen, the human figures that adorn many of the imported Chinese porcelains of our period are women, depicted either alone or in groups. They are sometimes accompanied by a gaggle of young boys, and an old man will occasionally appear in the scene, but from a European iconographic standpoint, the nearly total absence of virile young men from these gardens of sensual delight is remarkable. On one level the explanation for their absence is straightforward: the figures in these scenes represented wives, concubines, and maids in a domestic context that would have permitted little contact with men from outside of the household. Contemporary missionary accounts would have made such a reading available to English consumers of these images: the Jesuits vaunted the perfect modesty and virtue of Chinese women, associating it with the strict prohibitions on communication with men outside their household and the supposed absence of prostitution in Chinese society.[48]

Viewed from a perspective emphasizing female confinement and restraint, a Chinese depiction of an exclusively female world might well, in its suggestions of the dreaded convent, have horrified Behn's Hellena, Wycherley's Alithea, Haywood's Fantomina, or any of the other lusty heroines that populate the more familiar literature of the Restoration and early eighteenth century. The more emphatically feminocentric writings we have been considering here, however, suggest a strong reaction against the libertine sexual mores and the rakish celebrations of rape and whoremongering that color so many poems, plays, and even popular ballads of the period. The persistent literary counter-ideals of female friendship and the female retreat in the utopian visions and homoerotic avowals considered above can also plausibly be read, I am suggesting, as an imagined alternative to a rabidly patriarchal culture. Within such a culture, these ideals function not only as an affirmation of bonds between women, but also as a negation of male-dominated economies of sexuality and power. Given the ready availability, in the same domestic spaces in which the works of Cavendish, Philips, Behn, Astell, and others were read and perhaps even composed, of appealing visual representations of conspicuously female-only spaces, it seems most unlikely that women's responses to the porcelains on their mantelpieces and the books on their shelves did not inform and play off one another in this respect.

On a second, deeper level, however, the explanation for the absence of men in so many of these Chinese images may be considerably more complex. The ubiquitous leisured-women-in-the-garden motif might well reflect, to a certain degree, the very real experience of vibrant communities of women who actually succeeded in creating fulfilling bonds of friendship and poetry within and across Chinese garden walls. As Dorothy Ko argues in her pathbreaking study, *Teachers of the Inner Chambers*, the persistent and simplistic association of women in traditional China with "backwardness and dependency" obscures the historical richness of women's culture even as it reifies the nationalist historiography of the May Fourth movement and the Chinese Communist Party.[49] Ko complicates this picture by exploring the various forms of domestic, social, and public female communities that thrived in seventeenth-century Jiangnan (the prosperous region of present-day Shanghai) by deploying highly developed literacy in the "extension of an intimacy between women" based on "expressions of the emotional and intellectual concerns of their members *as women*."[50] The women of the Banana Garden in late seventeenth-century Hangzhou, for example, gained considerable fame for regular gatherings in their villas dedicated to drink, poetry, and painting. The wife of a government official in Suzhou composed and published admiring poems for the attractive local courtesans and singing girls with whom she regularly socialized. The centrality of literary pursuits to such groups is vividly illustrated by the description of a household's reception of a popular play left by a gentry wife in the early Qing dynasty:

> Ladies in the boudoir all collect the latest embroidery patterns and keep them pressed between the leaves of a book. In between cutting patterns, all our eyes are fixed onto the pages of *The Peony Pavilion*. . . . Once we read *The Peony Pavilion*, all of us are lured into the ocean of Classics and histories and are absorbed in poems and songs.[51]

At least some of these readings may have valorized women's affection for one another. A play called *Lian Xiangban* (*The Love of the Perfumed Partner*), by the prominent seventeenth-century writer Li Yu, centers on the impassioned attachment between two women who not only fall in love but contrive, in the end, to live together happily ever after. A short story in the famous collection *Liaozhai Zhiyi* (*Strange Stories from the Willow Cottage*) by Li Yu's contemporary Pu Songling tells the moving story of two beauties who become infatuated with each other and enjoy four months of love-making before their discovery and its tragic aftermath.[52] As in Restoration England, elite women in late seventeenth-century Jiangnan sought out the company of other talented women. As in England, they dedicated poetry to each other and saw the publication of their work during their own lifetimes. As in England, they explored a full range of intimacies on the friendship–love continuum, from the platonic and intellectual to the erotic and sensual.[53] In China as in England, in other words, women imagined, read about, created, and drew sustenance from exclusively female communities that prospered within or alongside traditional patriarchal structures.

Such parallels are as provocative as they are unexpected. Expanding networks of cultural and commercial exchange between China and Europe notwithstanding, there is no question of mutual awareness between the Banana Garden women of Hangzhou and the likes of Philips and Astell, let alone reciprocal influence. It may be that women's culture flourished in some similar ways in both locales at this time as a result of the comparable economic and social effects in England and China of the massive influx of Mexican and Bolivian silver in global trade networks beginning in the sixteenth century. To the (still considerable) extent that the study of English literary and cultural history retains vestiges of the exceptionalism that marked its disciplinary origins in the nineteenth century, an awareness of closely commensurable developments at the other end of the Eurasian continent may be helpful in dislodging assumptions about the uniqueness of England's trajectory and recognizing certain allegedly distinctive components of European modernity as in fact belonging to more broadly generalizable historical patterns. For our immediate purposes, however, the significance of such parallels might best be understood as a form of dramatic irony: they lend a depth and poignancy to the experience of a local spectacle that might well not have been available to the actors themselves. The resonance between textual and visual motifs that I am positing can be understood in its weak form as the merely arbitrary and contingent product of an entirely accidental alignment of entirely unrelated objects in a particular time and place. In its stronger form, enhanced by an awareness of historical convergences, the notion of resonance implies a historically grounded conduit of affective affinity, a palpable flow of meanings between worlds that enhances the concrete forms they assume at either pole.[54]

The thematic parallels of topography and gender delineated above point to resemblances in the representational content of seemingly disparate media. I turn now to consider modes of representation, which I suggest provide a third axis for mapping the analogy between Chinese porcelains and English feminocentric texts in the late seventeenth and early eighteenth centuries. Both media, I have argued, evoke a topos of female sociability. But while typically associated with a distinct setting – that of the enclosed garden – this utopian female space is also, quite pointedly, "not there." As an idealized, dream-like space, it is endlessly deferred from the here and now. This imaginative displacement of the promise of the garden may function as a form of nostalgia, preserving the sanctity of a cherished longing (for the intimacy of maternal affection, for example, or of love among social equals) from the dangers and disappointments of the everyday. Or it may open up a new and vital space of projection for the exploration of possibilities that exceed the representational constraints of a particular time and place. In either case, we can approach the "meaning" of the women's garden motif as usefully from the vantage point of its social function as of its semiotic reference.[55]

Recent scholarship by Terry Castle, Valerie Traub, and many others convincingly demonstrates that themes of intimacy and eroticism between women proliferate widely in the English (and French) literature of the early modern period. At the same time, there remained constraints on what could comfortably be imagined or expressed. Resilient taboos on explicit or public deviations from heteronormativity forced the regular displacement of potentially subversive imaginings and longings into less threatening channels, so that, as Kathryn King argues, "woman's desire for woman could appear only in oblique, ambiguous, and fragmentary forms."[56] Poetic ambiguity, as we have seen, provided one effective device for defusing intimations of sexual transgression while also potentially heightening, through the very experience of uncertainty, the reader's pleasure in a poem. Theatrical plot lines that resolved homoerotic attractions between women within a conventional heterosexual frame quarantined illicit desires within the doubly sealed space of a play within a play.[57] Fantasies of the exotic provided a third safe outlet for the sapphically inclined imagination. According to Valerie Traub, early modern English accounts of tribadism consistently inoculated themselves against charges of complicity by projecting the practice into the categories of the monstrous or the exotic: "travel accounts compose an exoticized body which often, though not inevitably, reveals the antithesis of (Western) normativity . . . Female homoeroticism is located somewhere *else*."[58] Imagining that Ottoman or Chinese ladies indulged in such practices provided a viable space for countenancing them without compromising the purity of English virtue.

Writers from across Europe provided ample opportunities for such imaginings. Visitors to Turkey from Robert Withers in the sixteenth century to Mary Wortley Montagu in the eighteenth delight in speculating on the pleasures indulged among the women of the harem. An English midwifery guide from 1671 asserts that the abnormally enlarged clitoris and its use in lesbian love-making is a frequent phenomenon "in the *Indies*, and *Egypt*."[59] A contemporary dialog by the French pornographer Nicolas Chorier ventures that among the women of Italy, Spain, and Asia, a leather dildo "is regarded as their most precious bit of paraphernalia." The anonymous author of *The Sappho-an* (*c.* 1735) ascribes its invention specifically to the women of China, to whom it afforded "new mirth" after tea.[60] While these projections of the sexually illicit onto the geographically foreign, like other literary tropes of displacement, reflected powerful constraints on acceptable configurations of female sexuality, at the same time, every instance of the imaginative recognition of alternatives, whether enabled through devices of poetic ambiguity, theatrical cross-dressing, or pornographic exoticism, contributed to their cultural currency and their availability to everyday thought, language, and experience.

It is difficult to imagine a more effective material catalyst for this process of meaning-making than the imported arts of late imperial China. As we have seen, one of the most immediately obvious features of the visual space they represent is a dreamy otherworldliness. Its serpentine dragons and contorted rock formations and suggestively homosocial scenes signal a representational register sufficiently alien and fantastical to be enjoyed with perfect complacency. The very neglect of naturalist conventions so deplored by English critics effected a displacement of forbidden forms of desire into a space of exoticism and fantasy that, like early modern literary allusions to same-sex attraction, provided the necessary condition of their conceivability. Nor is this effect in the Chinese case merely a product of uninformed misreading by English consumers: much of the literature and visual art of the late Ming dynasty is in fact characterized by a pronounced tone of ambiguity and fantasy and a notably fuzzy demarcation of the real and the unreal.[61] The fact that porcelain objects are themselves famously fragile – there is no end to the images of shattered and shattering china in eighteenth-century plays, poems, and prints – only heightens the sense of the medium as a transient and ephemeral one, a material substance with the seeming evanescence of a dream. In this respect, porcelain emblematizes the cultural status of the decorative arts generally in this period: namely, that they are merely ornamental fashion accessories, unworthy of any serious consideration or regard. To what extent, we are left to wonder, did the very insignificance and hence invisibility of porcelain as a cultural form enable its subversive possibilities, rendering its depictions of female community more potent by virtue of being hidden in plain sight?

4 William Hogarth and the gendering of Chinese exoticism

Once the exclusive domain of collectors and connoisseurs, the elaborate furnishings that adorned the homes of the eighteenth-century English elite have begun to interest scholars intrigued by the rich and varied contexts of their production and consumption. This period has proven especially fertile ground for a cultural history of domestic objects in part because of the unprecedented proliferation of such objects brought about by expanding consumer markets and the ever-increasing allure of novelty and fashion across all social strata. But these card tables and writing desks, candelabras and cellarets also acquired layers of meaning – and hence interest for cultural historians – from the ideas and debates that circulated alongside them.[1] As suggested in the first chapter, two of the most important of these discursive contexts were a fascination with the foreign and the exotic on the one hand, and with philosophical questions regarding the nature of taste and beauty on the other. The emergence of the Chinese taste in furnishings within the space of these intersecting concerns stamped Chinese objects with a set of profoundly gendered meanings that have persisted, in some degree, to this day.

In the previous chapter, I posited a productive resonance between the imported *shinühua* porcelains of the early Qing dynasty and the feminocentric writings that flourished in England in the late seventeenth and early eighteeenth centuries. The tensions, I suggested, between discourses of heteronormativity and female intimacy in England created a charged space within which Chinese iconography could function as a catalyst for the homosocial imagination. But this tension conditioned the reception of Chinese objects in less visually explicit ways as well. In this chapter I turn from a reading of Chinese images to consider the relation of female desire to the gendering of the Chinese taste in the works of one of the most prominent artists and aesthetic theorists of the eighteenth century, William Hogarth.

Commonplace conceptions of artistic beauty most clearly betray their eighteenth-century origins in their emphatic insistence on disinterestedness as a precondition of aesthetic enjoyment. Theorists from Shaftesbury to Kant argued that a pure experience of the beautiful required a state of transcendent aloofness from the yearnings of the flesh and the pull of ideological attachments.[2] Aesthetic experience is meant to be a chaste, strictly non-partisan affair; the depth of pleasure it can afford is owing precisely to the freedom it offers from the merely contingent and material. The fact that, for so many modern viewers, erotic art always teeters precariously on the edge of pornography and that patriotic art hovers dangerously close to propagandistic kitsch suggests the lasting power of this conception. We are skeptical of the aesthetic value of images suggestive of overt sexuality or national pride because the primal and hence ostensibly vulgar and unrefined desires and attachments conjured up by such images would seem to preclude the disinterested experience of the formal qualities of the work.

The line from Shaftesbury to Kant, however, is not without its serpentine twists and detours. Edmund Burke struggles mightily, in his *Philosophical Enquiry into the Origin of Our Ideas of the Sublime and Beautiful*, to sustain a clear distinction between a pure aesthetic love for beauty and a patently corporeal lust for the attractive women in whom he seemed personally to find beauty most frequently incarnate. One reason, however, that we hear so much less about his account of the beautiful in the *Enquiry* than about his theory of the sublime is that, like Pygmalion, he is embarrassingly unsuccessful at sustaining this distinction. Whereas Kant has the good sense to limit his examples of beauty to such unproblematic objects as flowers and arabesque designs, Burke compromises his credibility as an impartial arbiter of aesthetic value by basing his catalog of the empirical attributes of beauty on his close observation of nubile young women, invoking their lisps, tottering steps, and even feigned distresses as emblems of a universal aesthetic ideal. In his discussion of the importance of "gradual variation" as a formal quality of beauty, for example, he writes with the air of a seasoned connoisseur,

> Observe that part of a beautiful woman where she is perhaps the most beautiful, about the neck and breasts; the smoothness, the softness; the easy and insensible swell; the variety of the surface, which is never for the smallest space the same; the deceitful maze, through which the unsteady eye slides giddily, without knowing where to fix, or whither it is carried.[3]

To corroborate his argument, Burke cites the opinion of "the very ingenious Mr. Hogarth," pointing to Hogarth's famous line of beauty – an elongated S-shaped curve that was meant to represent the highest aesthetic ideal – as if to vindicate his otherwise perhaps too obvious delectation of the female form.[4] But Burke's more important debt to Hogarth goes conspicuously unacknowledged, and that is precisely the invocation of the beautiful, living woman as the cornerstone of an empiricist aesthetic theory. Hogarth's *Analysis of Beauty* (1753), more than any other aesthetic treatise of the period, rejects the Shaftesburian requirement of disinterestedness as a precondition of the experience of beauty, and indeed revels in the possibilities of sensuality and eroticism as components of aesthetic pleasure. According to Ronald Paulson, "Hogarth is attempting to create an aesthetics that acknowledges that if we place a beautiful woman on a pedestal we will inevitably and appropriately desire her and may discover, moreover, that she is not strictly virtuous." It is an aesthetics of "novelty, variety, intricacy, [and] curiosity" that foregrounds the pleasures of the chase and the tantalizing deferral of discovery, an "aesthetics of seeing under or into" that vindicates the natural wantonness of the wandering gaze.[5]

Not surprisingly, this aspect of Hogarth's theory has troubled not only adherents of the doctrine of aesthetic disinterestedness, but also students of the artist's famous moral satires – such as the *Harlot's Progress* and *Industry and Idleness* – which often convey a decidedly more somber tone. As Paulson points out, "an aesthetics in which sensation and pleasure replace moral judgment apparently contradicts the tenor of [Hogarth's] major works." Thus, Wallace Jackson dismisses the *Analysis of Beauty* as "a strangely eccentric document," while other art historians attempt to neutralize its radical eccentricity by reading it merely as a "rationalization of observed rococo principles."[6] Joseph Burke, who produced the first scholarly edition of the *Analysis* in 1955, likewise tries to redeem the text from the unsettling charge of voyeuristic licentiousness by proposing a reassuringly chaste reading of one of the most pivotal and suggestive phrases in the work. Formal intricacy, Hogarth famously asserts, gives rise to the pleasurable experience we know as beauty by leading the eye on "a wanton kind of chase." Joseph Burke asserts that the word "wanton" here is without any moral or sexual connotations, and rather means simply "free and frolicsome."[7]

Such a reading might plausibly account for the eye's pleasure in wandering over the stylized forms of an intricately carved rococo ornament. But it is disingenuous, in the context of a period manifestly obsessed with the pleasures of the flesh and their often unguarded pursuit, to deny the sexually charged overtones of the phrase itself and of the imagery Hogarth deploys in illustrating and explaining it. The *Oxford English Dictionary* quotes Shakespeare, Arbuthnot, and Samuel Johnson, among others, using the word "wanton" in the sense of lascivious or given to amorous dalliance. And the intricate objects that most frequently catch the eye, in Hogarth's account, are not ornamental carvings, but beautiful women. Nor are these the idealized beauties of classical statuary, held safely aloof from the realm of earthly desire by their transcendence of the particularities of actual bodies, but rather the living, breathing women of Southwark Fair and Covent

Garden. "Who but a bigot," Hogarth famously asks, "will say that he has not seen faces and necks, hands and arms in living women, that even the Grecian Venus doth but coarsely imitate?" These women, moreover, consistently appear as the objects of an explicitly eroticized gaze. Like the wanton ringlets adorning the fair head of Milton's Eve, "the many waving and contrasted turns of [their] naturally intermingling locks ravish the eye with the pleasure of pursuit." The fashionable adornments of Eve's post-lapsarian progeny serve only to heighten the effect: while a naked body soon satiates the eye, Hogarth says, "when it is artfully cloath'd and decorated, the mind at every turn resumes its imaginary pursuits concerning it."[8]

The unabashed eroticism that informs Hogarth's conception of aesthetic experience poses a problem for those who would preserve the phenomenology of beauty from the tyranny of desire. Within the context of Hogarth's text, however, it also presents a second, less frequently considered conundrum. Not the least of Hogarth's radical departures from the established norms of contemporary aesthetic theory is his insistence on the universal accessibility of the aesthetic experience he describes. Whereas Shaftesbury and later Hume depict a sanctified realm of high art whose full enjoyment is limited to an elite cadre of cultivated men of taste, Hogarth insists "that no one may be deterr'd, by the want of... previous knowledge, from entering into this enquiry." This anti-academic, populist gesture is clearly intended to undercut the monopoly on taste claimed by that wealthy class of elitist connoisseurs who were the consistent object of Hogarth's disdain. But Hogarth appears sensitive to the exclusions of gender as well as class implicit in the received ideal of the man of taste, and he holds out the promise of aesthetic edification to all readers of his book, "ladies, as well as gentlemen."[9] Given this conspicuous commitment to inclusiveness, it is striking that women are entirely absent as aesthetic subjects throughout the remainder of the text. When the gaze is gendered at all in the *Analysis*, it is inevitably gendered male. And when a human body figures as the object of aesthetic contemplation, it is, without exception, female. The hegemony of the male gaze is, as noted in the previous chapter, an all-too-familiar dynamic in any number of European art historical contexts. Within the specific context of an iconoclastic work, however, that explicitly claims to present a universally valid theory of beauty to readers of both sexes, an eroticized aesthetic so closely modeled on the dynamics of an exclusively heterosexual male desire seems especially problematic. Where, we are left to wonder, do the eyes of Hogarth's women turn in their own pursuit of aesthetic pleasure? And how can one account for Hogarth's resounding silence on this point?

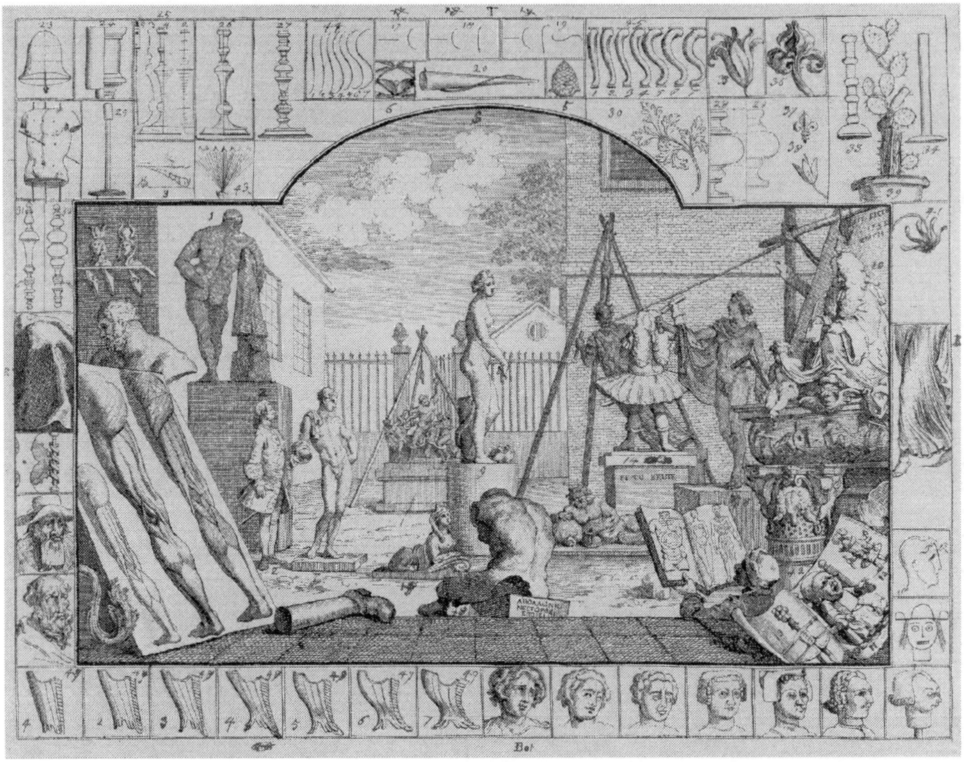

Figure 7 William Hogarth, *Analysis of Beauty*, Plate I, 1753.

Though the well-documented excesses of male foppery in the eighteenth century suggest that the eloquently bantering beaux of the period expected a certain reciprocity of aesthetic desire between the sexes, Hogarth's adjudication of the human physique according to the serpentine line of beauty rules out a strict equivalency of pleasure. A simple comparison of the relative appeal of a series of increasingly curvaceous lines illustrated in one of the two plates accompanying the text proves for Hogarth "how much the form of a woman's body surpasses in beauty that of a man" (Figure 7).[10] Should the female reader be disheartened by this revelation, she will find in the same plates no shortage of suitably curvaceous alternatives – including corsets, table legs, candlesticks, fingers, and leg bones – provided for her own delectation. As captivating as some of these quotidian emblems of the line of beauty surely are, one cannot escape the conclusion that those readers who may not share Hogarth's lusty delight in the spectacle of a consummately attractive woman are somehow getting the short end of the stick.

Figure 8 William Hogarth, scene from the *Rape of the Lock*, engraving for the lid of a snuffbox, date unknown.

If Hogarth is silent on the question of women's aesthetic proclivities in the *Analysis of Beauty*, a review of his visual *oeuvre* suggests that it is not for a lack of information. Not surprisingly, the attractive woman figures prominently as an aesthetic object in many of his paintings and engravings. What is surprising, however, are the number of women Hogarth depicts in these images as aesthetic subjects and the uniformity, in one crucial respect, of their aesthetic preferences. The most important literary source for popular conceptions of female taste in the early eighteenth century is, without a doubt, Pope's *Rape of the Lock*. Hogarth's early illustration of the poem, showing a distracted Belinda seated with her companions at tea, reminds us that the taste of wealthy women, at least, tended toward the foreign and the exotic (Figure 8). Within the poem, Belinda's tea-drinking habit is famously associated with vanity, extravagance, and luxury, to be sure, but it is also the mark of a particular aesthetic sensibility privileging rare foreign commodities that tend, according to Pope, to glitter, glow, and shine. The historical context of the reference to tea-drinking is the rapidly expanding China trade of the East India Company, a trade which by the 1720s had established the tea party as the preeminent site for the conspicuous display of a woman's taste and social status.[11] Hogarth's early conversation pieces conspicuously illustrate the importance of both tea-drinking as a social ritual and of the tea service itself as a marker of wealth and refinement. But imported porcelains and other examples of the fashionable Chinese taste crop up regularly in the satirical works as well, most frequently as a symbol of corrupted taste and, by implication, debauched morality, as in the second plate of *Marriage à la Mode*, or as an exemplar of the absurd excesses of modern fashion, as in *Taste in High Life*.

So if Hogarth was clearly aware of a widely held belief in the affinity of both elite and middle-class female taste for a particular category of exotic commodities, why is there no mention of this taste in the *Analysis of Beauty*, intended as it was for budding connoisseurs of both sexes? A shapely Chinese vase or teapot, after all, would surely have provided a more visually appealing exemplar of the formal principles of alluring curvature he describes than would a human leg bone, and it would have offered the further advantage of being a familiar object that many of his readers would have recognized as reflecting their own decorative tastes.

Indeed, Chinese import wares of the period perfectly exemplify many of the aesthetic values Hogarth champions in the *Analysis*. The unique qualities of porcelain itself – purity, smoothness, translucence, delicacy – bespeak the refined elegance and gentility that are, as Paulson argues, at the very center of Hogarth's creed. Many of the shapely objects into which Chinese and, later, European potters fashioned this magical material likewise demonstrated the truth of Hogarth's claims for the visual power of the serpentine line of beauty. Even the vivid imaginative exercise he suggests to help his reader recognize the lines of beauty in complex three-dimensional objects immediately evokes the visual experience of a thin, translucent porcelain vessel: "let every object under our consideration, be imagined to have its inward contents scoop'd out so nicely, as to have nothing of it left but a thin shell, exactly corresponding both in its inner and outer surface, to the shape of the object itself."[12] A delicate, translucent Chinese vase or bowl surely lurks beneath this prescription as the unacknowledged prototype of sensual allure in the plastic arts.

As an outspoken champion of the rococo style, moreover, Hogarth would presumably have found in Chinese and Chinese-styled wares more generally a set of decorative principles much in accord with his own. The designers of the exotic silks, fire screens, wall hangings, furniture, and even garden buildings that were colonizing contemporary English sitting rooms and country gardens adhered fastidiously to the rules of intricacy, variety, asymmetry, and non-linearity that Hogarth would promote in the *Analysis*, and indeed, rococo and chinoiserie motifs are regularly conflated in contemporary design. While these compositional attributes guaranteed the formal complexity necessary to engage the Hogarthian gaze in its wanton wanderings, Chinese goods in their inescapable exoticism also invited imaginative play on another level entirely. As I argued in the first two chapters, the radical unfamiliarity of their visual language and the obscurity of their local meanings and cultural points of reference would have presented to the Hogarthian viewer an occasion for imaginative pleasure every bit as alluring as their surface design. For Hogarth, after all, it is not only the eye that seeks diversion in art but the mind as well:

> The active mind is ever bent to be employ'd. Pursuing is the business of our lives; and even abstracted from any other view, gives pleasure. Every arising difficulty, that for a while attends and interrupts the pursuit, gives a sort of spring to the mind, enhances the pleasure, and makes what would else be toil and labour, become sport and recreation.[13]

The essence of exoticism as an aesthetic attribute, as I have suggested, is that it erects precisely such a pleasing barrier to the immediate assimilation of a visual spectacle, a teasing sense of alienation from the familiar every bit as captivating as the wanton ringlets of a lover's flowing hair.

For a variety of reasons, then, one might reasonably expect Hogarth to recognize and acknowledge the considerable aesthetic appeal of the Chinese goods his readers purchased and admired. And indeed, scholars have established that he owned a number of decidedly chinoiserie pieces himself.[14] Yet in the *Analysis of Beauty*, when the Chinese style is mentioned at all, it is summarily dismissed as an absurd and foolish taste unworthy of the least serious consideration. In a passage about the ubiquity of his line of beauty in depictions of the deities of Greece and Rome, Hogarth remarks on the sad contrast presented by the Chinese case. "How absolutely void of these turns are the pagods of China, and what a mean taste runs through most of their attempts in painting and sculpture, notwithstanding they finish with such excessive neatness."[15] Hogarth's manuscript notes on academies and the Society of Arts confirm this disparaging view of Chinese artistic production: in a discussion of the appropriate education for young artists, he praises English fabric designers for copying "the objects they introduce from nature; a much surer guide than all the childish and ridiculous absurdities of temples, dragons, pagodas, and other fantastic fripperies, which have been imported from China."[16]

In light of the seemingly compelling reasons why Hogarth should have looked more kindly on these fantastic fripperies and the circumstantial evidence that, in his own purchases, he occasionally did, why does he lash out with such uncompromising fury against the popularity of the Chinese taste? A number of explanations suggest themselves. To begin with, Hogarth's criticism of Chinese art on the grounds that it did not adhere to conventions of naturalistic representation was a commonplace one at the time. Although Hogarth rejected a classicist conception of nature as idealized form, he believed strongly that nature, in its infinite variety, was the artist's most trustworthy guide. To the extent, then, that certain genres of Chinese and Chinese-inspired art seemed to flout familiar standards of verisimilitude, they were beyond the pale of even Hogarth's post-classicist sensibilities. Furthermore, the popularity of the Chinese style surely grated on Hogarth's keenly developed sense of aesthetic nationalism. While perhaps weakening the claims of the highbrow connoisseurs to being the sole arbiters of fashionable taste, Chinese imports, like old Italian paintings, nonetheless threatened the livelihood of the native-born English artists Hogarth saw it as his mission to promote. To the extent that Chinese art seemed to replicate the rococo stylistics he espoused, there was all the more reason forcefully to repudiate it as a foreign usurper of English artistic glory.

I am more intrigued, however, by a third, less immediately obvious explanation for his disdain, an explanation that returns to the problem in the *Analysis* I raised at the beginning of this chapter. Hogarth's repeated insistence on the worthlessness of the Chinese style, I would like to suggest, is intimately bound up with his perplexing silence on the question of female aesthetic agency. A closer look at some of the many contemporary literary and visual representations of Chinese goods and their domestic consumption will help to elaborate this connection. As in the *Rape of the Lock*, Chinese import goods figure prominently in these works as emblems of female vanity and extravagance. More intriguingly, though, their physical qualities are often compared to those of the women who collect them. Both fine ladies and fine porcelain, the familiar simile goes, are prized for their smooth surfaces and radiant splendor, but they are equally fragile as well, and are soon despised for the appearance of a crack or flaw. The analogy could, at times, appear so compelling as to elide any remaining differences between them. In *Royalty, Episcopacy and the Law*, for example, Hogarth imagines a courtly lady as a metonymic pastiche of exotic commodities, including a fan for a body and a teapot for a head (Figure 9); in a contemporary poem entitled "Tea, or Ladies into China-Cups" the anonymous poet effects a like transmutation of English women into the porcelain vessels of which they are so enamored.[17]

From the perspective of female aesthetic agency, the implications of an imagined identity between female consumers and the objects of their

Figure 9 William Hogarth, *Royalty, Episcopacy and the Law*, 1724. Engraving.

consumption are suggestive, to say the least. If women, in their pursuit of beauty, turn to objects that either resemble or are understood as synecdochical extensions of themselves, the result is an entirely self-contained, self-reflexive economy of female desire, not unlike that of the female friendships and communities discussed in the previous chapter. Whether this economy is figured as narcissistic or homoerotic, it inevitably leaves male participants in the drama in the unaccustomed role of passive, powerless spectators. And indeed, those writers who imaginatively pursue the consequences of women's infatuation with Chinese goods invariably figure men as frustrated and jealous rivals, deprived by porcelain vases and teapots of attentions that might otherwise have been their own. An enigma-solving contest in an issue of the *Woman's Almanack* of 1741 features an intricate, rhymed riddle about a Chinese teapot: "Here the fair Nymphs with each becoming Grace, / And studied Art, my varied Charms embrace; / Oh!

what wou'd Lovers give, cou'd they command / So warm a Pressure from their fair one's Hand." John Gay's poem, "To a Lady on her Passion for Old China," similarly laments a lover's displacement by imported exotica: "What ecstasies her bosom fire! / How her eyes languish with desire! / How blessed, how happy should I be, / Were that fond glance bestowed on me! / New doubts and fears within me war: / What rival's near? A China jar."[18] In a poem by Anna Williams satirizing several women's abortive plan to form a nunnery so as to avoid the fetters of matrimony, the conspirators' strategem to banish men from their lives takes shape around a collection of chinaware:

Round the tea-table many a time they sate,
Th' important scheme at leisure to debate.[19]

This dynamic of masculine displacement is taken to its logical conclusion in a long pornographic poem called *A Chinese Tale* published in 1740. Described as "a tale in the Chinese taste," the mock-heroic fantasy recounts the adventures of the coy and beautiful maid of honour Cham-yam as she repels the advances of legions of desperately adoring mandarins. One of these suitors bribes a maid to conceal him in his tormenter's private chambers, where he watches from inside a large china jar as she fondles herself in front of a mirror. The sight sets his soul ablaze, and he bursts from his jar to ravish her. But what is most remarkable about the poem is the setting Cham-yam chooses for her self-pleasuring and the state of mind the decor seems to induce. The room is furnished in the height of the Chinese taste, with motifs of dragons and gilt flowers adorning the ceiling and, as we see in the accompanying frontispiece, the furniture (Figure 10). These are juxtaposed with lavishly described lewd paintings lining the walls, cabinets full of erotic curiosities, and bookshelves lined with novels and romances.

Reclining on a sofa amidst all this splendor, Cham-yam's mind wanders over scenes of the triumphs of her sex:

All languishing, supine she lay,
Revolving over all that's gay:
The Charms of Woman, and her Pow'r,
From the Creation to that Hour:
What Ravages! what Devastations!
What Havoc caus'd among the Nations!
What Slaves they made of lordly Man!
When sudden thus the Dame began.[20]

While the theme of women's sexual power is a commonplace one, its triangulation here with vivid spectacles of chinoiserie and autoeroticism suggests

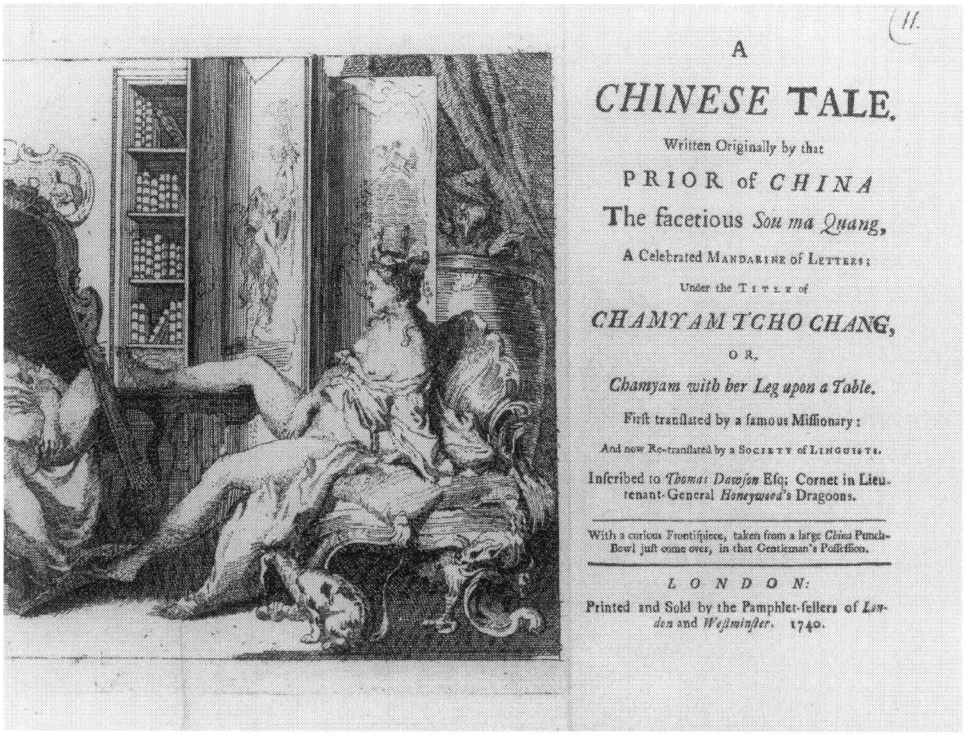

Figure 10 Frontispiece and title page from *A Chinese Tale*, London, 1740.

a powerful and deeply resonant association between the aesthetics of Chinese exoticism and the potentially unsettling specter of female autonomy and self-determination.[21]

As suggested by the Williams poem cited above, a more familiar and genteel locus of male anxiety about the wantonness of women's taste and power was the tea table itself. In an engraving called *The Tea Table* (1710), the social consumption of tea is depicted as a site of viciously malignant female gossip (Figure 11). The theme here is homosocial rather than autoerotic self-indulgence, but the iconography is familiar: just as in the *Chinese Tale*, male observers (here shown outside the window on the right) appear only as exiled, marginal figures, while a prominent display of Chinese porcelain suggests the aesthetic context of the women's transgression. The porcelain cabinet also draws our eyes to the devilish figure chasing Justice from the room, recalling, along with the allusion to "poison tongues" in the attached poem, contemporary associations between women's tea circles and the witches' covens of old.[22] Justice appears to have dropped her sword, which lies broken on the floor next to a curiously intact china teacup. This pair of objects

Figure 11 *The Tea Table*, 1710.

conspicuously inverts the iconic cliché of feminine china meeting its ruin at the hands of an impetuously phallic masculinity and provides a striking commentary on the reversal of roles enacted in this scene.

The same pair of icons appears again in the second plate of Hogarth's *Marriage à la Mode* (Figure 1). The broken sword on the floor at the husband's feet figures all the more obviously here as a sign of languid, frustrated masculinity; the wife's tea service, elevated and intact, provides a contrasting echo of her own wantonness and excess. It echoes as well the debauched taste revealed by the collection of Chinese figures on the mantelpiece above her head. Here Hogarth graphically illustrates his principal charges against the Chinese taste: that it is absurd, inelegant, and unnatural. But this well-known plate, read in the context of the period's rampant associations between Chinese goods and an extravagant, wanton femininity also suggests an answer to the question of female aesthetic agency in the *Analysis* with which we began. Hogarth rejected the Chinese style as an alternative to classicism, I would propose, not so much out of a considered repudiation of its underlying aesthetic values, but rather out of a sobering recognition that to grant the validity of the Chinese taste would be to legitimate a regime not only of female aesthetic self-determination, but also of the autonomy of female desire more generally conceived. As a theorist of art, Hogarth radically asserted the emancipatory power of a spontaneous aesthetic experience unconstrained by classicist pieties. But his gestures of inclusiveness notwithstanding, he stopped short of extending this freedom to women. While beauty could henceforth be safely admired in English as well as Italian paintings, it was still to remain the exclusive preserve of European artists and of a predominantly masculine gaze. To accommodate the errant wanderings of the wanton female eye would have been to invite a wholesale defection from the Western artistic tradition and from the social and sexual order of which it was a well-established part. And this was a travesty that our hero, canon-busting iconoclast and aesthetic libertine though he surely was, finally proved unable to countenance.

PART III

Of rocks, gardens, and goldfish

5 | The socio-aesthetics of the Chinese scholar's stone

From its inception in the seventeenth century, the Royal Society was no friend to poetry. The advancement of the new science, in the view of its champions, required the subordination of language to empirical observation, the unequivocal homage of inconstant words to the unchanging nature of things in themselves. Poets, needless to say, took a dim view of this development, as they staked their livelihood on the very malleability of language that the empiricists condemned. Satire provided sweet revenge: a team of scholars at Swift's Academy of Lagado make themselves ridiculous by taking Thomas Sprat's denunciations of figural language at face value. Rather than risk the ambiguity and semantic slippage attendant on verbal expression, these pedants have dispensed with words altogether and taken to communicating entirely with things, a collection of which they carry about with them in a handy satchel for deployment at academic meetings and cocktail parties.[1]

Three hundred years after Sprat published his seminal *History of the Royal Society*, figural language was chastened anew, as literary critics of the late twentieth century reminded us, with an insistence altogether worthy of intrepid seventeenth-century pamphleteers, that words rarely mean what they seem to mean, that they only sporadically mean what their authors meant them to mean, and that they offer at best a fleeting and highly mediated picture of the real world, if, that is, given our collective ideological hallucinations, such a thing can be said to exist. It is perhaps not surprising, then, that certain modern scholars, like the linguaphobic projectors of the Lagado Academy, have once again fled the crumbling prison house of language to take refuge in the reassuringly tangible verities of things. Recent years have seen rapid growth in the field now known as material culture studies, with influential books and articles bearing such titles as "Learning from Things," "The Meaning of Things," "History from Things," "The Social Life of Things," "Thing Theory," and "Material Cultures: Why Some Things Matter."[2]

The premise underlying such studies is that the objects that inhabit our everyday lives do matter in that they serve as repositories and conduits for a variety of individual and social meanings. The consumption of things, whether for use or display, is an act of creative expression by means of which personal identities and group histories emerge through the continual re-articulation and re-alignment of values such as taste, fashion, status, and individuality. Swift's satire on the language projectors notwithstanding, it is clear to anyone who has ever received a gift, admired a colleague's good taste in dress, or arranged knick-knacks on a mantelpiece that we do, indeed, communicate through things, and that these things, in turn, can structure our perception of the world in fundamental ways. By investing things with meanings and responding to the meanings others have invested in them, we gain access to a realm of signification that, like verbal language, provides us with the conceptual categories and cognitive tools by which we organize our mental lives.

The efficacy of any object in enabling thought or communication, however, depends on our ability to read it. Just as a Chinese character is illegible to the average European or, for that matter, its English equivalent to the Chinese peasant, so most meaning-laden things – whether martinis, brand-name clothes, or ritual objects more traditionally defined – are effectively limited to a single cultural context in communicating their original meaning. This is not to say that goods that move between distant cultures are necessarily stripped of their signifying function, but rather that they tend to lose their original signifying value. Anthropologists who have studied the migration of goods across cultural boundaries have found that the meanings attached to objects are neither permanent nor universal, and that, in fact, consumers confronted with an alien commodity for the first time are remarkably inventive in finding ways to assimilate it within their own local world of goods, giving it a completely new set of meanings in the process.[3] When Mary Wortley Montagu visited a Turkish bathhouse, to take a well-known eighteenth-century example, her bemused interlocutors interpreted her corset not as a marker of genteel femininity, but rather as the cruel contrivance of a jealous husband for preserving his wife's chastity.[4] In general, it seems reasonable to assume that in cases where the original meaning of an object, like a corset or a yellow ribbon or a judge's gavel, derives primarily from its relative position within a local semiotic system, that particular meaning will be lost in translation to another cultural context. Meanings that are purely the product of arbitrary convention, that is, do not travel well.

But what of a case where the original meanings of an object are not merely conventional, but rather are at least partially embedded within the object itself? Utilitarian objects fall into this category: the use value of a knife or a bowl is readily apparent from its shape to any viewer regardless of context. Decorated objects present a more complicated scenario. The figural scenes depicted on a painted dish can be interpreted to a certain extent, and as we saw in Chapter 3, such interpretations can resonate powerfully within the cultural contexts of the object's reception. But what of the manner in which such scenes are depicted? To the extent that an artist's style and the aesthetic tradition from which it derives can be understood as discrete features of a work that bear conceptual analysis, can such aesthetic ideas, encoded within a work, be recovered and, as it were, reactivated when a decorative object is transplanted into a new context? Foreign styles are often successfully imitated, of course, by local artists and craftsmen. The more interesting questions are whether and how the consumer of such an object might begin, in more subtle ways, to understand and respond to the aesthetic ideas inscribed in its design by its original creators.

The mania for Chinese and Chinese-styled goods that swept England in the first half of the eighteenth century provides a rich test case for the study of this question. The emergence of tea as a fashionable beverage created a demand for the accessories of the tea table, which in turn stimulated interest in the Chinese furniture, wallpapers, textiles, and architectural designs which became a ubiquitous presence in homes and gardens by 1750.[5] The artistic sensibility represented by Chinese goods and their European imitations was perceived, as we have seen, as a largely novel one. How might contemporary consumers have responded specifically to the stylistic dimensions of this alien aesthetic in their midst? In the previous two chapters, I considered the gendering of the Chinese taste with respect to the figural iconography of imported porcelains and the aesthetic agency of their (often female) collectors. In this chapter, I retain my focus on the interactions between English consumers and Chinese objects, but I shift from a consideration of the exotic as a catalyst of desire to an interrogation of its potential role in the transposition of aesthetic value. The second chapter in this section will address a similar question with respect to a particular instance in the literary arts.

The considerable scholarship that has been devoted to the phenomenon of the Chinese taste calls attention to four distinct forms of engagement and response, all of which I have touched upon in previous chapters. The most immediate response was no doubt that of wonder, the sheer delight in the spectacle of the unfamiliar that is the common currency of the exotic and that was typically subsumed, within eighteenth-century aesthetic theory, under the categories of the novel and the strange. The pleasures afforded by Chinese exoticism led to a second type of response: stylistic assimilation. English craftsmen responded to consumers' attraction to Chinese goods by first imitating their designs and motifs and then blending them with French rococo influences to create a new hybrid style. The rapid popularization of the Chinese taste led, in turn, to a sharp backlash against it on the part of critics who perceived it as an unwelcome foreign challenge to the dominance of the Palladian vision. And intermingled with all three of these was what we might call a proto-orientalist response, combining the smug pleasure of ownership of foreign goods with the construction of feminizing fantasies about Chinese culture on the basis of the playful garden scenes found on porcelains and lacquerware.[6]

These four types of responses – wonder, assimilation, repudiation, and fantasy – aptly characterize the most prominent effects of the appearance of Chinese goods in the English marketplace. But they would arguably apply equally well to the arrival of any exotic foreign style in any cultural context. They are responses, that is, to the exotic merely as cipher, without any specific reference to the social, historical, or indeed aesthetic particularities of their culture of origin. Recognizing these four types of responses, in other words, does not get us very far in addressing the central question I have posed here, namely, whether abstract aesthetic ideas – as opposed to decorative motifs, manufacturing techniques, vessel forms, or coloration schemes – embedded in decorative objects can be translated across cultural boundaries. The adaptation of a Chinese design by a Chippendale or Pillement no doubt entails a certain type of translation of influence, but whatever sustained engagement with the aesthetic ideas of the original work takes place in such a case is limited to the individual artist. I am more interested in considering the experience of the consumer, and in exploring the hypothesis that certain ways of seeing characteristic of the late Ming and early Qing dynasties might have been reconstituted upon the arrival of Chinese wares in English sitting-rooms.

In order to isolate a specific set of Chinese aesthetic ideas for discussion, I will focus on a single visual icon of particular importance within early modern Chinese literati culture: the contorted garden rock or scholar's stone (Figure 12). As elements in garden design, landscape painting, and decorative arts of all kinds, strangely shaped rocks and mountains have a prominence and significance that is nearly unrivaled in Ming–Qing iconography. The curiously twisted, pitted, and pockmarked rocks most famously associated with Lake Tai (*Taihu*) appear as central features in every manner of visual composition, their unusual shapes teasing the eye with the peculiar

Figure 12 Scholar's stone in a Suzhou garden.

contrast between their sheer physical mass and the sinuous lightness of their form.[7] Paintings depict scholars conversing in the company of large rocks. Garden pathways lead the visitor to a succession of vantage points contrived for the contemplation of rocks. A renowned magistrate from Wuhei province, Mi Fu, is celebrated for having kowtowed before a particularly impressive rock, which he thereafter addressed respectfully as *shixiong*, or "elder brother stone." To risk a sweeping generalization, the visual traditions we associate with early modern China would be inconceivable in the absence of these contorted heaps of pitted stone.[8] Certainly in eighteenth-century England, the vision of China that consumers derived from travel writings and from the decorated porcelains, lacquerwares, and wall hangings that crowded East India Company warehouses and fashionable sitting-rooms would have prominently featured these geologic curiosities. Readers of a well-known Dutch embassy account published in England in 1673 would have learned that:

> There is not any thing wherein the Chineses shew their Ingenuity more, than in these Rocks or artificial Hills, which are so curiously wrought, that Art seems to exceed Nature. These Cliffs are made of a sort of Stone, and sometimes of Marble, and so rarely adorn'd with Trees and Flowers, that all that see them are surpris'd with admiration. Rich and wealthy People, especially the great Lords and Mandorins, have for the most part such Rocks in their Courts and Palaces, upon which they squander a good part of their Estates.[9]

The fact that so many local imitations of Chinese wares replicated both the specific features and general style of this distinctive iconography suggests that the presence of strangely twisted rocks soon became, for contemporary viewers, a recognizable hallmark of the so-called Chinese style.

If the elite Chinese obsession with rocks and the veneration in which they were held by Ming–Qing artists and connoisseurs has any analogue in the Western tradition, it might be found in Pygmalion's legendary infatuation with a particularly well-turned piece of marble. And indeed, the centrality of the rock in Ming–Qing aesthetics invites a broader comparison with that of the statue or the statuesque human figure in contemporary Western art.[10] Both the contorted rock and the statuesque figure had, by the eighteenth century, long been prominent characteristic elements in both the paintings and the gardens of their respective traditions. Both were emblems of elite status display and objects of connoisseurship valued in part for the allusions they embodied to an ancient literary canon and a revered classical past. While both were emblems of a tradition of visual culture that prized disinterested aesthetic contemplation, they also participated as commodities in lively consumer societies in which the ownership and refined appreciation of objects of taste were widely recognized, if not infallible, markers of class status.[11] Like the cross-cultural analysis of the motifs and social practices of female intimacy in Chapter 3, the comparison provides a salutary reminder that the differences between Chinese and European societies in this period were not nearly so vast as subsequent commentators often made them appear.

Most importantly for our purposes, however, both Chinese rocks and the statuesque figures of Western painting and sculpture attracted the attention of the scribbling tribe. Writers in China and England concerned with codifying artistic norms and ideals in their respective cultures were drawn to these stony icons as paradigmatic expressions of the highest aesthetic values. If, in fact, abstract aesthetic ideas do travel through the medium of decorative goods, then comparing these two codifying discourses should help to identify some of the specific ideas that may have been transmitted to or resonated with Western consumers of Chinese wares in the seventeenth and eighteenth centuries.

Owing in part to the challenges posed to classical European conceptions of beauty by these East Asian imports, the eighteenth century, as we have seen, proved fertile ground for the early emergence of aesthetic theory in England. Beginning with Shaftesbury and encompassing writers as varied as Addison, Hutcheson, Hogarth, Hume, Burke, Gerard, Alison, and Gilpin, this century-long conversation on questions of taste and beauty charted the period's evolving conceptions of aesthetic value and of the faculties required to appreciate it.[12] The single most influential spokesman of this group, however, the figure who achieved the highest stature as both artist and theorist, and the one whose writings best express the contemporary art world's characteristic reverence for tradition, rigid hierarchies of value, and preoccupation with the statuesque human form is doubtless Joshua Reynolds. Reynolds' *Discourses on Art* is a series of fifteen lectures delivered to students at the Royal Academy in 1769 that at once summarize the art theory of the preceding three hundred years and lay down a set of precepts to guide the education of the serious aspiring artist. Highly regarded both in its own time and in ours, the work can be taken as broadly representative of the dominant strand of British aesthetic theory during this period.

When we turn to China, the situation is considerably more complex. It turns out that among the reams of art criticism published in seventeenth- and eighteenth-century China, there is no single work on the general principles of art that enjoyed the prominence of Reynolds' *Discourses.* There seems to be far less interest, in fact, in developing and arguing over abstract notions of beauty in the first place, with the result that one is hard pressed to identify a genre comparable to the European-style aesthetic treatise in China before the twentieth century.[13] As a result, modern historians of Chinese art have drawn upon a variety of works – including poetry, essays, connoisseurs' guides, and manuals of taste – in their attempts to reconstruct some of the dominant ideas associated with valued works of Chinese visual culture. While this is a vast and varied tradition and one about which it is hazardous to generalize, for the sake of a thought experiment designed to address some of the questions I have raised, I will venture to outline in broad strokes some of the crucial differences in the ways these two highly complex aesthetic paradigms seem to treat a central element in their respective iconographic traditions.

For Joshua Reynolds the fundamental purpose of every serious artist is to transcend the particularities of nature and the vicissitudes of local fashion in the pursuit of ideal beauty. In painting or sculpting the human form, which is the highest manifestation of this ideal, the artist draws upon his observation not just of the live model before him, but of all the models of humanity he has ever studied, whether in the flesh or in the best works of past masters. His task is to abstract from the incidental deformities of actual bodies an ideal form of which the most graceful of living creatures is but an imperfect approximation. To approach this timeless ideal, then, is to leave behind the accidents of time, place, and physical idiosyncrasy that separate the world of the artist from that represented in his art.[14] Reynolds is unequivocal in sustaining this distinction: "There are excellencies in the art of painting," he writes,

> beyond what is commonly called the imitation of nature . . . The poets, orators, and rhetoricians of antiquity, are continually enforcing this position; that all the arts receive their perfection from an ideal beauty, superior to what is to be found in individual nature . . . For the works of nature are full of disproportion, and fall very short of the true standard of beauty.[15]

Trying to extrapolate from contemporary Chinese sources a general theory of art comparable in purpose, scope, and cultural standing to that elaborated in Reynolds' *Discourses* is a task fraught with methodological potholes. Quite apart from the ever-present dangers of reductive generalization, the comparative framework itself may tempt us to impose decidedly non-Chinese patterns of thought and analysis onto the Chinese conceptual landscape. If we approach Chinese aesthetic theory, that is, with the aim of identifying specific features that are in some respect analogous to those that define aesthetic theory in the West, we may wind up with a picture that, while nominally Chinese in its particulars, will be decidedly Western in its priorities and principles of organization.[16] And though I will continue to use the term, I do so with the awareness that the very category of the aesthetic, being the product of a distinctly European cultural history, may itself introduce distortions of this kind in that it marks off a privileged space for a distinct and privileged type of experience that may not, *a priori*, be recognized as such within other cultural milieus. I will proceed with the comparison, then, from the premise that the two discourses may be fundamentally incompatible not only in the aesthetic values that they celebrate but also in the very questions that they pose about the nature and purpose of "aesthetic" value. It will quickly become apparent that Reynolds' theory, for all its implicit claims to universality, proves woefully inadequate as a description of Chinese artistic practice, and that its three foundational precepts would seem to have no legitimate place within early modern Chinese discourses about art.

To begin with, the unquestioned pre-eminence of the human form as the manifestation of the highest ideals of art makes little or no sense within the Chinese context. Rocks or mountains are more commonly the central subject of visual compositions in the most highly valued Chinese paintings of our period, and consequently receive considerably more attention than human figures in commentaries on works of art. Landscape, rather than anthropocentric history painting, was accordingly the most highly esteemed genre among elite classes in the Ming and Qing dynasties.[17] One of the central organizing principles in early modern Chinese landscape painting and gardening is the balance or tension between eternally opposed forces, *yin* and *yang*, water and rock, earth and sky. Human figures, like pine trees, typically represent a merely transient, intermediate state between these poles rather than the fully consummate pinnacle of divine creation.[18] For Reynolds and the tradition he represents, the human drama depicted in a painting is the source of its emotional resonance, while the disposition of human figures is the principle source of aesthetic pleasure. For his Chinese counterparts, the satisfaction to be found in gazing upon a painting is far more likely to be evoked by the juxtaposition of a rock and a tree and by the subtle delineation of their intricate forms.

The second Reynoldsian precept that falls flat in the Chinese context is the elevation of beauty as the gold standard for assessing the value of a work of art. Indeed, a concept commensurable with "beauty" as an aesthetic experience, let alone the abstracted notion of "ideal beauty" that animates Reynolds' theory, is rarely to be found among elite descriptions and assessments of artworks in early modern China.[19] The delicate court ladies of the *shinühua* paintings discussed in Chapter 3 may be described as beauties, and the experience of contemplating art is sometimes compared with that of gazing at a beautiful woman, but beauty does not appear as a primary category of aesthetic analysis *per se* (Figure 6).[20] Nor is there any analogous category of aesthetic description that organizes questions and ideas about art with the centripetal force exercised by the philosophical idea of beauty in the European tradition.

The concept that perhaps comes closest in its prominence in discussions of the pleasures of art and nature is that of *qi*, which is typically described in English as a form of cosmic energy or spirit that permeates all things. This is the same *qi* we hear about in connection with Chinese martial arts exercises, like *taiqi* and *qigong*, as well as acupuncture and other forms of traditional Chinese medicine, with their emphasis on regulating the proper flow of energy through the body. The term applies as well to the technique of Chinese painting and calligraphy, where it describes the flow of energy through the brush and the painter's goal of suffusing every brushstroke with the movement of life. In this context, it forms the compounds *moqi* and *biqi*, which connote the forms of *qi* manifested through the painter's ink and brushwork, respectively. The concept of *qi* is central to the six laws of painting first codified by the Daoist painter Xie He in his *Classified Record of Ancient Painters* at the end of the fifth century and later recognized as foundational to Chinese aesthetics. The first and most famous of these principles is *qiyun shengdong*, which has been translated as "rhythmic vitality, or spiritual rhythm expressed in the movement of life." According to commentator Eliot Deutsch, "the canon demands that the artist identify himself completely with a spiritual vitality or movement of life that is ubiquitous in nature and that this subtle natural-spiritual rhythm, by means of a highly disciplined spontaneous mastery of the medium, resound in his work."[21]

As such an account makes clear, *qi* is not merely an aesthetic category *per se*, but rather also a cosmological one that is manifest in effective visual compositions, whether natural or man-made. Rocks and mountains, whether in a landscape or a landscape painting, are often described as embodying this energy in its purest form. As one Ming commentator writes, "The purest essence of the energy of the heaven-earth world coalesces into rock. It emerges, bearing the soil. Its formations are wonderful and fantastic. Some with cavernous cliffs, revealing their interior; some with peaks and summits in sharp-edged layers."[22] The energy flow through the rocks and soil of a landscape is set in motion by the tension between the opposing *yin* and *yang* elements it contains. Like the flow of blood through the arteries of the body, the circulation of *qi* between these poles sustains and animates the landscape. Whereas beauty for Reynolds is a timeless, transcendent, and hence rather static ideal, *qi* is associated, then, with the idea of constant flux and transformation.

Finally, Reynolds' notion that the best art transcends the particularities of nature would have appeared utterly nonsensical to a Chinese counterpart, for the simple reason that the art–nature dichotomy is a false one within the dominant Ming–Qing aesthetic Chinese framework. Whereas Reynolds banishes the strange, deformed, or idiosyncratic from his aesthetic vision, the Chinese literati have traditionally embraced them. Singularity is, indeed, among the very highest of aesthetic values; a bizarre contorted rock formation is prized for its rarity and said to surpass the skill of the most accomplished artisan. "It is when a rock is lean, wrinkled, porous, and penetrated that it reaches the level of excellence," according to an inscription on a painting of a rock by the noted eighteenth-century artist Ying Bao.[23] Far from transcending nature in the pursuit of an abstract ideal, such oddly shaped rocks in a garden or a painting help to evoke the metonymic identity of the composition and the natural world. As the introduction to a catalogue by the twelfth-century collector Du Wan put it, "within the size of a fist can be assembled the beauty of a thousand cliffs."[24] The *qi* that animates the mountains and rivers of the earth surges with equal potency through their artistic representations, so that a miniature composition literally embodies on a smaller scale the forces of the cosmos.

The embrace of singularity in nature extended to the work of human artists as well. The prominent "wild and heterodox" school of the Ming dynasty originated, according to Richard Barnhart, with the works of Tai Chin (1388–1462), and developed through the art of a succession of independent master-painters including Wu Wei, Lin Liang, and many others. Adopting a painterly method described as "attacking directly," "brushing furiously," or "splashing and dripping," they achieved a virtuosic spontaneity that reflected both impatience with the limitations of contemporary academic art and a storied tradition of acclaim in China for *kuang* – wildness, craziness, or impetuousness – in art dating back to the foundational works of Confucius and especially the Daoist master Zhuangzi. Some of the painters of this school went so far as incorporating the character for *kuang* into their artistic names, providing them with such memorable monikers as "Pure and Wild," "Ancient and Wild," and "The Wild Master."[25] Biographers' descriptions of their technique suggest that they fully lived up to the aesthetic sensibility suggested by such names. Wu Wei, for example, who on at least one occasion painted in the presence of the emperor,

> was often inspired when he was drunk, and would brandish his brush and splash his ink with abandon, completing a painting in an instant. He wielded his brush as if it were flying... His techniques and ideas were bold and free, like a dragon leaping or a phoenix soaring... impossible to restrain.[26]

That such a description, aptly illustrated by his renowned *Celebration at the Fishing Village* (Figure 13), more readily recalls the work of Jackson Pollock than Joshua Reynolds suggests something of the distance that separated the dominant aesthetic principles of Ming China from those of eighteenth-century England. It reminds us, furthermore, that European "modernity," whether we date its arrival in the art world from the romantics or from the twentieth-century avant-garde, can make no exclusive claim

Figure 13 Wu Wei, *Celebration at the Fishing Village*, 1507–8.

to stylistic iconoclasm. From a more global perspective, indeed, it can appear rather belated in its spirited rebellion against artistic tradition.

While harboring no illusions that the thumbnail sketch I have offered here will be nearly as effective as the spectacle of a leaping dragon or of a lean and wrinkled scholar's stone in evoking the cosmos of Chinese aesthetics, I turn now to the question of how echoes of this system might have insinuated themselves into the aesthetic imaginations of Reynolds' contemporaries through the medium of Chinese export wares and their European imitations. A long succession of scholars from Arthur Lovejoy to Yu Liu have speculated on the influence of Chinese garden theory on developments in European cultural history from romanticism to Kantian aesthetics. The influence they posit is largely discursive: most of the many writers who discussed Chinese gardening practices in England had never set foot in China. Shifting to the material register allows us to contemplate the responses of the many consumers who directly encountered Chinese productions, but also compels us to do so in a more tentative mode, as the archives provide no direct evidence of tea-sipping connoisseurs waxing eloquent on the cosmic energy flow pulsating among the sinuous rocks depicted on their china teapots or on the lacquerware screens behind their chairs. We cannot

Figure 14 Louis-Philippe Boitard (active in England *c.* 1735–60), *A Very Lively Tea Party.*

say with certainty or precision what eighteenth-century consumers actually thought, in any more than a superficial way, of the Chinese-style goods they purchased and admired, nor can we establish definitively what kinds of perhaps unconscious meanings and ideas they associated with them. We can, however, conduct potentially revealing thought experiments based on what we know of the social contexts of this consumption and the reactions it provoked among contemporary cultural critics.

Imported Chinese goods, it is clear, were collected and enjoyed by both men and women in the early eighteenth century. But as noted in Chapter 3, a preponderance of evidence, historical and literary, suggests that their principal consumers were women.[27] Trade records, furthermore, along with a vast body of contemporary writings, corroborate the clichés, first, that the most commonly encountered vehicle for the Chinese pictorial style was porcelain tea-wares, and second, that one of the most common contexts in which these foreign artifacts would have been viewed, commented on, and potentially translated into the realm of social discourse would have been the preponderantly feminine space of the domestic tea party (Figure 14).[28]

Here, too, the gender lines are far from absolute. Men also drank tea, of course, and figure frequently in the many conversation pieces that portray as a domestic ideal a well-heeled family gathered around an elegant tea service. But certainly in the popular imagination, and, judging from letters, diaries, plays, novels, and popular prints, very often in daily practice, the tea table provided a privileged space for intimate conversation among English women of all social classes. We cannot, of course, recover the content of most of these tea-table conversations. We can, however, safely surmise that their purpose often included the casual exchange of news and views about other members of the participants' social circle, otherwise known as gossip.

The history of gossip obviously predates the seventeenth and eighteenth centuries. Gossip as a distinct discursive form, however, does emerge into a prominent notoriety during this period, through the commodification of information as "news" and the inevitable newsmongering it promoted, widespread satirical denunciations of women's talk, and the emergence of that immensely popular literary genre of scandal writing most closely associated with writers like Delarivier Manley who, according to one twentieth-century critic, "collected filth with the relentless energy of a dredger, and aimed it with the deadly precision of a machine-gun."[29] We flatter ourselves in our association of early modern news culture with the foundations of the liberal public sphere. But racy gossip columns, no less than hard-nosed political reporting, are a central legacy linking the earliest English newspapers with our own. In 1626 Ben Jonson's late play the *Staple of News*, which features scenes set in a news office and a chorus of four gossips arraigning the play between acts, satirized "the degree to which news was invented to suit the contemporary appetite for gossip." A century and a half later, news continued to serve much the same purpose: widespread complaints surfaced in the 1770s concerning the degree to which serial news publications such as *Town and Country* had taken over the role of *chroniques scandaleuses* in exposing private intrigues to public view.[30]

Taking gossip seriously as a historical or literary phenomenon requires that we acknowledge its prominent place in the history of print culture, but also that we peel away the moralizing judgments that for centuries have condemned and trivialized its oral forms as a vain and meddlesome folly, so much idle women's chatter. Once we consider gossip in a more objective light, we can begin to recognize it as a regular, rule-bound discursive practice that serves distinct social and even aesthetic functions. In her marvelous study of the cultural history of the practice, Patricia Meyer Spacks describes it as a structured and purposeful conversational form that, at its best, resembles a work of art.[31] Although Spacks does not pursue this analogy between

Figure 15 Fragment of a bed curtain. English or Scottish, late 17th or early 18th century. Linen and cotton twill embroidered with wool.

gossip and art, her suggestion raises the intriguing question of what sort of art gossip most closely resembles, and what kinds of aesthetic ideas gossip, viewed as art, might be taken to embody.

Without suggesting that every tea-sipping tatler in eighteenth-century England was, in her aesthetic predilections, a sinophilic petromaniac, I will venture the observation that the narrative structure and social function of gossip, as both Spacks and the early modern historian Bernard Capp describe them, suggest much closer affinities with Chinese rocks than with classical statuary and a more obvious kinship with the flux and flow of *qi* than with a static ideal of perfect beauty as the *sine qua non* of aesthetic experience. The tea-sipping tatler of the early eighteenth century may have found in her Chinese porcelains, fire screens, and needlework patterns (Figure 15) an imaginative vision that resonated deeply with her discursive habits and desires, that set the tone for her conversations, and that offered glimpses of an aesthetic ideology in which the transgressive undercurrents of women's chatter could, for once, be acclaimed and legitimized rather than piously condemned. John Richetti argues that the dominant ethos of this period tended to "value experience for its variety, curiosity, or intensity rather than for its status or propriety."[32] If a fluorescence of gossip marked the discursive expression of this ethos, the ubiquitous image of the Chinese scholar's stone provided a compelling visual analogue.

Such a claim might appear, at first glance, as overly conjectural. The empirical reality of an analogy between visual and discursive formations can rarely be "proven," and indeed analogies between Chinese art and other contemporary visual forms – the garden grotto, for example, the contortionist's entr'acte, or the painterly picturesque – might suggest themselves more readily. The methodology I am deploying here, in its exploration of potential convergences in unexpected places, is recognizable, however, as an application to broader extra-textual contexts of an imaginative reading process that is well established in literary criticism. What is literary interpretation, after all, but a structured exercise in identifying and reflecting on the significance of resonances, divergences, and other patterns within and between texts, whether of a phonetic, metrical, thematic, philosophical, historical, or ideological kind? The interpretive experiment in this chapter, as in Chapter 3, is to take as my source texts the distinctive iconography of a popular foreign aesthetic and the particular social contexts in which it was admired and assimilated in early eighteenth-century England. To suggest a possible connection between these two registers is not to make a definitive claim about historical causality, but rather to call attention to an unexpected convergence and to ask how the fresh perspective offered by this convergence can illuminate, like a well-shaped metaphor, familiar phenomena in an unfamiliar light.

And indeed, pursuing the conjecture a step further reveals a number of possible points of convergence between the aesthetics of gossip and of the Chinese taste. The first, and most obvious, is the manifest delight they both share in the strange, curious, or unexpected. The twisted rocks that provide the focal point and set the stylistic tone for so many characteristically Chinese images are undeniably bizarre. Both Chinese and Western writers, in spite of the differences in the aesthetic paradigms within which they operate, use strikingly similar adjectives to describe these rocks and the compositions built around them: they appear to both groups of writers as surprising, odd, wild, bizarre, singular, strange, and above all, curious. The moral judgment that inflects these terms tends to be far less favorable in the Western descriptions than in the Chinese, but the initial reaction of surprise and curiosity itself is universal.[33]

If we turn back now from the contorted landscapes painted on many an old china teapot to the conversation that once swirled around it, do we not find that curiosity and surprise, wildness and singularity are the essential affective principles of gossip as well? We gossip, according to Spacks, out of an insatiable desire to surprise ourselves and our friends with the unseemly excesses of human behavior, to vicariously gratify our curiosity about inaccessible realms of experience, to reveal in others the wild, untamed impulses we have successfully concealed in ourselves.[34] Scandal attracts us precisely because it flouts prescribed conventions and moral ideals. The scandalous transgression is the social equivalent of the physical deformity or singularity that Joshua Reynolds sought to banish from the canvases of the Royal Academy. As the subject of conversation, it is the nearly precise discursive equivalent of a Chinese garden rock. The congruency is captured by a satirical poem by Christopher Smart that juxtaposes a description of a porcelain teapot:

A Tawdry Tea-Pot, *a-la-mode*,
Where art her utmost skill bestow'd,
Was much esteem'd for being old,
And on its sides with red and gold
Strange beasts were drawn, in taste *Chinese*,
And frightful fish, and hump-back trees...

with a characterization of the scandalous conversation it enables:

To *you* each impious scandal's owing,
You set each gossip's clack a going.
How Parson *Tythe* in secret sins,
And how Miss *Dainty* brought forth twins:
How dear delicious *Polly Bloom*,
Owes all her sweetness to perfume;
Tho' grave at church, at cards can be,
At once a prude and a coquette.

The secret sins of Parson Tythe and his congregation are the moral equivalent, if not the consequence, of the monstrous aesthetic indulged by the patrons of the Chinese taste.[35]

The curiosity that animates gossip resonates on a second level with these geological masterpieces. The strangeness of many a Chinese garden rock is owing to the foraminate structure we see in the pockmarks and holes that penetrate its surface. These pits and craters, carved into limestone boulders by underwater currents, not only add to the singularity of the formation for Chinese connoisseurs, but also contribute to an effect of continual movement and transformation and an outward manifestation of inner structure highly prized among artists and collectors.[36] When we gaze upon a marble statue, the eye is soothed by the uniformity of a finely polished surface and invited by the smoothness of its contours to apprehend the insistent formal unity of the composition as a whole. When we contemplate a *Taihu* rock, in contrast, the eye is endlessly perplexed by the intricacy of surfaces, led in restless pursuit into and through boundless crevices and cavities, never permitted to settle or to proclaim its apprehension of the whole. It is this restless pursuit that suggests a second analogy with gossip. For if curiosity, as a desire to know, characterizes the motive force of gossip, as a mode of action curiosity also describes its method. According to Barbara Benedict, early modern curiosity was all about the restless pursuit of unsanctioned forms of knowledge; it was a form of transgressive penetration, a relentless, unseemly probing into matters best left untouched.[37] What better visual metaphor for this pursuit than a prodigy of pitted limestone? The English gossip, I would suggest, is the kindred spirit of the Chinese rock connoisseur in her privileging of interiority over superfice and in her imaginative revelation of hidden spaces dizzying in their fractal-like complexity.

It passed for a truism in early modern diatribes against gossip that female chatter was a profoundly anti-social form of behavior. Gossips tattled with poison tongues, maliciously destroying the reputations of their rivals through their relentless insinuations of scandal. As Bernard Capp points out in *When Gossips Meet*, the frequent attacks on gossiping "reflected a widespread concern that unsupervised female sociability posed a threat to the order and values of patriarchal society."[38] Whatever its social implications, the destructive potential of scandal mongering is only one half of a complex story. While gossip often sets out to destroy or undermine certain social bonds, it unquestionably strengthens others. As Capp notes, the original meaning of "gossip" was "godparent," but it later came to denote a woman's close female friend. As in any circle of friends, the participants in an early modern gossip session were bound together into an implicit, mutually supportive community through the exchange of advice and assistance, but also of news and judgments about those outside their circle.[39] According to Capp's analysis, while gossiping was fundamentally "about bonding and belonging," this solidarity "could be accompanied by a far more aggressive stance towards outsiders . . . [that] might translate into collective harassment," with the result that "female networks . . . played a key role in policing the boundaries of acceptable behavior."[40]

This simultaneous sustenance and destruction of social ties is, for Spacks, one of several facets of a fundamental dialectic that structures the psychological and social workings of gossip. Our delight in gossip, to point to another, requires an implicit set of shared norms against which the censurable behavior in question stands in a dialectical relation of willful transgression or ignorance. And in a final paradox, the very act of discussing the libidinous exploits of the shameless bed-hoppers among us provides a sanctioned outlet for vicarious sexual pleasure that owes much of its psychic charge to an uneasy tension between our vicarious pleasure and the moralizing posture that enables us to indulge it. Spacks links this recursively dialectical structure of gossip to its irresistible energy and generative force. Just as a novel like *Pamela* achieves an emotional charge by encouraging a reader's sympathy with the opposing voices of the heroine's mind and heart, so gossip attains both its narrative drama and verbal profuseness, she suggests, through a dynamic confrontation between principles of excess and control.[41]

Spacks' description of the relentless energy of gossip helps, I think, to illuminate her provocative claim that this most benighted of conversational forms may occasionally approach the status of art. The aesthetic implicit in such a conception, though, is far removed from the dominant eighteenth-century English notion of ideal beauty. It resembles far more closely the dialectical dynamic of *yin* and *yang* that animates a Ming landscape composition. This dialectic is, according to theorists of the tradition, often most visibly present in the juxtaposition of rock and flowing water (*shanshui*), but it is also expressed in the visual indeterminacy of particular rock formations or of the boundaries between water, rock, mist, and sky, which often seem to flow into or out of one another like a cloud brushing a mountain top. The experience of ambiguity and restless movement in such compositions brings with it the expectation of transformation and perpetual change. The energy flowing through rocks and mountains is linked to this transformative capacity, so that what may first appear an emblem of solidity is also a reminder of flux and decay, and there is a constant sense of transition between these two states. It is precisely this dialectical energy flow within the composition that generates the aesthetic charge of the work as a whole.[42]

I have suggested three parallels between the poetics of gossip and a type of Chinese artistic iconography and pictorial style widely disseminated in early eighteenth-century England. The mere existence of such parallels, as I have noted, proves nothing in itself, and it may, in the end, be simply a product of curious coincidence. But given the ubiquity of Chinese and Chinese-styled goods in England during this period, their demonstrable association with female sociability, and the ferocity with which the nation's self-proclaimed guardians of taste lashed out against the style and its partisans, one can imagine a significant flow of energy, so to speak, between the discursive and visual realms, a profound and mutually reinforcing resonance between the closely intertwined activities of looking and speaking within a particular social context. To suppose that an eighteenth-century consumer might have internalized something of the imaginative sensibility implicit in Chinese art would not necessarily require that she consciously understand, articulate, or imitate it. It might, however, entail a subtle recalibration of aesthetic values and proclivities, an adjustment which, in turn, could quite plausibly find expression or reinforcement in corresponding modes of social interaction. While we must finally concede to Swift the inadequacy of things, in many cases, as substitutes for words, it is clear that things can, nonetheless, speak to us in complex and compelling ways and affect us deeply in what they say. Aesthetics, it is often claimed, is a form of ideology. If eighteenth-century consumers were entranced by the visual charms of Chinese porcelains and lacquerwares, their pleasure may well have encouraged the cultivation of habits of perception and response that transposed elements of a Chinese value system into English social practice.

6 | Horace Walpole and the Gothic repudiation of chinoiserie

In a letter to a close friend in the spring of 1746, Horace Walpole describes a scandalous trial at the Old Bailey of which he has just learned. An elderly widow who for many years, it seems, had been surreptitiously minting coins in an attic room, appeared in court to denounce her maid for the crime of counterfeiting. It soon became clear that the accuser herself was the guilty party, and the maid at worst an unknowing accomplice. On being asked by the incredulous judge whether she had no scruples about accusing an innocent employee of a capital offense, the widow replied that she had trusted that the maid's innocence would be perfectly evident to the court, and that she had made the charge only to save herself from prosecution. The judge, Walpole reports, was furious with her ruse, and made it clear that he wished he could stretch the law to hang her. Walpole's own response is more ambivalent. "I think I never heard," he writes, "a more particular instance of parts and villainy."[1] While he condemns the widow for her cynical indifference to principles of justice and the neck of her servant, he also plainly admires the "parts," or shrewdness and intellectual acumen, she displayed both in her remarkable success as a counterfeiter and in her ingenious manipulation of the law to her own advantage.

Walpole's ambivalence towards the widow's masterpiece of duplicity is typical of his response to the forgeries that proliferated in the eighteenth-century literary world as well. On the one hand, he had little patience for the occasional frauds of which he found himself the dupe. Still smarting, perhaps, at having been taken in by Macpherson's Ossian poems in 1761, Walpole rebuked Thomas Chatterton with such violence upon discovering that he had been deceived by the sixteen-year-old's clever imitations of medieval poetry that he could be plausibly accused in the pages of the *Monthly Review* of contributing to the youth's desperation and suicide.[2] Twelve years after his ill-fated encounter with Chatterton, Walpole was still fuming about the mischief wrought by such literary sleights of hand in their erosion of public standards of taste. He writes to Lady Ossory in 1781, "When there is nothing so foolish and absurd that is not believed and adopted, what matters whether Ossian or Rowley or Mother Goose's Tales are canonized as classics?"[3] Yet ingenuity, as in the widow's case, often seems to compensate for the villainy of deceit. Once recovered from the sting of his own initial gullibility, Walpole fulsomely acknowledges the genius of Chatterton's Rowley poems and "the amazing prodigy" of their production, placing them in the same category as the notorious deceptions of the self-styled native Formosan George Psalmanazar, who by the age of twenty-two, as Walpole gleefully reminds his readers, had created "a language, that all the learned of Europe, though they suspected, could not detect."[4]

The mastermind of Strawberry Hill, one of the greatest architectural impostures of the period, could hardly afford to be too censorious of deception in the name of art. Walpole had purchased the villa at Twickenham in 1747, only one year after the counterfeiting trial he had reported to Horace Mann. Seventeen years later followed the first edition of the *Castle of Otranto,* with its widely credited preface asserting the tale's origin in sixteenth-century Naples. Though he had no doubt forgotten about the audacious widow by this time, surely his pleasure in these creations partook of the same roguish sensibility, attuned to the delightfully subversive possibilities of clever knavery, that had led him to an appreciation of her parts and wit. For the modern reader, the widow's stratagem and the curiously hedged reaction it evokes from Walpole is a reminder not only of the prevalence of numismatic and literary forgeries in Walpole's world, but also, perhaps, of the skepticism with which we ought to treat historical testimony from the hands of acknowledged masters of artifice and illusion. "History," as Walpole himself once quipped, "is a romance that is believed; romance, a history that is not believed."[5]

The historical problem I wish to explore in this chapter concerns the relationship between two of the most prominent, and, at the time, controversial, artistic developments in eighteenth-century England: the chinoiserie style and the Gothic revival. Like the previous chapter, this is a story of unexpected cross-cultural convergences. Like the subjects of the earlier chapters on Chambers and Hogarth, its central character displays a pointed ambivalence towards the Chinese style that can be seen to reflect the unsettling effects of such convergences on the eighteenth-century imagination. In using the term chinoiserie, I refer loosely here to the adaptation by European artists of Chinese motifs and design principles in elements of interior decoration such as wall hangings, porcelain, and furniture, in garden structures and the layout of grounds, and, to a lesser extent, in literary works.[6] As we have seen, the chinoiserie designs of the period are characterized by a distinctly rococo air of lightness and frivolity, a delight in playful or romantic scenes, and a clear preference for capricious incongruities over naturalistic representation. In the fantasy worlds it portrayed, chinoiserie expressed a fascination with the aesthetic possibilities of the unremittingly exotic, an aesthetic response, as I have argued in previous chapters, to a newly illuminated awareness of cultural difference.[7]

The emergent Gothic sensibility, meanwhile, which Walpole so effectively promoted in Strawberry Hill and *Otranto*, derived most recently from the antiquarian researches and Gothic poetry of the early eighteenth century. As the sentiment for appreciating and preserving ancient abbeys and other buildings became more commonplace, proto-Gothic topoi from Spenser and Milton were refashioned into a new poetic style by David Mallet, Thomas Warton, and the Graveyard Poets.[8] But while a certain fascination with scenes of wildness and gloom carries over into the Gothic fiction of the late eighteenth century and beyond, the architectural Gothic of the mid-century frequently exhibited a lighter side. If the owner of Strawberry Hill found satisfaction, as he claimed, "in imprinting the gloom of abbeys and cathedrals" on his house, it was surely a lighthearted gloom, tinged with an irony that placed it at a considerable remove from the somber, brooding melancholy of an Edward Young or a Thomas Gray.[9] While the Gothic revival as a whole was informed by historical research and a patriotic identification with the values of a heroic past, like chinoiserie it also represented an escape from the banalities of history in its fanciful evocations of a distant and exotic world.

The mid-eighteenth century in England, indeed, saw a remarkable convergence between the forms of historical and geographical exoticism represented by the Gothic and chinoiserie. Like the delicate neoclassicism of Robert Adam, both of these styles borrowed from the rococo an air of lightness and nonchalance; both styles expressed a reaction, in their emancipated sensibility and their very novelty, against the staid and rigorous order of earlier classical forms. The authors of architectural pattern books contributed to the popular conflation of the two styles. The year 1752 saw the publication of William and John Halfpenny's handsome folio edition of *Chinese and Gothic Architecture Properly Ornamented*, in which ornate pagoda roofs sporting dragons and dangling bells appear to be largely interchangeable with Gothic turrets and battlements (Figure 16). Two years later, Thomas Chippendale's the *Gentleman and Cabinet-Maker's Director* interspersed unlikely Gothic and Chinese fantasies among its predominantly rococo creations (Figure 17). As an anonymous satirist, no doubt acquainted with one or both of these volumes, quipped in a 1754 edition of the *World*, "It has not escaped your notice how much of late we are improved in architecture; not merely by the adoption of what we call Chinese, nor by the restoration of what we call Gothic; but by a happy mixture of both."[10] This bizarre

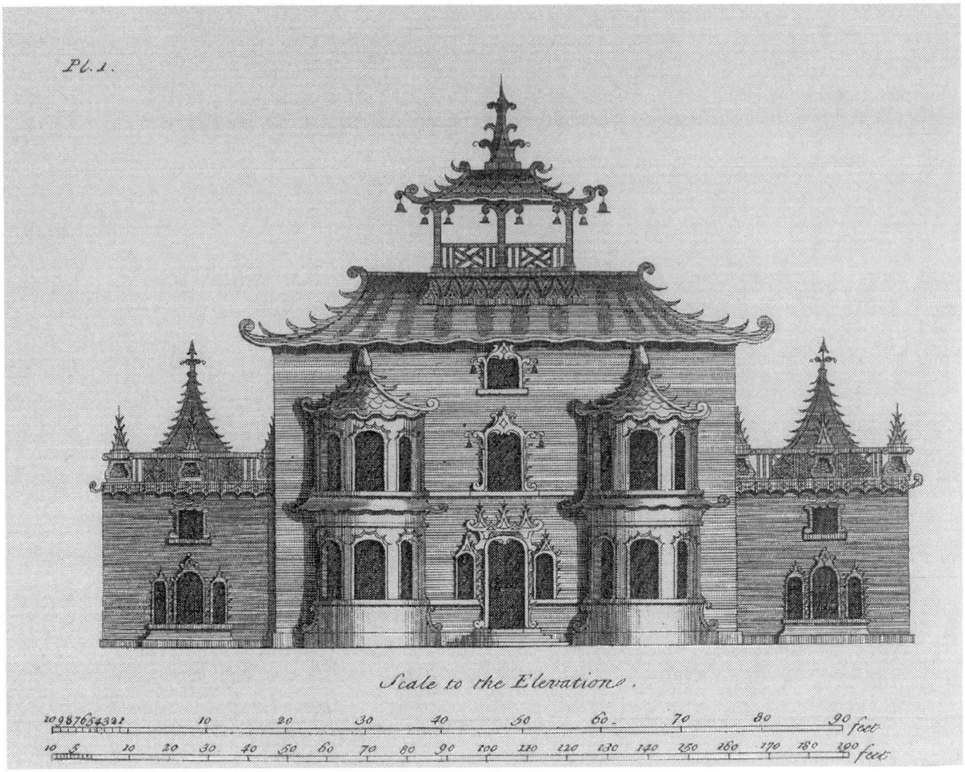

Figure 16 William and John Halfpenny, "Plans for a Design to a House and Offices," in *Chinese and Gothic Architecture Properly Ornamented*, London, 1752.

syncretism was encouraged by the fact that both the Gothic and Chinese styles partook of a spirit of architectural experimentation loosely informed by distant, quaintly exotic, and distinctly anti-classical models.

Observers and critics of the two trends, like the architects themselves, tended to group their productions into a single broad category of aesthetic non-conformity. A contributor to the *World* in 1755 writes of taking a visiting gentleman and his lady on a tour of "all the Gothic and Chinese houses in the neighborhood."[11] With somewhat less equanimity, John Shebbeare observes later in that year that "the simple and sublime have lost all influence almost every where, all is Chinese or Gothic." And it is not just the monstrous figures on Chinese wallpaper and the incongruity of Gothic porches affixed to country manors that he laments; the corruption of taste extends even to music:

To my unpolite ears, the airs which are sung at present have no longer the imitation of any thing which would express passion or sentiment, and the whole merit lyes in

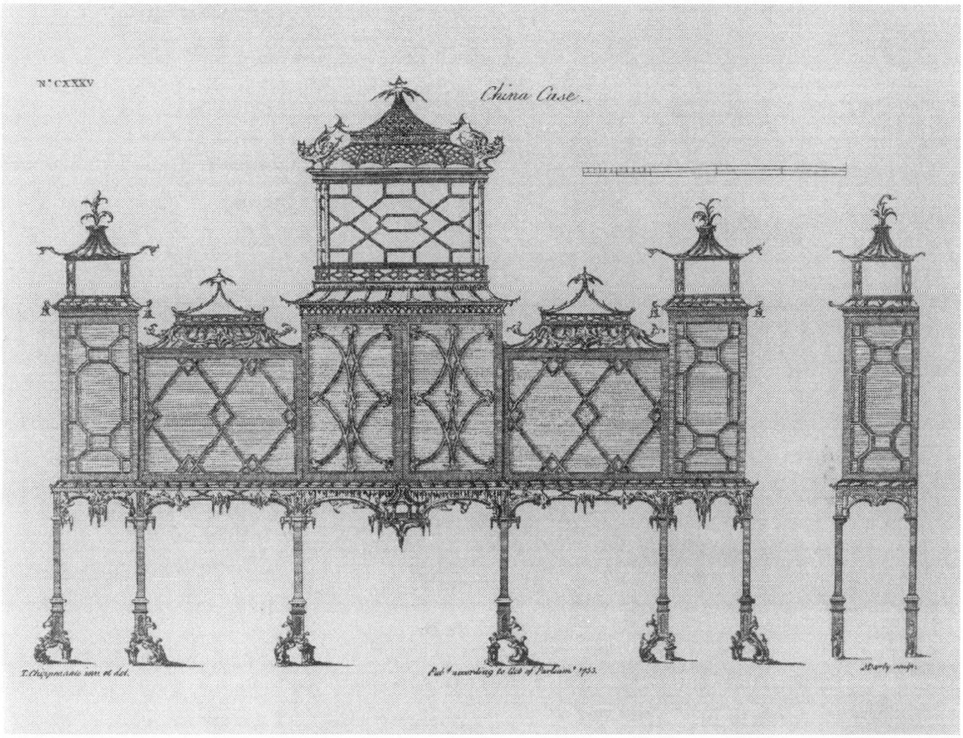

Figure 17 Thomas Chippendale, "China Case," in the *Gentleman and Cabinet Maker's Director*, London, 1754.

the Gothic and Chinese closes and cantabiles, frithered into niceties and divisions, which, like minute carvings, are the certain characteristics of a little taste, that delights more in difficulties than truth.[12]

To the classicist critic, in other words, the Chinese and Gothic styles can be logically grouped together because they offend in the same manner against good taste. To delight in such gratuitous difficulty and intricacy of ornament is, in the words of a Mr. Marriott writing in the *World*, "to threaten the ruin of that simplicity which distinguished the Greek and Roman arts as eternally superior to those of every other nation."[13]

By the late 1760s the Chinese component of this hybrid threat to classical taste had begun to drop out of view. The Gothic revival, of course, continued in full force well into the nineteenth century, but the chinoiserie style gradually fell from vogue, and its later productions no longer occupied the same aesthetic register as those of the increasingly well-defined and self-assured Gothic sensibility. The decline of chinoiserie in the later eighteenth century can be attributed to a number of factors, including simple satiety with a novel fashion, its relative paucity of meaningful historical associations for a Western audience, growing hostility to foreign imports in general, and a broader but clearly perceptible decline of China's standing in the European imagination over the course of the eighteenth century.[14] Whatever the ultimate cause, the clear triumph of the Gothic over the Chinese as the dominant mode of anti-classical, proto-romantic innovation in the later eighteenth century has tended to eclipse the historical fact of their striking and unmistakable convergence during the 1750s and to obscure the early kinship between the two styles in standard genealogies of the Gothic aesthetic.

If the insistently nativist Gothic style is, as I am suggesting, haunted by the sprightly ghosts of chinoiserie, Horace Walpole will prove an indispensable, if not entirely disinterested witness to the fact. As the first successful popularizer of the Gothic creed in both fiction and architecture and a connoisseur known for the omnivorous eclecticism of his taste, he is uniquely positioned to speak to us of the myriad aesthetic and intellectual currents that fed into the Gothic stream. A number of these have been thoroughly documented: the influences of the Grand Tour, Italian landscape painting, antiquarianism, trends in lyric poetry, and the emergence of theories of the sublime are incontestable and need not be rehearsed here. Chinoiserie, however, perhaps because of the seeming incompatibility of its essential lightness with the more forbidding affective timbre typically associated with the Gothic, rarely receives more than an incidental mention. My contention is that it warrants more than this, and that Walpole himself was largely responsible for the subsequent historical oversight.

Walpole's own interest in chinoiserie describes a trajectory similar to the general trend in the style's reception in England during his lifetime. Although crucial letters from this period are missing, he seems to have been an early and ardent convert to the new fashion for all things Chinese. In 1735, during his first year at Cambridge, he received from Lord Hervey a copy of the Jesuit compiler Jean Baptiste Du Halde's monumental *General History of China*, the standard source for eighteenth-century sinophiles in both France and England. He must initially have shared in the general enthusiasm over the marvels of this newly accessible civilization, for Lord Hervey writes to him, "[I] am extremely glad to hear the History of China has so strong an effect upon you . . . You describe in a very entertaining manner the change it has made in you." Hervey seems to have feared that the impressionable young student would don a mandarin's garb and in a moment of misguided Confucian reverie ship off to Canton, for he continues this passage, "notwithstanding my partiality to China, I advise you if you can to continue an Englishman."[15]

There is little further mention of matters Chinese in the letters until 1750, but in this and several subsequent years Walpole resurrects his youthful fascination with the East and is thoroughly swept up by the chinoiserie craze. He calls the goldfish pond at Strawberry Hill *Po Yang*, after a reference in Du Halde to a large lake in Jiangxi province celebrated for its plentiful fish. He refers playfully to a boar and sow on his estate as "the Chinese pair," and describes an overweight acquaintance as resembling "Ticchi Micchi . . . the Chinese god of good eating and drinking."[16] In 1756 he composes two unpublished letters for the *World* drawing upon the story of the notorious book-burning Chinese emperor Qin Shihuang in order to mount a playfully satiric assault on the excesses of the publishing industry.[17]

When he turns to the description of houses and grounds in this period, Walpole follows the architects and critics cited above in conflating the Chinese and Gothic styles. A letter written in 1750 from Strawberry Hill to Horace Mann, then in Florence, conveys the appeal of the new vogue to the trendsetters of the age:

> I wish you could see the villas and seats here! The country wears a new face; every body is improving their places, and as they don't fortify their plantations with entrenchments of walls and high hedges, one has the benefit of them even in passing by. The dispersed buildings, I mean, temples, bridges, etc. are generally Gothic or Chinese and give a whimsical air of novelty that is very pleasing.[18]

In another letter of the same year, also to Mann, he specifies more precisely the nature of the Chinese contribution to this new stylistic synthesis. In explaining the limited usefulness of the Palladian style outside of stately public buildings, he makes use of a new aesthetic term recently imported from the Chinese:

> Columns and all their beautiful ornaments look ridiculous when crowded into a closet or a cheesecake house. The variety is little, and admits no charming irregularities. I am almost as fond of the Sharawaggi, or Chinese want of symmetry, in buildings, as in grounds or gardens. I am sure whenever you come to England, you will be pleased with the liberty of taste into which we are struck, and of which you can have no idea.[19]

The term "sharawaggi" (more frequently spelled "sharawadgi") which Walpole associates in this passage with irregularity, asymmetry, and freedom from the rigid conventions of classical design, was introduced by Sir William Temple in his 1692 essay *Upon the Gardens of Epicurus* and by the time of Walpole's letter had become a common term in the lexicon of eighteenth-century aesthetic theory. Possibly derived from the Chinese phrase *sa luo wei qi*, literally meaning careless grace employed for an impressive and surprising effect, it typically referred to the principle of planned naturalness of appearance in garden design.[20] What is particularly striking in Walpole's appropriation of the term is that he extends its accepted horticultural usage to encompass the variety and charming irregularity that characterize his vision of Gothic architecture. In those very principles, in other words, that mark its departure from cold classical symmetries, the spirit of the Gothic is for Walpole in this letter unmistakably Chinese.

Within two years, however, the novelty of the Chinese style as such had begun to fade. There are no further ebullient accounts in Walpole's letters of Chinese bridges and temples and the glories of sharawadgi, and he never moved forward with a proposed Chinese house at Strawberry Hill for which Bentley had provided a plan.[21] He seems increasingly troubled, indeed, by the very conflation of styles that had once seemed so stimulating. In 1752 he describes to Bentley a pyramid he had seen at Lord Westmorland's Mereworth estate, "which by a most unnatural copulation is at once a grotto and a greenhouse." He continues with a telling comparison: "Does it not put you in mind of the proposal for your drawing a garden-seat, Chinese on one side and Gothic on the other?"[22] Where once variety and syncretism had been the hallmarks of stylistic panache, purity of form is now privileged as the mark of cultivated taste. In another letter to Bentley of the same period he reiterates his growing impatience with hybrid architectural pedigrees: "When I every day see Greek and Roman and Italian and Chinese and Gothic architecture embroidered and inlaid upon one another, or called by each other's names, I couldn't help thinking that the grace and simplicity and truth of your taste, in whichever you undertake, is real taste."[23] It should be noted that in these passages Walpole is not so much rejecting the Chinese style *per se* as repudiating his earlier belief in the possibility of productive architectural synthesis between East and West. Simplicity and truth can, after all, be attained within the Chinese style; it is the potential mongrelization of forms that raises the alarm.

In later years, Walpole definitively breaks off his flirtation with chinoiserie, positing the Gothic not only as a distinct style but as a clearly superior one. Recalling, perhaps, Lord Hervey's admonishment that he remain an Englishman, he boasts in several letters about "having converted Dicky Bateman from a Chinese to a Goth," noting with smug satisfaction that "though he was the founder of the Sharawadgi taste in England, I preached so effectually that his every pagoda took the veil."[24] But Walpole's most dramatic and stinging repudiation of the sharawadgi taste is prompted not by a travesty in architecture but in gardening. In May of 1772, Sir William Chambers, royal architect and designer of Somerset House and the gardens at Kew, published the controversial *Dissertation on Oriental Gardening* discussed at length in Chapter 2. As we saw there, the burden of his argument in this lengthy treatise is that the prevailing style in garden design, the literalist naturalism of Lancelot "Capability" Brown with its predictably undulating walks and hills, had fallen into dullness and insipidity, and that the Chinese approach, with its emphasis on variety, surprise, and an active engagement of the viewer's imagination, supplied the perfect remedy. In his fanciful and rather far-fetched descriptions of an elaborate Chinese garden, Chambers deliberately stretches the principle of sharawadgi to the point of absurdity in order to make the serious point that the guiding purpose of garden design ought to be to stir and engage the passions and imagination of the viewer.[25]

Walpole's response to the *Dissertation* is swift and implacably hostile. Within weeks of its publication, he writes to William Mason that he has read the book, and finds it "more extravagant than the worst Chinese [wall]paper." Nor does he find himself alone in this view. The book "is laughed at," he adds, "and it is not likely to be adopted, as I expected, for nothing is so tempting to fools, as advice to deprave taste."[26] That same summer he collaborates with Mason in composing an anonymously published satirical rebuke, *An Heroic Epistle to Sir William Chambers*, a small masterpiece of parody and pugnacious political pasquinade that went through fourteen editions in five years, thoroughly discrediting Chambers' position, and contributing in no small measure to the continuing decline of the Chinese vogue in England. As if to nail the lid on the coffin, Walpole inserts a brief entry on Chambers in the final volume of *Anecdotes of Painting in England* that dismisses the dissertation as "a work that tended to bring back all manner of bad and whimsical taste."[27]

Why did Walpole turn so sharply against this witty and entertaining manifesto of a style that he once had so admired? Long-standing personal animosity towards the author was clearly not at issue: in 1771 he had written to a friend that he was "slightly acquainted" with Chambers and had "a good opinion of him," and in the preface to the first volume of *Anecdotes of Painting* he had described Chambers' treatise on civil architecture as "the most sensible book and the most exempt from prejudices that ever was written on that science."[28] Nor does it seem plausible to reduce the quarrel to a simple difference in taste. Attacks on the *Dissertation*'s extravagance and whimsicality are, frankly, difficult to take seriously from an author who had penned both *Otranto* and the playfully absurdist *Hieroglyphic Tales* within the previous eight years. The model of true taste in gardening, moreover, that Walpole proposes as a felicitous alternative to Chambers could hardly be exempt from similar criticisms. Mason's long poem the *English Garden*, lavishly praised by Walpole in his notes to a collection of Mason's poetry, indulges in Gothic fantasies every bit as wild and extravagant as Chambers' paeans to chinoiserie. Mason's idealized vision of a garden in the "antient English" style includes a barn guarded by a mock portcullis, a dairy and ice house veiled in "moss grown stone" to resemble a "time struck abbey," and various other structures "in Gothic-semblance" that would stir the viewer with "those bold feudal forms that fancy loves to gaze on."[29] Mason, as Isabel Chase has pointed out, "criticized Chambers for doing essentially the same thing that he himself was attempting to do," with, we might add, the aid and abetment of Horace Walpole.[30]

It is clear that politics played some role in the outburst against Chambers: Mason and Walpole, in addition to being admirers of Chambers' rival Capability Brown, were both confirmed Whigs, and found in Chambers, that favorite of the Tory court, a safe and suitable target for their vituperative attacks on the administration of George III. But given Walpole's earlier endorsements of Chambers and his work, partisan political antagonism alone would seem an insufficient explanation for Walpole's hostility towards the *Dissertation.*

Political considerations of another kind, however, do seem likely to have affected Walpole's assessment of Chambers' work. Throughout his life, the son of Britain's longest-serving prime minister was an unabashed patriot in matters of aesthetics, and one who occasionally allowed his chauvinism to cloud his better judgment. In the first volume of *Anecdotes of Painting*, Walpole ventures in a highly speculative aside to claim the invention of oil painting for England. Though he acknowledges that his hypothesis is "nothing more . . . than mere conjecture" that is "unsupported by any of the writers on painting,"[31] he continues to entertain it over the course of the next decade, until his eagerness to uncover corroborating evidence leads him to his initially credulous reception of Chatterton's forgeries. In March of 1769 Walpole receives from the young poet an essay purporting to give a history of painting in England, supposedly penned by one T. Rowleie in 1469. He replies the same day, asking for a clarification of dates that he hopes will confirm "what I had guessed . . . that oil painting was known here much earlier than [its] discovery or revival [by John Van Eyck (1385–1441)]."[32] Walpole was led, in other words, into one of the more embarrassing and ultimately tragic mistakes of his career in part by the seductive appeal of a nationalist historiography.

Unrepentant, Walpole composes in the following year the fourth volume of *Anecdotes of Painting*, covering the history of the arts in his own era from a similarly partisan perspective. In a chapter on architecture under

George II, he seems intent on redeeming the honor of his country from the humiliating collapse of his painting hypothesis by proclaiming in decidedly jingoistic tones its triumph in another sphere:

> Before the glorious close of a reign that carried our arms and victories beyond where Roman eagles ever flew, ardour for the arts had led our travellers to explore whatever beauties of Grecian or Latin taste still subsisted in provinces once subjected to Rome; and the fine editions in consequence of those researches have established the throne of architecture in Britain, while itself languishes at Rome, wantons in tawdry imitations of the French in other parts of Europe, and struggles in vain at Paris to surmount their prepossession in favour of their own errors.[33]

A final, striking instance of Walpole's nationalist proclivities as a cultural historian arises in a 1791 discussion of Western civilization's historical debts to the East. Though he grants the greater antiquity of the East, he argues – anticipating a common nineteenth-century refrain – that its later stagnation left it with little of value to offer the rapidly advancing West. The Egyptians and notably, for our purposes, the Chinese count among those "nations who made early progress in sciences and arts, and stopped short . . . like forward children who have quick parts at five years old, were advanced no farther at fifteen, and at thirty are blockheads." A blockhead nation, clearly, could have had nothing to offer the Greeks, and Walpole dismisses the possibility of any early cross-fertilization out of hand:

> You will not wonder that I have not the least enthusiasm for the East – much less do I believe that the country, and a very diminutive one, that engrosses all my admiration, learnt almost anything from their orient predecessors. When Greece in so few centuries that they scarce form a number, could establish standards of perfection in so many various kinds, I cannot think they borrowed from such rude and barbarous elements as the East furnished.[34]

This passage represents a logical culmination of Walpole's earlier anxieties over the promiscuous blending of Chinese and Gothic styles in architecture. From the time of his initial repudiation of the chinoiserie style in the 1750s, Walpole is preoccupied – in a manner familiar from our discussion of Hogarth and that we will see again in the case of Thomas Percy in Chapter 8 – with a vision of aesthetic supremacy for England and its classical patrimony based largely on notions of cultural purity that explicitly exclude any vestige of oriental influence.

In this light, the motivation for Walpole's hostile response to Chambers seems far more readily apparent. The English, after all, had made great strides in gardening over the course of the century, as Walpole himself had proudly documented in his *History of the Modern Taste in Gardening.* In 1748, he had lamented living in "so barbarous an age, when we are come to so little perfection in gardening."[35] By 1771 he can hardly contain his enthusiasm over the influence of the now well-established English style in France. He writes from Paris, "It is with great satisfaction I inform your Ladyship that the taste of English gardening makes great progress here . . . I have been to see a garden almost out of Paris, which has been laid out in our taste at a vast expense . . ."[36] When the *Dissertation* appeared in the following year, it must have been for Walpole a most unwelcome reminder that this newly triumphant English taste in gardening in fact owed a substantial debt to the Chinese in the now thoroughly assimilated idea of sharawadgi. Already in the first edition of his history of gardening he had caricatured Chinese gardens as marred by excessive artificiality and "unsubstantial tawdriness" in an early attempt to discredit this putative model for English innovations.[37] But as he no doubt had feared, many of Chambers' readers, chief among them the French, recognized the connection between Chinese theory and English practice and cast aspersions on English celebrations of their supposedly original achievements. In 1775 Walpole complains to Mason "that by the help of Sir William Chambers' lunettes [the French] have detected us for having stolen our gardens from the Chinese,"[38] and in the 1782 edition of the gardening history he attempts to set the record straight on precisely this point, appending a lengthy footnote defending England's laurels:

> The French have of late years adopted our style in gardens, but chusing to be fundamentally obliged to more remote rivals, they deny us half the merit, or rather the originality of the invention, by ascribing the discovery to the Chinese, and by calling our taste in gardening Le Gout Anglo-Chinois. I think I have shewn that this is a blunder . . .[39]

In his notes to Mason's *Satirical Poems* he presses his claim still further, asserting that "the imitation of Nature in Gardens . . . is Original, & indisputably English," and that, moreover, owing to its dependence on vast accumulations of wealth sanctioned by the state, "the English Taste in Gardening is . . . the growth of the English Constitution, & must perish with it."[40]

Arthur Lovejoy has argued persuasively that Walpole was wrong in his assessment of the essential Englishness of the new style, and that the French were largely justified in referring to it as an Anglo-Chinese taste. Chinese ideas in gardening, filtered most notably through Temple and Chambers, but also, less directly, through Addison, Pope, and others, shaped in significant ways some of the most prominent aesthetic theory and practice of the eighteenth century.[41] Walpole refused to see, or at least refused to acknowledge this influence for the same reason that he rejected the architectural syncretism of the 1750s and the possibility of classical debts to oriental civilizations: a misplaced patriotism and an accompanying distaste for cross-cultural hybridity of any kind.

This much, at any rate, can be reliably ascertained from the materials Walpole chose to leave us. But what if, following Walpole's example with regard to the origins of oil painting, we venture beyond the limits of the historical record to engage in some conjectural speculation of our own? It is here that we return to the genealogy of the Gothic and to the opening story of the counterfeiter's false charge. For what if it was not just chauvinistic zeal that prompted Walpole's willful blindness to Chinese contributions, but a more deeply rooted authorial vanity as well? What if Walpole, like the cunning widow he had described with admiration and disgust, turned against a former ally in order to safeguard his own name and place in literary history? One would not expect Walpole to have been troubled by imitations of his work, as they would only testify to his pre-eminence as the founding father of a style. Given what we have seen thus far, however, one would expect him to have been horrified by even a veiled suggestion that his own writings had oriental inspirations, or that any but the purest English ink, as he once put it, flowed through its author's veins.

Yet on reading Walpole's fiction alongside Chambers' writings on Chinese gardening, one cannot fail to be struck by profound similarities, suggesting that Walpole's work shared with Chambers' a common proto-orientalist genealogy stemming from his earlier infatuations. Most obviously there are the prominent stage effects, the machinery of sublime supernatural spectacle engineered to entrance and terrify the viewer. *Otranto* boasts animated portraits, bleeding statues, and rambling giants; Chinese gardeners, according to Chambers, compose "scenes of terror" featuring not only gloomy woods and implements of torture by the side of the road, but also smoking volcanos, fiery explosions, and simulated earthquakes. On reading the two books side by side, a reader might well surmise that labyrinthine passages, secret caverns, beautiful maidens, and an atmosphere charged with thinly veiled eroticism were common accoutrements of both medieval Italian castles and Chinese pleasure gardens. Both authors, in other words, recognize the aesthetic limitations of a strictly naturalistic vision and reach to the supernatural as a means to escape the stifling conventions of established genres. For Walpole, the dominant paradigm to be contested is that of the modern romance, or novel, in which, as he writes in the second preface to

The Castle of Otranto, "nature is always intended to be . . . copied with success," with the result that "the great resources of fancy have been dammed up, by a strict adherence to common life."[42] Similarly, Chambers objects to the prevailing style of gardening among the English on the grounds that nature tends to be copied so closely, and with so little guidance from the imagination, that "our gardens differ very little from common fields."[43] Walpole's solution to the problem of the modern novel is to inject naturalism with an animating dose of fantasy, to "[leave] the powers of fancy at liberty to expatiate through the boundless realms of invention" in order to "[create] more interesting situations." Chambers' remedy to the slavish adherence to "inanimate, simple nature" is likewise to enliven it with the powers of fancy. "Gardeners, like poets, should give a loose to their imagination, and even fly beyond the bounds of truth, whenever it is necessary to elevate, to embellish, to enliven, or to add novelty to their subject."[44]

The list of congruities in the two writers' understanding of aesthetic practice continues. Both writers explicitly privilege original invention over imitation and adherence to rules. Both recognize and capitalize on the value of variety as an essential component of the aesthetic experience. And both, finally, fly in the face of classical convention in advocating an appeal to the passions as a legitimate component of artistic expression. When Chambers writes in the *Dissertation* that the aim of Chinese gardeners "is to excite a great variety of passions in the mind of the spectator; and the fertility of their imaginations, always upon the stretch in search of novelty, furnishes them with a thousand artifices to accomplish that aim,"[45] he recalls Walpole's famous distinction between the Grecian and Gothic styles in the *Anecdotes of Painting*:

> It is difficult for the noblest Grecian temple to convey half so many impressions to the mind, as a cathedral does of the best Gothic taste . . . [Their creators] exhausted their knowledge of the passions in composing edifices whose pomp, mechanism, vaults, tombs, painted windows, gloom and perspectives infused such sensations of romantic devotion . . . One must have taste to be sensible of the beauties of Grecian architecture; one only wants passions to feel Gothic.[46]

In the second preface to *Otranto*, Walpole claims Shakespeare as his model in order to justify his wild deviations from accepted generic conventions. Shakespearean license notwithstanding, however, the affective foundations of his novel consist in large measure of those passions evoked by the pomp and gloom of the Gothic cathedral. But the Gothic of *Otranto* is not all pomp and gloom. There is a tincture of frivolity, of absurdity, of ironic delight in incongruity that is entirely absent in the Graveyard Poets. This tincture of absurdity is the spirit of chinoiserie that haunts Walpole's Gothic, and bubbles exuberantly to the surface of his *Hieroglyphic Tales*. The Gothic sensibility, for Walpole, was intimately bound up in his early life with his interest in chinoiserie. Later, he struggled to separate the two strands of aesthetic innovation in the hopes of purifying the Gothic of its vestiges of Eastern influence, just as he would attempt to free English gardening from its embarrassing association with chinoiserie. The publication of Chambers' *Dissertation on Oriental Gardening* raised his hackles not only because it cast aspersions on the cultural purity of the English country estate, but also because it reminded him of his personal debt to the Chinese taste in liberating his own aesthetic vision from the shackles of conformity.

Walpole's most recent biographer, Timothy Mowl, has argued persuasively, if controversially, that the famous account of *Otranto*'s origin in a fantastic dream and a subsequent frenzy of spontaneous composition was, in fact, a convenient lie contrived by Walpole in part to conceal his anguish over his ignominious outing as an effete homosexual at the hands of William Guthrie in 1764.[47] If the shame of a forbidden passion is, as Mowl suggests, concealed among the twists of guilt and vengeance that shape the plot of Walpole's tale, there are vestiges in the novel, too, of another kind of secret love, an infatuation with the sheer extravagance, ironic incongruities, and playful insouciance of a style imported not from the Middle Ages but from a distant and quaintly exotic East.

PART IV

China and the invention of Englishness

7 Chinaware and the evolution of a modern domestic ideal

The material turn of cultural studies notwithstanding, the professional disposition of the text-oriented scholar makes it difficult to grant to material objects the same potency as sources of cultural meaning that are so readily attributed to text and language. It remains tempting simply to subsume isolated objects within the categories of the textual (where they can be "read" or "decoded") or the aesthetic (where they are given license to "evoke" or "inspire"), to interpret them, that is, merely as secondary instances of language or art, rather than carving out discrete theoretical categories in order to understand their distinctive role in meaning making. If there is any truth to Weber's claims regarding the progressive disenchantment of the modern world, it stems in large measure, I suspect, from our deeply entrenched post-Enlightenment and, indeed, post-Reformation insensibility to the inner life of things.

In this chapter I will reach beyond familiar textual and aesthetic frames to elaborate on the kinds of cultural work that enchanting objects can perform when they are set loose in an unsuspecting world. As I have attempted to show throughout this book, the Chinese objects imported in vast quantities in the seventeenth and eighteenth centuries were never simply passive objects of consumption, evaluation, and symbolic appropriation, but rather functioned also as active catalysts for the transformation of sensibilities and social identities. To borrow the lingo of material culture theorists, porcelain objects were good to think with.[1]

In particular, they were useful in thinking about gender. Chinese ceramics take on a wide range of meanings and associations in England during the early modern period, but as several earlier chapters have made clear, there is a pronounced clustering of these meanings around ideas of the feminine. In this chapter I will address two specific questions that emerge from my previous observations concerning the gendered reception of Chinese goods in the British context. First, and most generally, how does porcelain acquire the array of specific cultural meanings that it does over the course of its striking metamorphosis from exotic novelty in the early seventeenth century to quotidian necessity and paradigm of Englishness by the end of the eighteenth? Second, and more specifically, by what narrative logic do the commonplace associations of Chinese ceramics with women evolve over the course of this period?

In considering these questions I will attempt to steer clear of the language of symbolism. Porcelain objects can and do function as relatively straightforward symbols within certain works of the period. But the notion of a symbol typically suggests a sense of stasis and intentionality that can be deeply misleading insofar as it obscures the flux and flow of an object's meanings in real life, deriving as they do from the largely arbitrary and provisional ways in which we actually use objects to forge new thought structures or to accomplish psychological tasks. To read a rose simply as a symbol of love, for example, may blind us to the more subtle ways in which the rose enables us to focus, amplify, preserve, or reflect on experiences of affection, passion, loss, nostalgia, and the like. In interpreting depictions of porcelain in early modern visual and textual artifacts, then, I will resist the temptation to ascribe to them a fixed, predetermined symbolic meaning or value, and try to grapple instead with the question of how these objects might have worked to catalyze and thereby bring into being new, perhaps inarticulable ways of seeing and knowing for those who traded, owned, or admired them.

Whereas the symbolic value of objects within a particular tradition is often understood to be relatively stable and even quasi-universal, this catalytic function of objects is by definition historically contingent. The clusters of associations that gather about a given object depend on what kinds of still-formless ideas, aspirations, longings, and anxieties are emerging into consciousness at a particular moment and are therefore seeking with the greatest urgency a material habitation and a name. As Jules Prown writes, "[w]hen style is shared by clusters of objects in a time and place, it is akin to a cultural daydream expressing unspoken beliefs."[2] So, to take another example, the booming popularity in the United States of oversized sports utility vehicles like the Hummer and the Navigator from the late 1990s into the early years of the second Iraq war might be understood, at least in part, as a result of their ability to catalyze – to give a reassuring shape, form, and substance to – an increasingly solipsistic conception of American triumphalism that emerged in the post-Cold War period.

Whereas a ceramic vessel in the 1690s certainly can appear as unmistakable and unambiguous a symbol within a Freudian lexicon as any monumental obelisk, it can also function, like a rose or a sports utility vehicle, in considerably more nuanced and less predictable ways. In an effort to foreground the contingency of this catalytic function and to begin to answer the question posed above concerning the evolution of the meaning of porcelain, I will frame my observations as a three-stage history of depictions of Chinese porcelain in England from roughly 1615 to 1760. While my three stages do overlap chronologically and the narrative connecting them invites further elaboration, I hope the rough schema they provide may help to make better sense of the otherwise bewildering variety of gender-inflected responses to Chinese wares evident across this period.

It is difficult to overestimate the wondrous novelty of Chinese porcelain when it first began arriving in significant quantities on English shores in the seventeenth century. For the past thousand years, according to Robert Finlay, porcelain had been the "most universally admired and most widely imitated product in the world."[3] In English domestic spaces where the spartan surfaces of wood, pewter, and coarse earthenware goods had long been the norm, Chinese porcelain surely delighted the senses in its dazzling luminosity, pearl-like smoothness, and sonorousness when struck. The captivating blue and white designs common to the late Ming and early Qing porcelains exported from China during this period were of an intricacy and clarity unlike anything that had been seen in the European decorative arts up to that time. While some of the designs were based on abstract floral motifs, others, copied in China from woodblock prints and popular editions of novels and plays, vividly illustrated the extravagantly exotic garden scenes discussed at length in Chapter 3.

It is important to stress here the extraordinary novelty, in England, of these designs and images and the distinctive aesthetic they embodied. When we think of eighteenth-century chinaware, we most often think of chinoiserie, that tremendously popular but decidedly European amalgam of rococo, Gothic, and Chinese influences that gave us willow-pattern dinner sets and the Brighton Pavilion. Chinoiserie is, as I have suggested, a thoroughly hybrid style, representing the local domestication of an alien visual sensibility. In contrast, the first porcelain wares to reach the English marketplace and to stimulate the imaginations of consumers were bona fide Chinese goods reflecting contemporary Chinese rather than European tastes. The significance of this distinction is that it allows us to regard Chinese porcelain as something more like a genuine *tabula rasa* when it first enters the British semiotic field. Because such objects had rarely, if ever, been seen before and their alien aesthetic had not yet been stylistically assimilated to a European sensibility, their imaginative valences and uses within a Western context were as yet largely unsettled and indeterminate.

It is also worth recalling that, contrary to the kind of orientalist cliché of Chinese cultural stagnation that we saw Walpole espouse in the previous chapter, the Chinese wares imported during the seventeenth century represented neither a changeless Chinese aesthetic nor even a particularly venerable tradition. As it turns out, the types of porcelain that arrived in East India Company warehouses during this period were nearly as much of a novelty in China as they were in England. In Chapter 3 I described how the collapse of the Ming dynasty in 1644 led Jingdezhen craftsmen to turn away from the formal, non-representational designs favored by the court to a more figural iconography, often borrowed from illustrated novels and plays, that appealed to the increasingly prosperous Chinese merchant classes. By what seems a remarkable historical coincidence, popular vernacular fiction first flowered in China at nearly exactly the same time and for many of the same social and demographic reasons as it did in England. It is perhaps not altogether surprising, then, that the porcelain accessories to the rise of the Chinese novel in the early Qing dynasty found such a favorable reception among the readers of Aphra Behn, Eliza Haywood, and Samuel Richardson.

But we hardly need a hypothesis of cultural convergence to account for the instant popularity of Chinese wares when they arrived on European shores. Their pure sensual appeal, exotic novelty, and luxury pricing were surely sufficient to ensure that porcelain objects would become highly desired commodities in seventeenth-century England and its neighbors, and that Chinese blue and white wares would be regularly depicted in contemporary still lifes as emblems of sumptuousness and wealth. One of the first and most obvious uses of these alien artifacts, in other words, was no doubt in the service of status display. In the homes of the wealthy, the massing of porcelain objects was a clear instance of conspicuous consumption. The problem with any account that stresses the status value of objects, however, is that it reduces their myriad potential sources of appeal and interest to a single, overriding concern with social prestige. I will suggest that the specific contexts of the consumption of porcelain in this period invited a clustering of considerably more nuanced and volatile associations.

In the modern popular imagination porcelain carries decidedly domestic connotations. If home is where the hearth is, it is also where, at least for a certain demographic segment, the tea set is laid out, where the family china is displayed, where elegant vases and collectible figurines adorn bookshelves and knick-knack stands. Prior to colonizing the bourgeois ideal of domestic space, however, Chinese wares had first to find their way from London's East India Company warehouses on Leadenhall Street to the private homes of the elite. Inevitably they did so through the very public space of the marketplace.[4] And it was within this mercantile space, I will suggest, that the idea of Chinese porcelain first took shape as a versatile and potent talisman in the cultural lexicon.

We know that in seventeenth-century London, porcelain wares were sold in so-called china-houses, many of which were clustered near the New Exchange, a fashionable shopping mall that first opened in 1609. We also know that these shops seem often to have been owned and regularly frequented by women, suggesting that the site of London consumers' early, formative encounters with this strange and alluring new class of goods was both a very public and a decidedly female space, and one that often carried an erotic charge. Addressing the New Exchange in 1619, one commentator observed, "Thy shops with prettie wenches swarm, / Which for thy custome are a kind of charme / To idle gallants."[5] While true porcelain would not be fired in Europe for another hundred years, as a cultural construct it was first forged in a crucible combining a volatile mixture of sensuality, novelty, femininity, desire, and exchange. The richly cathected artifact that emerged served as a powerful catalyst for an increasingly commercial society's constructions of female sexuality in the literature and visual culture of the seventeenth and early eighteenth centuries. The familiar ceramic vessel of Catholic iconography, a symbol of virginal purity, was transformed through the English china trade and the urban literary and visual culture that accompanied it into an eroticized vehicle for imaginings of illicit and commoditized desire.

An early sign of this transformation appears in Ben Jonson's play *Epicene*, first performed in London in 1609. The play is set in the neighborhood of the Strand and the New Exchange, a newly fashionable address and a part of town known for conspicuous consumption. The character Sir Amorous La Foole, we learn, has taken a lodging in the Strand in order "to watch when ladies are gone to the china-houses or the Exchange, that he may meet 'em by chance and give 'em presents."[6] Note the interpellation of multiple forms of desire and exchange even within this single sentence. Sir Amorous is as entranced by the visual spectacle of colorfully bedecked ladies as the ladies are by the dazzling porcelain. Pursuing the object of desire in each case requires stepping out of the safety and privacy of a home into a relatively anarchic public space. And obtaining that object, in each case, involves an exchange, whether of silver coins for porcelain jars, or flattering presents for sexual favors.

The china-house becomes, by implication, a site of seduction, exchange, and sexual commodification, so that we are hardly surprised when in the following scene we learn about a "rich china-woman" – the proprietor of another china-house – who is regularly frequented by male courtiers drawn by the "rare entertainment" that she offers.[7] Southerne's play *The Maid's Last Prayer* of 1693 picks up this connection by introducing another china-woman, Mrs. Siam, who is likewise suspected of being a bawd, suggesting that the wondrous novelty of these women's exotic wares captured metonymically the curiosity and thrill attending their trade in female bodies.[8] As late as 1724, a young woman selling china still carries an erotic charge: a tottering Oxford don in a poem by Nicholas Amhurst falls for

Fair RAGGABEL, that near his college-gate
Fine china sells, and tea, and chocolate . . .
Oft to her shop the feeble lecher strays,
Toys with her hand, or with her bubbies plays.[9]

Once again, the spectacle of china in a public space evokes illicit sexual desire. Chinawares and the women who traffic in them are conflated as alluring playthings whose accessibility is guaranteed by their appearance in the public marketplace. The implicit analogy linking women and porcelain vessels as both commodities and objects of desire that runs through these examples becomes fully explicit in a song Fielding provided for his adaptation of a play by Molière in 1731:

A Woman's Ware like China,
Now dear, now cheap is bought;
When whole 'tis worth a Guinea,
When broke not worth a Groat.[10]

In each of these cases, one might be tempted to posit a simple transformation of the religious symbolism of the ceramic vase in annunciation paintings for a Protestant, mercantile context: the precious vessel is still a female body, but now it has become an explicitly eroticized and commodified one. As Christopher Smart's scrubbing brush lambasts a "tawdry tea-pot" in a mid-century poem, "*You're* fair without, but foul within, / With shame impregnated, and sin."[11] But the transformation turns out to be more complicated than this, and the pleasures of porcelain more polymorphously perverse. While Sir Amorous La Foole may regard the china-house as a place to meet attractive women, the women, we might assume, are drawn to the china. The playwright William Wycherley famously seizes upon the metaphorical possibilities of this attraction when, in the *Country Wife*, he casts porcelain in the role of a rakish hero's sexual potency. Horner famously gains access to married women by claiming to be a eunuch; while the ladies are delighted by his abundant store of precious china, there never seems to be quite enough to go around.[12] While the most famous metaphor of the play may inflect our response to cylindrical porcelain jars and certain curious Delftware drinking vessels excavated from the site of seventeenth-century London brothels (Figures 18 and 19), the metaphor is, finally, less about the phallic attributes of ceramic forms than about the potent conflation of sexual and material appetites. A female character in a comedy by Fielding suggests the durability of the connection when she remarks, "I have heard there is not a more dangerous place than a China-Shop."[13]

China again serves to catalyze these two destabilizing forms of desire in the *Lady's Triumph*, a 1718 play by Elkanah Settle in which a jealous alderman takes issue with a china merchant's presentation of a porcelain figure of cupid as a fine and pretty ornament for his wife: "Does your rascalship intend to adorn my virtuous Lady's Bedchamber with naked Boys, Villain!" The lady's protestations of her innocence in selecting the object are in vain. The alderman falls to cudgeling a crate of china, cursing the offending merchant with every blow. "This wicked varlet, this sly seducer, to bring his profane China to lead thy chaste Eyes astray, and snare thy virtuous Modesty into temptation and vanity. Cupids, Rascal! I'll do your business for a China-Merchant." Here the china merchant morphs into a consumer society's rendition of the serpent of Eden, with his enchanting, colorful porcelains serving as the forbidden fruit in a sly plot to lead virtue into the profane temptations of sexuality and commerce.[14]

Chinese porcelain, when it appears in the London marketplace in the seventeenth century, makes a conspicuous entry into the world of goods as a material whose power in the popular imagination derives not from any fixed or autochthonous meaning but rather from its relational position as the locus of deeply fraught ideas of sensuality, novelty, desire, femininity, temptation, and exchange. Porcelain provided the occasion for thinking these ideas together, giving form through its very materiality to fears and pleasures which, in the absence of a suitable substitute, might otherwise have remained hauntingly inchoate.

By the early eighteenth century Chinese porcelain was commonplace in middle- and upper-class homes. The English were importing and consuming tea in ever-increasing quantities, and porcelain tea-wares were essential accessories to the newly fashionable beverage. In the second stage of my history, then, porcelain has lost some of its original associations with exotic novelty and the marketplace, and also, as a result, some of its erotic charge. No longer viewed primarily within the context of luxury commodity exchange, it becomes familiar, domestic, quotidian. It retains strong associations with the feminine, but as the principal setting of women's interactions

Figure 18 Covered jar of inverted ballaster shape, Qing dynasty, Kangxi Reign.

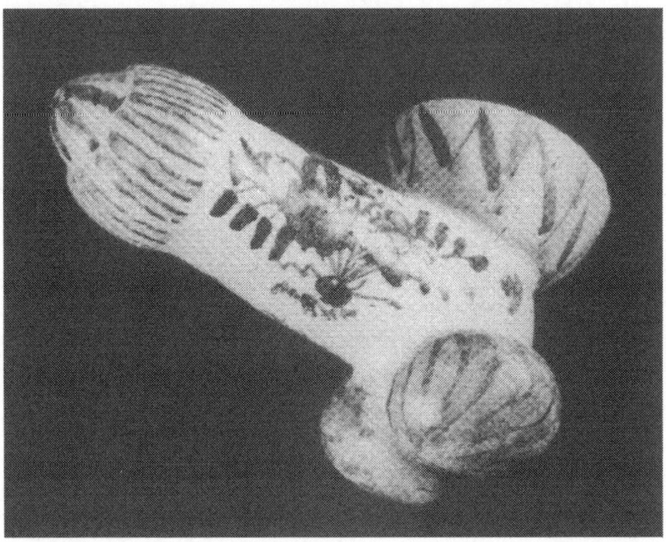

Figure 19 Late Stuart phallic drinking cup, London, 17th century.

with china shifts from the public marketplace to the private interior, the specific configuration of ideas around and about femininity that is enabled by its presence shifts as well. The private woman safely ensconced within the home is far less available to readings as a transgressive subject or common object of desire than the public woman in the marketplace. Within the popular imagination the domestic woman remains, however, a potentially unsettling presence, chafing at the bonds of matrimony and the strictures of meek obedience promulgated by countless conduct books, determined to upset god-given hierarchies through her exercise of power as a gossip, a virago, or a shrew. Indeed, the contemporary proliferation of these moralizing tracts might well be seen as a response to the unwillingness of many women, accustomed to exercising more substantial forms of power in the realms of politics and print culture, to abide by increasingly restrictive norms of appropriately modest feminine behavior.[15] Porcelain, as a universal accoutrement of the married woman's domestic sphere and one which still carried echoes of the untamed appetites of her past, was ideally positioned as a cathexis for these fears of feminine subversion within the home. In an early eighteenth-century print called *Matrimonial Fisticuffs*, the distinctly Chinese porcelain figures – including a long-sleeved mandarin and a round-bellied laughing buddha – lined up on the mantelpiece behind the quarreling couple highlight the durability of this association (Figure 20).

This new role for chinaware in the popular imaginary appears most dramatically in the spectacle of its own shattering, repeated in novels, poems, plays, and prints throughout the eighteenth century. Whereas the simile in Fielding's song compares women and china as passive objects of breakage, women in the company of china are more commonly depicted as the agents of violence. With striking regularity, the demise of Chinese blue and white in eighteenth-century depictions comes at the hands of enraged or manipulative housebound women. Couplets such as these from a 1698 poem by Thomas D'Urfey are typical:

She rants, and swears, and stares, and flings
About her Clothes, and tears her Things;
Breaks China, clatters Looking-glasses,
And calls him Twenty thousand Asses.[16]

These lines call to mind the most famous contemporary depiction of a woman's rage, in the climactic scene of Pope's *Rape of the Lock*. While Belinda is not the actual agent of the china's breakage here, Pope, like

Figure 20 Hubert Gravelot (1699–1773), *Matrimonial Fisticuffs, with a Portrait of the Pugilist John Broughton, in the background.* Early 18th century.

D'Urfey, deploys the spectacle of its shattering figuratively to dramatize the violence of virulent anti-male sentiment:

Then flash'd the living Lightnings from her Eyes,
And Screams of Horror rend th' affrighted Skies.
Not louder Shrieks to pitying Heav'n are cast,
When Husbands or when Lap-dogs breath their last,
Or when rich China Vessels, fal'n from high,
In glittring Dust and painted Fragments lie![17]

The tumbling vases, seemingly jarred from their perch by Belinda's livid laments, echo the vengefully precipitous double deflation of a man's household status in the fantasy of his demise and his pairing with a spaniel in a lady's menagerie. In Hogarth's treatment of the "glittring Dust and painted Fragments" motif in the second plate of *Harlot's Progress*, Moll kicks over a tray of tea-wares in order to create a distraction while her lover slips out of the room (Figure 21). In this case, the violence is more measured, even choreographed, suggesting not anger but rather a woman's self-assured mastery over the fates of both men in the scene. While the hapless hen-pecked husband in a mid-eighteenth-century print by that title is being assaulted with his wife's shoe, the weapon's close juxtaposition with the chinaware on the mantlepiece suggests that porcelain is once again an accessory to

Figure 21 William Hogarth, *Harlot's Progress*, Plate II, 1732.

the crime (Figure 22). In each of the last three images we have considered, the emphatic presence of chinaware at the scene of female violence seems to explain to the savvy viewer a woman's forceful subversion of the sexual order. Whether we are meant to infer that the presence of porcelain enables this subversion or rather that women's fashionable consumption is analogous to this subversive impulse remains unclear, but a correlation between the two ideas is inescapable.

The reach of a powerful woman's subversions extended, in popular lore, well beyond her home through the medium of gossip. As we saw in Chapter 5, a common contemporary cliché held that women drank tea together for the sake of scandal mongering and articulating social hierarchies in contexts that pointedly excluded men. In the *Tea Table* print introduced in Chapter 4, the relation of calumnious rumors among tea-drinking dames sends Justice fleeing from the room, where, according to a poem printed below the original image, "At each sip a lady's honor dies" (Figure 11). Once again, Chinese porcelain is implicated in a topsy-turvy inversion of the "natural" order of things at the hands of potent, autonomous, and unruly women.

While these and other instances demonstrate that china was regularly associated with subversive forms of female agency, it is not immediately

Figure 22 *The Hen Peckt Husband*, 1768.

apparent why this should be the case. Imbuing a porcelain vase with sexual overtones may appear, after Freud, a reasonably plausible and even predictable move; reading spite and vitriol into a common teapot would seem considerably less so. Two additional observations can help account for this rather unexpected connection. The first derives from my argument in Chapter 3 that Chinese depictions of women in gardens are remarkably free of the signs of impetuous, phallic masculinity that so typically intrudes upon depictions of women in early modern European paintings. I reflected in that chapter on the striking circumstance that these Chinese images of a utopian female space became fashionable in England at roughly the same time that we see a proliferation of poetic, polemic, and fictional works by prominent English women, including the Duchess of Newcastle, Mary Astell, Katherine Philips, Jane Barker, and Aphra Behn, exploring the themes of female friendship, female community, and other alternatives to the stifling norms of heterosexual marriage. In light of this cross-cultural confluence of visual and textual themes and the likely contemporary association of certain Chinese wares with feminocentric topographies, it may not be altogether surprising that contemporary English satirical prints depicting the resistance of women to the traditional domination of men invoke Chinese porcelains as a visual correlative to this resistance.

A second kind of connection between women and their porcelain comes into view when we look a little more closely at some of the engravings reproduced above. In the spousal battery scene, while it is the shoe's proximity to the tea-wares that immediately implicates the latter, the fact that the teapot and cup closely echo the color, shape, and size of the wife's exposed breasts seems to corroborate their guilt. In Hogarth's scene, Moll's bared breast, too, precisely mirrors the spherical form of the teapot she has just sent clattering to the floor. Even in the *Tea Table*, the appearance and position of the teapot and teabowl held by the central figures evoke a similarly suggestive analogy between anatomy and accessory. The Amazonian self-assurance of all three of these virago dames is reflected in their unconcerned and defiantly immodest self-display, which in turn finds an echo in conspicuously juxtaposed porcelain props. The British artists who created these engravings were drawing, of course, upon a well-established and entirely respectable painterly tradition in Europe. Formal, almost academic comparisons of human breasts to all manner of vaguely spherical fruits and other round objects had been for centuries so entirely commonplace as to be almost unremarkable; many of these objects of comparison, furthermore, bear considerably less resemblance to the painterly ideal of the body part in question than the basic form of the small, smooth, spherical, white teapots characteristic of the late Ming and early Qing dynasties.[18] I am not suggesting that the teapot or teacup becomes a symbol of the breast in any stable or consistent or even conscious way – sometimes a teapot, after all, is only a teapot – but rather that the availability of such a potent visual analogy contributed to the efficacy of porcelain tea-wares as a material catalyst for figuring certain versions of the feminine within the early eighteenth-century domestic interior.

British artists would not, in any case, be the first to have imagined a visual resemblance between mammary anatomy and household vessels. The familiar form of the teapot emerges in China from a tradition dating back several thousand years of incorporating breast- or udder-like forms in the design of utilitarian and ceremonial objects associated with preparation of food and drink. Hollow-legged bronze and ceramic vessels from the Shang

Figure 23 Red pottery tripod vessel (*Li*). Neolithic (*c.* 4500–2000 BCE). Pottery.

dynasty and earlier periods, known as *li* or *ding*, were used to cook food or heat wine over an open fire (Figure 23). The *kendi* drinking and pouring vessel, with its characteristic mammiform spout, originated in India but was later widely manufactured in China and was common throughout Southeast Asia during the sixteenth and seventeenth centuries (Figure 24). In Indonesia the *kendi susu* or breast *kendi* has long been associated with the sustaining powers of mother's milk and is often used as a fertility symbol during marriage rites. Such historical precedents, of course, do not definitively prove anything about the imaginative resonances of the Chinese teapot in Britain. They do, however, establish that such visual analogies have had a powerful and lasting appeal in other societies no more or less susceptible, perhaps, to the enchanting evocativeness of the human form.[19]

Figure 24 *Kendi*, Wanli period, *c.* 1610–20.

This brings us to the third and final stage of the journey of Chinese porcelain through the early modern gender imaginary. In the first stage, porcelain provided a means for representing and thinking through the public commoditization of female sexuality and desire. In the second stage, tea-wares in particular helped to catalyze a vision of domestic space as a site of social constraints against which the unruly woman incessantly rebelled. In the third stage, they appear to broker a thoroughgoing domestication of the woman herself, a taming of her shrew-like spleen, a channeling of the abrasive power of the discontented wife into the nurturing roles of complacent mother and hostess. The public women of the New Exchange have been restored to the home, their rebellious spirit tamed, their spite and bile transformed into the virtuous and good-humored industry of the contented homemaker. The domestication of the dominant womanly ideal over the course of the long eighteenth century in England is a well-recognized historical phenomenon. It can be traced in conduct books and in the evolution of literary heroines from the wayward, autonomous, and delightfully scandalous heroines of Aphra Behn's *The Rover*, Haywood's *Fantomina*, and Defoe's *Roxana*, who captivated playgoers and readers in the early decades, to their considerably more staid descendents Pamela and Jane Bennet, who set the standard of respectable femininity from mid-century onward.

The causes, implications, and the scale of this shift, it should be noted, all remain deeply contested. In what is perhaps the most influential book on the subject, *Desire and Domestic Fiction*, Nancy Armstrong traces this process of domestication to the invention by eighteenth- and nineteenth-century women writers – both real and fictional – of a model of female identity that conformed to the purposes of middle-class cultural hegemony and the formation of the modern state. An emergent individualist social ideology, she argues, required the foregrounding of sexual differences (as opposed to those of class, religion, etc.) as the basis of personal and collective identity; by creating female characters and domestic spaces that exemplified an exaggerated vision of such difference, women writers effectively authored middle-class subjectivity itself. "The modern individual," as Armstrong claims, "was first and foremost a woman."[20]

Armstrong's revisionist reworking of the history of the novel has been criticized on a number of grounds, including its relative inattention to (non-literary) historical evidence, the narrowness of some of its readings, and an over-emphasis on the social power of language. Later critics, such as April Alliston, have demonstrated that substantial numbers of lesser-known women's fictions of the later eighteenth century significantly resist the domestication plots and regressive sexual contracts more common to the novelistic canon.[21] Whatever the complexity of its meanings and contexts, however, there remains a discernible shift towards the domestic in the predominant representations of women's social roles over the course of the eighteenth century. And this discursive shift, I would argue, has distinct and potentially enabling correlatives in the realms of material culture and social ritual.

While the breathless escapades of earlier heroines leave them little time for leisure, Jane Austen's women are forever drinking tea: eight separate tea-drinking occasions are described in *Pride and Prejudice*. Indeed, by the Regency period the afternoon consumption of tea seems to have become so natural and indispensable a part of the daily household routine in England that we tend to overlook the historicity of the ritual and its role in the consolidation of the modern ideology of maternal domesticity.[22] I use the term ideology quite intentionally here, in order to call attention to the way the very naturalness and taken-for-grantedness of English tea contributes to the construction of one particular fantasy of feminine essence precisely by obliterating its own history, in the forgotten figures of those commercially active, outspoken, vigorous, defiant, and lusty women who inhabit the poems, plays, and prints we have considered up to this point.

Figure 25 Francis Hayman, *Jonathan Tyers and his Family*, 1740.

Chinaware, as these earlier representations make clear, did not always conjure up images of homey tranquility; in fact, it is only in the 1730s that porcelain begins to take on this new maternal valence. In painted conversation pieces by Hogarth, Francis Hayman, and other contemporary artists, the porcelain tea set figures prominently in scenes of domestic bliss, as an emblem of fashion and status, yes, but also of the woman's sway over the domestic sphere and role as a provider of warmth and nurturance (Figure 25). "To do away with the tea-table," we learn in a later novel by Mary Elizabeth Braddon, "is to rob woman of her legitimate empire."[23] And indeed, in many such images, the lady of the house does preside like an empress over the men, women, and children gathered around her tea service. The unseemly and illegitimate passions and appetites evoked by Chinese wares in our first two stages have here been sublimated into a benign and peaceable sovereignty over a decorous domestic sphere. Woman's power has been legitimated, to be sure, but its once unruly energy has also been confined and disciplined through an aestheticized regimen of poised self-control and ritualized hospitality.

As Ruth Perry has argued, the domestication of the womanly ideal over the course of the eighteenth century was accompanied by an increasingly essentialized view of the woman's role as mother.[24] During the Restoration and early eighteenth century, the majority of elite women sent their babies out to wet nurses, suggesting that the value accorded to nursing one's own children may have been less than the interest in recovering their figures, accommodating their husbands, or resuming an active sexual life. In subsequent decades, an emerging consensus on the benefits of natural childrearing practices reversed this trend, so that women of all classes were increasingly expected to nurse their own offspring in the home.[25] At the same time, the development of natural science and the corresponding interest in classification and taxonomy led human females increasingly to be regarded through the reductive lenses of biological functionalism: as God's manifest purpose for the females of lower mammalian species was obviously sexual reproduction and the nurturance of offspring, so too the rightful role of human females could be read definitively in their anatomical particularities.

Chief among these, of course, was the female breast. The rather extraordinary degree of contemporary fascination with this organ can be ascertained, as Londa Schiebinger points out, from the rapid acceptance, in the mid-eighteenth century, of Linnaeus' otherwise entirely arbitrary designation of the entire taxonomic class of warm-blooded vertebrates – mammals – solely on the basis of the presence of mammary glands in the females of these species.[26] The elevation of the breast and, by implication, of the maternal function to the primary distinguishing characteristic of the higher animal species thus essentializes the scientific conception of femininity at roughly the same historical moment that the increasingly domesticated novel tames its popular conception.

Had the English been a Catholic people, we might expect to have seen a resurgence of images of nursing madonnas to accompany this emerging reconception of the domesticated mother's proper role. The English were Protestants, however, and increasingly prudish ones at that, so that instead of a cult of Mary we find the new emphasis on motherhood accompanied by a cult of tea. There is a certain correlative logic to this substitution. What is tea, after all, but a warm, sweet, nurturing fluid served in shapely smooth white vessels by the loving hand of a beneficent mother goddess? The visual resonances between breast and ceramic wares had, as we have seen, already been well established in popular prints of the early eighteenth century. The analogy was more subtly suggested now, in keeping with the shift from a context of willful subversion to one of dutiful decorum, but it remained in

Figure 26 Alphonse Mucha (1860–1939), *Chocolat Idéal*, 1897.

play through the eighteenth and even into the twentieth century, providing a material embodiment, at once comforting and evocative, of both a primal longing and bourgeois domestic ideal (Figure 26). To this day, the phrase "Shall I be mother?" still connotes, in many an English household, an offer to pour the tea.

A passage from Charlotte Brontë's 1853 novel *Villette* serves as a reminder of both the durability of this maternal ideal and the depth of its saturation in the history of the porcelain imaginary I have sketched out here:

While she read, I perceived she listened – listened for her son. She was not the woman ever to confess herself uneasy, but there was yet no lull in the weather, and if Graham were out in that hoarse wind – roaring still unsatisfied – I well knew his mother's heart would be out with him.

"Ten minutes behind his time," said she, looking at her watch; then, in another minute, a lifting of her eyes from the page, and a slight inclination of her head towards the door, denoted that she heard some sound. Presently her brow cleared; and then even my ear, less practised, caught the iron clash of a gate swung to, steps on gravel, lastly the door-bell. He was come. His mother filled the tea pot from the urn, she drew nearer the hearth the stuffed and cushioned blue chair – her own chair by right, but I saw there was one who might with impunity usurp it. And when that *one* came up the stairs . . . and strode straight in

"Is it you, Graham?" said his mother, hiding a glad smile and speaking curtly.

"Who else should it be, mama?" demanded the Unpunctual, possessing himself irreverently of the abdicated throne.

"Don't you deserve cold tea, for being late?"

"I shall not get my deserts, for the urn sings cheerily."[27]

This scene is remarkable for its condensation of the thematics of maternal empire I have associated with the final stage of my narrative. We have a female character defined, first and foremost, by her unwavering affection for an errant and rather irresponsible son. At the same time, she is a woman of emotional discipline, whose ability to suppress unwanted feelings and expressions – she would never confess herself uneasy, and could conceal a smile beneath curt words in a moment of gladness – has earned her the undisputed right to her hearthside throne. And most importantly, we find that her maternal function – her boundless reserves of unconditional affection and nurturance – is both anchored and naturalized through the figure of a teapot and urn: the merry singing of the latter belies her stern and scolding tone and guarantees a supply of warmth and sustenance invulnerable to the fickleness of undomesticated femininity.

At the same time, the scene offers a striking retrospective vantage point from which to reconsider the seventeenth-century theatrical scene with which this narrative began. A number of parallels invite the comparison: Graham's mother and our old friend Sir Amorous La Foole are both, after all, anxiously awaiting the appearance of their beloved, in the hopes of bestowing on them tokens of their affection. And, as we have seen, the women in both scenes are largely defined through their association with porcelain objects. What is most striking, however, is the gender reversal between the two scenes and its implications for what the clichéd association of women and porcelain comes to mean in these two periods. In Ben Jonson's play, after all, rather than a cloistered mother waiting for her errant son from the hazardous outside world, we had an amorous playboy waiting patiently inside his private rooms, while the women occupied the public sphere, coming and going freely within the exposed spaces of the marketplace. And rather than a maternal character defined through her porcelain as having a boundless capacity for giving, we had in the play women whose lives were defined, again through porcelain, as the pursuit of pleasurable consumption.

Looking back from our nineteenth-century novel to this seventeenth-century play allows us to recognize just how radical are the transformations of affect and identity that took shape over these two hundred years. That such a reversal can be closely traced through the semiotic machinations of as seemingly trivial a material object as a porcelain vessel strongly suggests that certain kinds of objects can, in fact, play an unexpectedly significant role in the evolution of sensibilities. It suggests, moreover, that they do so not in the manner of authored texts or static symbols but rather as free-floating catalysts of that ongoing process of cultural bricolage by which each generation fashions anew its own understandings of gender, self, and the ten thousand things that make up, in Chinese philosophy, the inseparable and mutually constituting spheres of the human and material worlds.

8 Thomas Percy's sinology and the origins of English romanticism

Thomas Percy's *Reliques of English Poetry* is widely credited with being a seminal inspiration for the English romantic movement. In a recent study of the work's compilation, Nick Groom declares the *Reliques* the "epoch-making work of English romanticism." Romanticist Stuart Curran concurs, arguing that Percy's collection of old ballads "indelibly altered Britain's sense of its literary heritage." According to Percy biographer Bertram Davis, they "fired the imaginations of Blake, Scott, Wordsworth, and Coleridge," and through these poets "effected a revolution in English poetry."[1]

While it is well known that Percy was engaged in sinological research and writing during the same years that he was preparing the manuscripts of his famous ballad collection, little effort has been made to explore the possible connections between these projects. Percy's proposal for a volume of "Specimens of the Ancient Poetry of Different Nations" makes clear that he considered both the Chinese and English poetic traditions as falling within the rubric of what we might today call world literature. But none of the modern scholars quoted above sees any significance either in the simultaneity of the projects or in their formal resemblance. In an unpublished essay, Eun Min calls attention to some of these striking similarities: the stories behind both the *Reliques* and the sinological publications involve serendipitously rescued texts, incomplete or damaged sources, and a prominent role for Percy himself as a mediator and cultural guide.[2] That such common features should fail to inspire a closer comparison of his responses to the two ancient cultures that so captured his imagination is not entirely surprising: the apparatus and outlook of the *Reliques* are so insistently and defiantly anglocentric that they would seem to allow little room for an alien genealogy of any kind.

Reading Percy's Chinese writings alongside his *Reliques*, however, reveals significant intertextual dynamics between the two projects. For all of his pointed claims to detachment and objectivity in his presentation of "the Chinese mind," Percy is at once thoroughly captivated and deeply disturbed by his sinological discoveries. His ambivalence is dizzying: at one moment Percy seems to identify deeply with Confucius, like himself a moral teacher and antiquarian collector of ancient songs; the next moment he heaps scorn upon Chinese claims to antiquity and moral virtue. This ambivalence, I will suggest in the first part of this chapter, reflects a struggle on Percy's part to redeem his emerging conception of English national identity in the face of plainly superior Chinese cultural achievements.

In the second part of the chapter, I will argue that the *Reliques* can be read as a product of this struggle. While fastidiously avoiding any explicit mention of China, Percy creates, in the essays and notes that accompany the ballads, a myth of Englishness and England's literary past that is profoundly indebted to his Chinese studies. Like Hogarth, Chambers, and Walpole, Percy finds in Chinese productions a model that is at once inspiring and unsettling, leading him simultaneously to repudiate Chinese claims to cultural greatness and to appropriate them for his own purposes. Like his compatriots, he draws upon Chinese examples to expand his aesthetic imagination, only to disown them when faced with the implications of this debt within a cultural sphere increasingly constrained by considerations of nationalist exclusivity. In the case of each of these figures, then, we find evidence of what might be termed an instrumental amnesia with respect to China's role in the production of eighteenth-century British aesthetic culture.

Percy's interest in things Chinese, as earlier chapters have suggested, was by no means unusual for his time. The publication of Jesuit missionary reports from China beginning in the seventeenth century had generated considerable interest in the philosophy, political system, language, and customs of the great empire at the far end of the Eurasian land mass. Prodigious quantities of imported tea, silks, and porcelain had given the luxury marketplace of early eighteenth-century England a decidedly Chinese cast. Within the literary world, Elkanah Settle had exploited the tragic possibilities of the overthrow of the Ming dynasty in his 1675 melodrama *The Conquest of China by the Tartars.* Daniel Defoe had sent his famous shipwrecked hero on a voyage to China in the 1719 sequel to *Robinson Crusoe.* Four decades later, popular interest in the Far East was still lively enough to inspire Percy's close friend Oliver Goldsmith to pen a collection of letters to and from a fictional Chinese visitor to London for the *Public Ledger* that would be published as *The Citizen of the World* in 1762.[3]

So when in 1758 Percy discovered a manuscript translation of a popular seventeenth-century Chinese novel produced thirty years earlier by an East India Company representative in Canton, he knew there would be considerable interest in his find, and immediately set out to identify a suitable publisher. He revised the original translation in early 1759, and may also have translated some additional portions of the manuscript from the Portuguese.[4] His major contribution, though, was in his extensive annotations to the text of the novel, in the form of often lengthy footnotes illuminating the customs and beliefs of the upper-class Chinese with detailed reference to the dozens of published sources he consulted for the project. He borrowed further from these sources to round out his manuscript with a synopsis of a Chinese play, a collection of Chinese proverbs, and a brief selection of Chinese poetry with an accompanying essay by the Jesuit Nicolas Freret. He seems to have been pleased with his work: his diary records that he read portions of the novel aloud on several occasions for friends during a visit to London later in 1759.[5] Robert and John Dodsley published the four-volume work – Percy's first – in 1761 under the title *Hau Kiou Choaan; or, The Pleasing History*, ordering a large print run in the hopes of cashing in on contemporary interest in the topic, but, alas, many copies remained unsold.[6] Perhaps the oft-vaunted virtue of the Chinese and their strict separation of the sexes dampened the appeal of a putatively Chinese novel to the looser-laced readers of Cleland, Fielding, and Sterne.

Whatever the reason for the book's disappointing sales, it offered a first glimpse of Chinese fiction that in its basic premises, anyway, must have seemed oddly familiar to mid-century English readers. The novel's heroine, Shuey-ping-sin, is an uncommonly beautiful, clever, and virtuous girl who attracts the unwanted attentions of a rakish schemer, inspiring him to desperate measures, including trickery and abduction, in order to force her into marriage. The Richardsonian rape plot takes a turn towards French romance with the appearance of a chivalric scholar-hero who saves and is saved by the heroine in turn, forging a bond that will eventually lead to a more suitable union once a series of trials have provided the requisite proofs of their determination and the purity of their love.

Before the *Pleasing History* had even been published, Percy was planning its sequel. *Miscellaneous Pieces Relating to the Chinese*, which would appear in 1762, was a two-volume collection of both Chinese writings and European writings about China, nearly all of which had been previously published in Europe. The two Chinese pieces, a Qing conduct guide and a tragedy from the Yuan dynasty which Percy translated from French Jesuit compilations, furthered Percy's project of introducing English readers through Chinese literature to "the workings of the human mind under all the peculiarities of a Chinese education."[7] The anthologized essays, three of which he translated from French and German accounts, can be seen as an extension of his mammoth annotation project for the *Pleasing History*, representing some of the more memorable selections – on the Christian church in China,

Chinese gardening, and Chinese imperial birthday rituals – from the numerous sources he had assembled in preparing his Chinese novel. The one original essay in the collection was his "Dissertation on the Language and Characters of the Chinese," an extended reflection on the idiosyncrasies of the written and spoken forms of the language and their implications for the understanding of Chinese culture.

In the prefaces to both of his China books and in his private correspondence, Percy takes pains to position himself in the disinterested, mediating role of a dutiful scribe, faithfully transmitting what he has learned of Chinese civilization to his English readers. He offers the *Pleasing History* as a "curious specimen of Chinese literature," attempting neither "to conceal nor extenuate its faults," and "leav[ing] it to the critics to decide its merit."[8] The book's literary merits, though, are less important, for Percy, than the insider's view it can provide on Chinese ways of being in the world. Just as a foreigner can learn more about the "genius and spirit of the English" from a page of Fielding than from volumes of expository works, so too English readers can gain a better understanding of the Chinese from their own writings than from the comparatively superficial accounts of visiting outsiders. Percy extends the self-deprecating hope, then, that his efforts will allow the Chinese to speak for themselves, and that the novel will be considered as "a faithful picture of Chinese manners, wherein the domestic and political economy of that vast people is displayed with an exactness and accuracy to which none but a native could be capable of attaining." The most faithful of pictures, however, occasionally requires interpretation, and Percy apologetically explains the unusual frequency and length of his footnotes on the grounds that "the manners and customs of the Chinese, their peculiar ways of thinking, and modes of expression are so remote from our own, that they frequently require a large detail to render them intelligible."[9]

In describing the project to his friend William Shenstone, Percy borrows from the language of natural philosophy and Enlightenment universalism to frame it in even more explicitly rationalist, ethnographic terms. The book is worthy of attention, he suggests, primarily for the "history of the human mind in China" that it provides. Understanding the Chinese mind, in turn, gives us deeper insight into "our common nature" and "the mind of man," which we cannot know except by studying "the manner of its operation under every possible combination of ideas."[10] The Chinese, for all their peculiarities, represent simply another permutation of that set of basic qualities that make up our common humanity. To understand them is to grasp the richness and capaciousness of this category, all the better to understand ourselves.

By the time Percy wrote the preface to his *Miscellaneous Pieces*, he was less intent on making such grand claims for the importance of his sinological work, and seems rather almost to trivialize it. He describes having translated "two or three entertaining articles" simply "for his amusement," and having then been persuaded to compile them with "a few other small pieces" for the benefit of the public.[11] His dismissive tone is a conventional gesture of editorial humility: he had, after all, expended much less effort assembling these two volumes than the previous four. But it also manages to preserve the studied air of disinterestedness that he had cultivated in preparing the *Pleasing History*. The suggestion that he had undertaken the project almost as a lark implies that he was invested neither in the content of the essays nor their reception. High-minded scientific objectivity has here given way to a casual nonchalance, but the underlying premise that China is a curious specimen to be regarded from afar remains unaltered.

Percy's implicit claims to a disinterested position with respect to China are significant precisely because they are so unusual. Far more typically, the China watchers of the previous century had deployed the example of China in the service of heated partisan polemic. Jesuit missionaries had an interest in celebrating the cultural achievements of the Chinese as a means of justifying their controversial policy of religious accommodationism. A generation of language reformers exalted the Chinese written language as an example of a rational, systematic language whose principles might be applied to addressing the shortcomings of contemporary European vernaculars. Voltaire joined Leibniz and others in suggesting that the Europeans had more to learn from the Chinese in matters of philosophy and religion than Christian missionaries could possibly offer them. In England, meanwhile, the best-selling account by Walter and Robins of Anson's circumnavigation rivaled Defoe's *Farther Adventures of Robinson Crusoe* in the venom of its jingoistic diatribes against Chinese merchants and pretensions to military might, while Shaftesbury and other self-appointed guardians of proper taste lambasted Chinese and Chinese-inspired design as monstrous and absurd.[12] None of the other major figures treated in earlier chapters of this book, it should be noted, so much as pretends to an objective stance when China is the subject.

Against this background, then, for Percy to decline to pass judgment on a Chinese work's literary merits, or to suggest that Chinese fiction might be a more reliable source on China than European accounts, or to claim that his own interest in translating writings on China amounted to no more than mere intellectual amusement was refreshingly unorthodox, to say the least. But it was also, as we shall soon see, deeply misleading. In the course of his

China researches, Percy developed strong, even impassioned views about his subject that reveal his framing claims to neutrality to be little more than a pious façade. Given the weight of precedent among his predecessors, why, we might reasonably ask, should he have troubled with such claims at all?

The short answer is that unlike those of many of his contemporaries, Percy's ideas about China admitted of no easy summary. His extensive reading probably left him with a more thorough and nuanced understanding of China than any other British armchair traveler of his century. Not surprisingly, then, his responses were complex, ambivalent, and even deeply conflicted.[13] But they were also frequently impassioned, suggesting that for Percy something more than a merely academic argument was at stake. His claims to aloofness, it seems clear, provided a convenient and decorous means both of papering over the ruptures and contradictions in his China writings and masking the intensity of personal engagement with his subject that produced them. Far from attaining the detachment of the philosopher or casual ease of the dilettante he tried to project, the author of the *Reliques* was consumed by his sinological studies and ultimately transformed by them.

Percy's ambivalence towards his subject registers most plainly within individual notes whose tone vacillates, even within the space of a few lines, between praise and condemnation. In his comment on a prenuptial gift-giving ceremony in the *Pleasing History*, Percy remarks, "There is nothing for which the Chinese have higher veneration than their ceremonies," citing a book that prescribes no fewer than three thousand rules of civility. Though he finds such a number absurd – he finds the "higher" abstract principles of the Christians preferable as guides to moral conduct to the proliferation of concrete rules among the Chinese – he also recognizes the usefulness of such a pragmatic approach: "Ridiculous as these punctilios may appear, to them is owing in a great measure the wonderful stability of the Chinese empire, and its having subsisted above 4,000 years."[14] Nor is this a merely rhetorical concession: the storied stability of the Chinese political system had long been a source of wonder and admiration for Europeans whose unceasing religious and political conflicts regularly decimated populations and institutional structures.

Perhaps the best known of these "ridiculous" punctilios, and the most conducive to social stability, was the Chinese penchant for looking after their elders, living and dead. Here again, Percy finds both virtue and absurdity in their beliefs: "As the Chinese are distinguished for filial piety beyond all other nations, so they seem to carry this to an idolatrous excess. Various and excessive are the honours which they pay to their deceased parents and ancestors."[15] But if the honors paid to parents are too great, the honors paid by valiant heroes to attractive maidens can be found wanting. Commenting on a scene in which the male protagonist declines, on grounds of propriety, even to discuss the possibility of a match with the heroine, Percy remarks, "As in this, and some of the following pages, the Hero of the piece cannot but suffer in the opinion of every fair Reader, for his seeming Indelicacy and want of Gallantry." Once again, though, there is another side to the story: gallantry, after all, cannot properly be expected "among a people, who admit of no intercourse between the two Sexes" and among whom arranged marriages are common.[16]

The most striking of Percy's equivocations appears in a note responding to an otherwise sympathetic character's adamant declaration of his unwillingness to forgive or forget past injuries even after his enemies have been punished. Percy, an ambitious vicar of the Anglican church, takes issue with the novel's apparent endorsement of the speaker's resolve. "The Morality of the Chinese author in this and the preceding page appears in a very contemptible light compared with the Christian, which so strongly recommends the forgiveness of injuries and the return of good for evil." As if concerned, however, that his condemnation might be mistaken for a rejection of Chinese morality generally, Percy abruptly softens his tone: "Yet he might have learnt better from the great doctor of his nation Confucius; who will be judged to have made no mean proficiency in ethics from the following position; 'To recompense hatred with benefits is the virtue and piety of a noble [or enlarged] breast.'" This ritual kowtow to the much-vaunted hero of the Jesuit accommodationists must have struck Percy, on further consideration, as venturing too far in the other direction towards the theological promiscuity of the detested Catholic order, as he promptly executes a second about-face: "It ought however to be observed, that even this great Philosopher doth not insist upon this, as a duty: and hath neither backed it with any sanction nor recommended it upon adequate motives."[17]

As if to reaffirm his Christian credentials, he concludes his painfully equivocal note with an affirmation of the "glowing benevolence" and "sublime and affecting motives" with which the virtue of forgiveness is taught by "the SAVIOR of the world," followed by a series of illustrative passages from the gospels of Luke and Matthew. Percy unwittingly rehearses in an extended footnote, then, the dramatic conflict that inflamed the controversy over accommodationism in the previous century. On the one hand, the Chinese were manifestly possessed of an admirable, full-bodied ethical code that resembled Christianity in many key respects. Yet on the other hand, any non-Christian approach to morality had to be considered *a priori* as fundamentally flawed and demonstrably inferior to Christian thought. It seems clear that Percy inhabited both of these positions simultaneously, and had a difficult time reconciling them. But this, as we will see, would eventually appear the least of his dilemmas.

The pattern of ambivalence that appears in these and other local instances anticipates a deeper and more systematic tension that informs Percy's Chinese writings as a whole. At first glance, the alternation of admiring and critical remarks might appear to vindicate his claims to being an objective, dispassionate observer. The comments do achieve a kind of balance, and at times may seem to array themselves neatly into a symmetrical ledger of pros and cons, virtues and vices. Percy encourages this kind of reading in the fastidiously assembled index to his Chinese novel, which includes, under the heading "CHINESE (the)," a subheading for "the dark side of their character" with fourteen entries (affected, crafty, corrupt, cowardly, etc.) and another for "the bright side of their character" with twelve (complaisant, decent, dextrous, dutiful to their parents, etc.).[18] The appearance of detachment conveyed by such a careful moral accounting is undermined, however, when one turns to some of the passages indexed by these entries. To begin with, many of his remarks have a rhetorical force that extends beyond the needs of mere description. Complicating matters further, Percy's tidy Manichean schema of bright and dark sides begins to fracture, on closer examination, into a multifarious array of at least four distinct modes of response, each of which, ultimately, reveals less about the nature of the Chinese character than about the inclinations, aspirations, and fears of the first English sinologist.

The most straightforward of these modes of response, and the one most in keeping with the spirit of his predominantly Jesuit sources, is admiration. As the several examples above suggest and as his index heading amply confirms, Percy finds much to praise in Chinese customs and values. In addition to the traits mentioned above, Percy comments favorably on the "uncommon modesty" of the Chinese in their looks and dress, the usefulness of the prevalent attitude of "mild civility" in the avoidance of conflict, and the many remarkable instances of "exemplary courage, fidelity, and public spirit" recorded in the historical annals.[19] I am less interested in the specific attributes Percy singles out for acclaim, however, than in the rhetorical uses to which he puts his commendation. The basic point I want to establish here is that far from sustaining the pose of a detached observer, Percy becomes intimately engaged (as most of us do, I suspect) with the object of his research, incorporating his insights into his larger worldview, and experimenting with the possibilities they provide for seeing his own heritage anew.

The first instance of such a rhetorically pointed tribute appears on the second page of the *Pleasing History*, in Percy's dedication to the Countess of Sussex. His opening assertion of his work's moral character, its tendency to "countenance virtue and to discourage vice," is entirely conventional for the eighteenth century. His elaboration of the claim, however, is not:

> At a time when this nation swarms with fictitious narratives of the most licentious and immoral turn, it may have some good effect to shew what strict regard to virtue and decorum is paid by writers amongst the Chinese, notwithstanding the deplorable ignorance they labor under of those sublime and noble truths, which we enjoy to so little purpose.[20]

In a gently satirical gesture reminiscent of Montesquieu, Diderot, or Voltaire, Percy deploys the cliché of a virtuous heathen to expose the moral hypocrisy of his own countrymen. The modern novel was widely condemned in Percy's time for leading young readers astray; Percy is surely the first, however, to recommend Chinese fiction as a suitable antidote. The unusual vantage point provided by his familiarity with a Chinese novel allows Percy to regard English literary productions with fresh eyes and to invoke a Chinese moral perspective for criticizing current English trends.

Percy's admiration for Chinese literati extends to the social and political institutions in which they play such an important role. Percy comments with approval on the use of a government newspaper, the *Chinese Gazette*, to report on the activities of public officials throughout the empire and the reasons for their promotion, punishment, or dismissal. "It is easy to imagine," Percy reflects, "what excellent purposes of government this must serve, and what influence it must have on the Mandarins." Should officials fail to take this guidance to heart, the privileges of rank provide little protection. "The greatest ministers," Percy notes elsewhere, "are not beyond the reach of punishment; upon detection of their guilt the Emperor treats them with as little ceremony as the meanest of his subjects."[21] In a British context where the greatest ministers were notoriously corrupt and seemingly immune from prosecution, and where, indeed, the prime minister could be satirized in the figure of the legendary highwayman Jonathan Wild, Percy's account of the Chinese civil service surely contains an ironic subtext of its own, a barbed commentary on the deficiencies of comparable British institutions.

The most striking rhetorical use of the trope of admiration for China in Percy's notes, however, appears in his challenge to the unique status of the Bible and the works of classical antiquity as the gold standard of civilized attainment in philosophy and literature. To the extent that their stature depends on their antiquity, it pales in the relativizing light of Chinese history. In a note introducing Confucius, Percy points out that "the great philosopher of the Chinese" lived "five hundred and fifty-one years before Christ . . . and somewhat earlier than Socrates," while a note introducing the "Elegiac Verses" from the *Book of Songs* avers that "this is the most ancient piece of poetry extant in the world."[22] Nor does the Western canon, Percy discovers, hold a monopoly on poetic attainment. In the second volume of the *Pleasing History*, after noting the biblical resonances of a particularly apt metaphor, Percy alerts the reader that "many other Chinese expressions exactly correspondent to those in Scripture will occur in this History." In the postscript to a selection of Chinese poetry he appends at the end of the novel, he quotes Du Halde's assessment that the Tang dynasty poets "Lee-tsaupe and Tu-te-muey did not yield to Anacreen and Horace."[23] Such claims for the precedence of Chinese antiquity would have been taken in stride by continental sinophiles of the likes of Leibniz or Voltaire, but in an England where sermons outsold novels and leading poets cut their teeth on imitations and translations of Horace, they most likely would have received a cooler reception. No other major eighteenth-century writer in England ventured so far as Percy in asserting commensurability between the great ancient civilizations of East and West, and thus in subtly undermining a nascent Anglo-European exceptionalism that would become increasingly evident in subsequent decades.

To those of Percy's contemporaries who identified, through Pope and Dryden, with the legacies of classical antiquity, or through Bunyan and Wesley with a biblical heritage, Percy's bald assertions of comparable Chinese achievements might have uncomfortably undermined their pride in this identification. It comes as little surprise, then, that claims of this kind are not widely repeated in this period. So how did our Oxford-trained clergyman himself overcome what one might imagine would be a deep-seated resistance to the notion that the glories of ancient civilization were not limited to the western end of the Eurasian continent? We find a clue in Percy's remark, quoted above, concerning the exact correspondence of expressions in his Chinese novel to those in scripture. The assertion of equivalence here produces a curious ambiguity. For while it might readily be glossed, by a Eurocentric reader, to suggest – perhaps troublingly – that Chinese writers occasionally reach biblical heights of rhetorical sublimity, it could equally well imply – perhaps reassuringly – that the Bible periodically attains to Chinese standards. Admiration brings with it the risk of anxious self-deprecation. But admiration expressed as an identification with its object preempts this danger, in that it elevates the admirer to the stature of that which is admired. Percy's admiration for what he finds in Chinese culture frequently works in just this way: his gestures of identification with Chinese models suggest a desire to share in the worthiness that he reflexively ascribes to them.

This second mode of response appears most clearly in Percy's fascination with Chinese proverbs. He appends a heavily annotated and alphabetized collection of these colorful and pithy sayings, painstakingly assembled from a dozen different sources, to the end of the third volume of the *Pleasing History*, where they span a full seventy-seven pages. The advertisement to this collection opens with an assertion of its importance to a full understanding of the Chinese character: "No truer judgment can be formed of the temper and genius of any nation, than from their common Proverbs. These could never have prevailed, and become universal, if they had not expressed the general sense of the people, who adopt them." His selections run the gamut from moral maxims ("Temperance is the best physic") to pedagogical principles ("A man never opens a book without reaping some advance from it") to political advice ("Is a prince entirely upright, every thing succeeds well with him; doth he belie himself, though but in one instance, it may lead to his ruin").[24] Percy inserts editorial notes for more than half of the entries. While some of these explicate obscure allusions with reference to Chinese history, geography, and beliefs, a large proportion of the notes situate the Chinese proverbs by pointing out equivalents in European languages. Thus, under the entry "A fault acknowledged is half amended," Percy notes, "This is the same with the French, *Faute confessée est à demi pardonée*." The Chinese proverb "He who suffers, hath some comfort in singing his pains," Percy remarks, "seems equivalent to the Spanish proverb, *Quien canta sus males espanta*."[25]

Given the tendency of proverbs, in Percy's view, to reflect "the temper and genius of [a] nation," the implication of his discovery of these hundreds of aphoristic equivalents is clearly that the temper and genius of the Chinese and European nations are in many respects very much alike. While one might be tempted to view this implicit conclusion as a grudging concession, one can equally well imagine that, from the perspective of an English country cleric awed by the cultural achievements of a distant civilization renowned for its antiquity and moral wisdom, there might be something reassuring in the demonstration that one's own culture, broadly defined, possessed comparable resources of popular wit and wisdom. In striking contrast to the prevalent outlook today, according to which a "backward" Chinese society is forever playing catch up with the "modern" West, Percy seems in his proverb collection to take Chinese cultural production as the standard against which those of other nations can be measured. On the Chinese proverb, "Heaven and hell are seated in the heart," Percy remarks,

This fine saying is common with the Chinese. To the same effect our celebrated poet,

The mind is its own place, and in itself,
Can make a heaven of hell, a hell of heaven.[26]

His note on the proverb "Honour the dead, as you would honour them if they were alive" makes explicit the precedence he grants to Chinese popular wisdom. "This is the favourite maxim of the Chinese: and seems more founded on justice and good sense, than that maxim so current with us, '*De mortuis nil nisi bonum.*'" Other Chinese proverbs are compared with a "coarse but expressive saying of Oliver Cromwell," a "trite saying of ours," or a "homely proverb" of our own.[27] Far from condescending to the Chinese in noting these equivalents, Percy seems almost embarrassed by the lack of expressive dignity he finds in so many English and European idioms.

Percy often seems to identify with the more generally literary aspects of Chinese culture. In his advertisement to a brief collection of Chinese poetry appended to the fourth volume of the *Pleasing History*, he explains his interest in this subject: "The Chinese are known to bestow great attention on literature: this must excite our curiosity to examine their productions."[28] The Chinese concern with literature must excite "our" curiosity because "we," after all, are concerned with literature as well. Nor is this a merely casual resemblance: the Chinese concern with poetry is of a kind that elevates "us" in our identification with it. Later in his introduction to the collection, Percy excerpts a Jesuit memoir which attests that poetry "hath been no where in higher request, than in China, where it was the first vehicle of their morality, religion, and politics, and where it hath always been regarded with peculiar reverence and esteem." For a clergyman possessed of a notable aptitude for editing and composing verse, it is hard to imagine a more flattering account of the poet's calling. One can almost, indeed, detect a note of envy in Percy's account of why the study of literature in China is afforded such great respect: "As all civil offices in China are bestowed according to personal merit, no wonder that the study of letters is held in the highest esteem, and that the examinations of students are conducted with the greatest decorum, solemnity, and exactness."[29]

Percy's identification with the literary intellectualism of the Chinese reaches a peak in his tributes to Confucius. The moral maxims of this "prince of the Chinese philosophers" bear a "striking resemblance" to those of "the ancient Hebrew sages" of the Book of Proverbs.[30] But more importantly, Confucius was a sage after Percy's own heart. By a considerable margin, the longest footnote in all of Percy's Chinese writings is a three-and-a-half-page eulogy midway through the second volume of the *Pleasing History* that offers striking resonances with Percy's own life and self-image. Confucius, Percy notes, was "descended from an Emperor of a former dynasty"; Percy himself took pains to claim an affiliation with the aristocratic Percy clan, changing his given family name (Piercy) in 1756 to match their "more ancient and correct spelling," demonstrated his fealty by including numerous ballads about the Percys in his *Reliques,* and dedicated the collection to the matriarch of the clan, the Duchess of Northumberland. Confucius, in Percy's account, "discovered an uncommon gravity and wisdom" from a young age, "and about the fifteenth year gave himself up to the study of the ancient books." Percy, too, was an unusually conscientious schoolboy with precocious literary tastes: by the time he was seventeen, he had amassed a library of 265 books and earned a scholarship to Christ Church, Oxford, to study the classical and clerical traditions.[31] Confucius married at nineteen, but soon divorced his wife, according to Percy, "that he might pursue his studies with the greatest application." During his own years at Oxford, according to Percy's biographer, he was so preoccupied with his studies of Homer, Cicero, Euclid, Virgil, and the Greek Bible that he had no time for drink or women.

The youthful application of both men paid off in their later careers. Confucius, "on account of his admirable qualities, his learning and virtue . . . was several times invested with the magistry in different places, which he only accepted of as the means of promoting his intended reformation both in morals and government." Percy, too, had built a successful career as a moral teacher, having preached sermons at multiple churches from an early stage, and was granted a "living" as an Anglican priest in 1753. Confucius wandered the empire as a "private sage"; Percy served as a tutor to the sons of the nobility. Confucius would eventually be honored as "the great master, the illustrious king of letters," Percy as a Doctor of Divinity at Cambridge. Most importantly, though, Confucius edited and compiled many "philosophical and historical works, which compose the canonical books of the Chinese."[32] Percy, at the time he was writing these lines, had already begun collecting the ballads that would shape his own legacy as a creator of the English literary canon. It is impossible to imagine that Percy did not notice these parallels; it seems far more likely that he shaped his account of Confucius and gave it the prominence he did precisely in order to stress them, and implicitly to associate himself with an historical figure in whose life, work, and values Percy clearly found much to admire.

I referred above to another footnote in which Percy tempers his enthusiasm for Confucian moral sagacity with the hasty qualification that a Chinese philosopher could never hold a candle up to the saintly luminescence of Christ. As the China Jesuits had discovered before him, for a Christian to claim common cause with a heathen, however virtuous, was to totter on the edge of blasphemy; Percy's rhetorical backpedaling reflects his sensitivity to the limits of cross-cultural identification. Nor is this an isolated instance. Percy's earnest embrace of Chinese literati values is matched throughout the Chinese writings by an equal and opposite reaction, an adamant disidentification with Chineseness, a determined pulling away from an Other with which he risked becoming too closely intertwined. These repeated gestures of repudiation are not just personal or religious but are more broadly cultural, suggesting an attempt to define Englishness oppositionally as that which the Chinese are not. For an Englishman, it seems, to claim common cause with an Asian, however civilized, was to totter on the edge of treason.

The impulse of disidentification appears most starkly when Percy attributes to the Chinese qualities that represent the negation of supposedly quintessential English virtues. In the preface to the *Pleasing History*, just a few pages after his paean to the virtue and decorum of Chinese writers, he offers a pointed qualification that distinguishes them in unmistakable terms from their English counterparts:

> That there is a littleness and poverty of genius in almost all the works of taste of the Chinese, must be acknowledged by capable judges. This at least is evident in their writings; and in a narrative like the following, would make a writer creep along through a minute relation of trifling particulars, without daring to omit the most inconsiderable. The abjectness of their genius may easily be accounted for from that servile submission, and dread of novelty, which enslaves the minds of the Chinese, and while it promotes the peace and quiet of their empire, dulls their spirit and cramps their imagination.[33]

Genius, of course, was the hallmark of the English literary tradition. It was native genius that distinguished the plays of Shakespeare, in the age of bardolatry, from their slavishly rule-abiding French counterparts. And it was genius that distinguished the age's leading poet from the legions of dunces he so reviled. Samuel Johnson's assessment of Pope illustrates the standard against which Percy is judging the Chinese: "Pope had likewise genius; a mind active, ambitious, and adventurous, always investigating, always aspiring, in its wildest searches still longing to go forward, in its highest flights still wishing to go higher."[34] In such a comparison, the Chinese muse cuts a pathetic figure indeed. The muse of Albion has genius on her side, that of the Chinese, mere abjection. The English embrace political and by extension imaginative freedom; the Chinese know only servile submission. The English aesthetic spirit, at least since Addison, adventurously seeks out the new and the strange, while the Chinese live in dread of novelty. By characterizing Chinese literature in these terms, Percy quite intentionally portrays it as a perfect inversion of the tradition of which he is a part. But at the same time, of course, he is reaffirming a conception of literary Englishness that in equal measure derives its contours from its juxtaposition with its imagined opposite.

This gesture of radical disaggregation, of constructing each muse as the opposite of the other, is a necessary counterpoint, I am suggesting, to the strong centripetal pull of the attractions for Percy of so many aspects of Chinese culture, and indeed of his inescapable desire to identify closely with them. Just as he is forced to renounce the virtue of Confucius in order to reaffirm his identity as a Christian and a propounder of the Christian faith, so he is bound to renounce the merits of Chinese literature in order to preserve his identity as an English writer and promulgator of the English literary tradition. Neither Christianity nor Englishness, Percy's gestures seem to suggest, has any coherence as an idea in the absence of a sufficiently radical Other against which it can be defined.

Portrayals of the Chinese in terms that suggest an inversion of prized English virtues appear regularly throughout Percy's notes. During the early eighteenth century, the figure of the honest English merchant had become a well-worn literary trope: think of Lillo's Thorowgood in the *London Merchant*, or Roxana's "thorowly honest . . . true-bred merchant" advisor Sir Robert Clayton and Robinson Crusoe's "honest and plain-dealing" captain friend in Defoe's novels.[35] This is the cultural self-conception against which Percy describes the Chinese, in a note to the *Pleasing History*, as "the most subtle crafty people in the world," and hence a people we may naturally suppose "to esteem and admire subtilty and craft." In contrast to an English tradition of martial valor embodied in warrior heroes from St. George to Beowulf and Henry IV to Bunyan's dragon-slaying pilgrim, the Chinese, for Percy, "are the most cowardly people in the world, [and] are much addicted to suicide." While the English imagined themselves as without peers in their love of liberty, according to Percy "no people live under more political restraints than the Chinese."[36]

While each of these characterizations implicitly defines the Chinese in opposition to imagined English virtues, they further compound the effect of distancing or differentiation through their use of the superlative. The Chinese are not just the bearers of generically antithetical traits, they are "the *most* subtle," "the *most* cowardly," and the *most* politically restrained people in the world (emphasis added). Even if one were to harbor some doubt that every Englishman was an exemplar of political freedom, courage, and integrity, that is, the Chinese would still be irredeemably Other by virtue of their own exemplarity as negative models. The superlative degree flatly rules out the possibility of congruence or identification, positioning its object as a unique and matchless paradigm case, while simultaneously confirming that all other contenders possess a lesser measure of the quality in question. We are reaffirmed in our belief in the (relative) courage and honesty of the English by the knowledge that some other nation occupies the nadir of cowardliness and craft.

Even when Percy describes Chinese qualities that might well bear comparison with recognized English traits, he often uses a superlative formulation to preclude the possibility of identification. Discretion and reserve were the corollaries of social dignity in England, but "the Chinese affect a privacy and reserve beyond all other nations." Though the prophetic arts remained alive and well in eighteenth-century England, China was a case apart: "diviners, soothsayers, and astrologers nowhere meet with greater encouragement than in China." For all the dance and comportment lessons subscribed by the English, "The Chinese are the most ceremonious and complaisant people in the world . . . [and] affect an exterior beyond all other nations." Though brevity was recognized as the soul of wit, "Chinese is the most concise language in the world." In the age of the Grand Tour, antiquarianism remained a powerful force in English life – not to mention Percy's own work – and yet "No people have such blind veneration for antiquity as the Chinese."[37] The Chinese, we might conclude, are taken to excess in all things, while the English, by implication, are a people governed by sensible moderation. There is no question of identification between them.

Nor can there be any question, at other moments, that, for all its vaunted achievements, China is worthy of anything but contempt. Just as Percy's impulse to identify with certain features of Chinese culture is counterpoised with frequent gestures of disidentification, so his admiration for those features he deems superior appears to engender a countervailing response of condescension and disdain. We get a taste of this already in his repeated denunciations of supposed Chinese affectedness and dishonesty, examples of which are cited above. A far more caustic and even venomous tone, though, emerges when Percy turns his sights on the sin of pride. The exalted self-image of the Chinese is a frequent irritant to Percy. In a note explaining the tragic implications of a novelistic character's punitive exile to Tartary, Percy remarks, "How grievous a punishment banishment must be to them, we may easily conceive from their excessive fondness for their own country."[38] This same excessive fondness accounts for their supposed lack of interest in travel even of a more profitable kind:

As all the nations bordering upon China are barbarous and uncivilized compared to themselves, they have no inducement to travel abroad. And hence they have learnt to hold all other countries in most sovereign contempt, supposing their own Empire to comprize not only the best, but the greatest part of the habitable world; on which account they call it *Tianhia*, or *all under heaven*. They likewise give it the name of *Chong-que*, or *the kingdom of the middle*, from its supposed situation in the midst of the earth, which they believe to be four-square.

The Middle Kingdom's subsequent acknowledgment of Europe's existence at the far reaches of the habitable world only adds insult to injury, as "they have added it to their maps, as if it were one of the Canary islands, or some little barren spot." A seventeenth-century Chinese official had apparently confirmed as much in a memorial to the throne: "We find very plainly, that Europe is only two little islands in the middle of the sea."[39] The national pride of the Chinese vexes Percy because it quite explicitly insults his own. Like Swift's image of Lemuel Gulliver sailing a toy boat in a Brobdingnagian bathtub, Chinese geography deflates English pretensions to dominion over anything more than a little barren spot. The prime meridian would not be established at Greenwich for another hundred and twenty years. In Percy's time the Chinese claim to occupying the center of the world was still unnervingly plausible – and, it increasingly seems, largely true.[40]

Percy was itching for a way to even the score, and in 1762, as he was preparing the preface to his *Miscellaneous Pieces*, he found it. In the June issue of the *Critical Review* he stumbled upon extracts of a book by John Turberville Needham that claimed to demonstrate the derivation of Chinese characters from Egyptian hieroglyphics. Needham, it seems, had noticed that the characters carved into the face and breast of a bust of Isis at Turin bore some resemblance to Chinese writing. He made copies of these symbols, along with several Egyptian characters from surviving monuments in Rome, and passed them along to a Chinese librarian at the Vatican who claimed to find close matches for most of them in his Chinese dictionary. Percy concludes that the ancient Egyptians communicated their writing system to the early Chinese and seizes on this curious discovery to deflate at a stroke the aggravating historical hubris of the Chinese:

Of the inferences to be drawn from it at present, one of the most important is, that it demolishes at once all the pretences of the Chinese to that vast antiquity, which has been wont to stagger weak minds, and which has with so much parade been represented by certain writers as utterly incompatible with the history of the bible.[41]

The Middle Kingdom, which for millennia had exacted tributes from the barbarous outposts on its peripheries, turns out, according to Percy, to be a mere upstart, indebted for its proudest cultural relic to one of these same Western kingdoms.

Percy continues with this project of deflation in his opening essay on the Chinese language. Not only are the fabled Chinese characters a merely derivative invention, they have subsequently proven a hindrance to progress and creativity in other areas, notably science and literature. They require so much time to learn to read and write that by the time a scholar has achieved any degree of mastery, he has most likely reached that age when "the spirit of inquiry is dulled and blunted" and interest in innovation has waned.[42] During the previous century, the Chinese language and the vast literary and historical canon that had been erected upon it had been revered by European commentators in a tumultuous age as models of stability, continuity, and rationality.[43] Percy hacks away at both ends of this earlier conception, belittling the Chinese, on the one hand, for a relatively late emergence into literacy and, on the other hand, for a failure fully to capitalize on it when they had the chance. Lacking both the dignity attending true antiquity and the dynamism that comes with progress, the Chinese remain mired in a medieval swamp of mediocrity. The state of the Chinese spoken language only confirms Percy in this contemptible vision of stagnation. Because the literary language developed independently of the vernacular and monopolized the attention of the literati, the oral language had been utterly neglected and "therefore remains in its original state of barbarism and rudeness," a "barren and contracted" collection of "a few undeclinable and uncompounded monosyllables."[44]

The entire essay on the Chinese language is structured according to a dichotomy of barbarism and civilization. The barbaric state of the oral language is exemplified by sounds such as that rendered by the Portuguese as "usto" and sounding like "a kind of cry fetched from the hollow of the stomach." The Chinese were still in a "wild and barbarous" state when they first received the gift of writing from the Egyptians. A writing system based on the "picture or hieroglyphic" suited Chinese barbarity as "the first and most obvious kind of writing" likely to be adopted by the "savage" and men living "in a state of wild nature." The use of an alphabet, in contrast, is reserved for the truly civilized as a practice "too refined and artificial to have been the first expedient of untutored man." The rhetorical motive behind this narrative is transparent. As we have seen, Percy is well aware that the Chinese designate as "barbarous and uncivilized" those nations beyond its borders. Percy's tirade on China's linguistic failings enables him neatly and decisively to turn the tables, restoring to civilized Europe the dignity that is its due, and consigning the Chinese barbarians to the company of the "savages of North America."[45]

Percy's allusion to biblical history in the preface to *Miscellaneous Pieces* reminds us that his China-bashing moments are never just about China. To debunk Chinese claims to a staggeringly vast antiquity is simultaneously to redeem not only the literal truth of biblical chronology but also the historical primacy of "Western" civilization. To assert that Chinese science and literature have long been essentially static is implicitly to invoke Bacon, Newton, Shakespeare, Dryden, and Pope as the torch-bearers of a contrasting English tradition of progress. To dismiss spoken Chinese as a rude, barbarous, and barren tongue is to remind the English reader of his birthright, confirmed by street corner ballads, playhouse repartee, and the refined conversation of elite sitting rooms, as the heir to a vigorous and long-cultivated oral tradition. These workings of cultural geography are doubly reciprocal. Percy, in his attempts to "other" and degrade China, grasps at tropes that represent the antithesis of Englishness. At the same time, positing these specific Chinese failings as quintessential features of otherness reifies the identification of Englishness with their opposites. In constructing, however ambivalently, a certain vision of Chinese culture in the *Pleasing History* and *Miscellaneous Pieces*, Percy simultaneously anticipates the invention, in his *Reliques*, of a distinctive new paradigm of Englishness.

Before turning to this later work, it is worth pausing to consider the rather remarkable equivocation we have seen in Percy's attitudes towards things Chinese. I have suggested that the degree of enthusiasm and disdain that animates many of his comments on Chinese culture belies his framing assertions of both anthropological objectivity and amateur nonchalance. Rather than providing a disinterested accounting of the strengths and weaknesses of Chinese civilization, Percy's observations seem rather to reflect the aspirations and anxieties of a reader who had not only become thoroughly absorbed by his research but also personally invested in its conclusions. The source of the tension we find in the Chinese writings, then, is less the product of a doubleness to the Chinese character, as Percy suggests with his "dark side" versus "bright side" index entries, than of a doubleness within Percy's response to China as an overwhelming spectacle at once enchanting and threatening.

Percy himself seems conscious of the possibility of China evoking this kind of intensely interested, double-faced response in other Western observers. The first volume of *Miscellaneous Pieces* includes Percy's English translation from the French version of the Chinese tragedy, *The Little Orphan of the House of Chao*. Immediately following the play, Percy appends a commentary by Richard Hurd that praises it for the "great art and probability" of its dialogue, the exemplary beauty of its climactic scenes, and the remarkable degree to which the *Little Orphan* adheres to the conventions of classical Greek tragedy.

> The two essential rules, before spoken of, are observed in it with a degree of exactness, not always to be found in the works of more knowing dramatists. For 1. the action is strictly one . . . [And] 2. The action proceeds with almost as much rapidity, as Aristotle himself demands.

Several further congruities corroborate Hurd's claim that the "general plan or structure" of the play "agrees very well to the Greek form," leading him to the conclusion that the Aristotelian rules must simply be the products of common sense, equally accessible to thoughtful writers in all times and places.[46]

To assert an equivalence between Chinese and Greek tragedy is to deny the uniqueness and exemplarity of Greek genius. Percy responds to this apostasy not by denying it outright, but by claiming that the author had subsequently retracted his views. In the "advertisement" that serves as a preface to Hurd's essay, Percy imagines a psychological motivation for this apparent about-face:

> As much as the reader may be disposed to admire this ingenious piece of criticism, the author hath shewn himself so dissatisfied with it, that he hath wholly dropped it in the latter editions of that masterly work [*The Discourse on Poetical Imitation*]. His reasons for this he hath no where given us, yet, if we may be allowed to hazard a conjecture, it was because he found upon a cool revisal that he had expressed himself rather too warmly in favour of the Chinese attempts, and had fancied design, and resemblances of the Grecian drama, in a much higher degree than they were found to possess.[47]

The reversal Percy ascribes to Hurd closely resembles that which, I have argued, Percy repeatedly enacts in his Chinese writings. The "warmth" Percy expresses in favor of certain of his Chinese subjects is, as we have seen, likewise bound up with a recognition of congruities and a desire to identify with a foreign symbol of admired values. And, like Hurd's, Percy's warmth rapidly cools once this identification approaches a threshold of self-abnegation. In Percy's case, however, this shift is not an isolated event but an ongoing dialectical process that structures the work as a whole.

The China Jesuits who were the original sources of most European knowledge about China at the time had themselves undergone a similar reversal during the early years of their mission. As they sought to construct an appropriate social role for themselves in their host society, they had initially found local Buddhist monks to be amenable models. The Jesuits noted striking similarities between the rituals, habits, and lifestyles of the two orders, and attempted to present themselves as only slightly foreign variations on a familiar religious theme. Soon discovering, however, that their Buddhist counterparts commanded little respect and occupied a low social position in their own communities, the Jesuits swapped their Buddhist trappings for the robes of the Confucian literati, and eventually turned upon their earlier compatriots with the kind of venom typically reserved for those adversaries most unnervingly similar to oneself.

Percy devotes a long footnote early in the *Pleasing History* to the peculiar relationship between the Chinese Buddhists and the Jesuit priests. He quotes the Jesuit Premare's account of the uncanny resemblance between the orders:

> [The Buddhist monks] have long robes which reach to their ankles, with vast sleeves, which exactly resemble those of some of the religious [orders] in Europe. They live together in their Pagodas, as in convents; they go about the streets a-begging as the mendicants. They rise in the night to worship, they sing together in their choirs in a tone, which very much resembles our psalmody or chanting.

And yet these Buddhist monks, for all their outward trappings of piety, appear to Premare as "priests of Satan." The resemblances are so strong, according to Percy, that the Jesuit "can no otherwise account for it, than by supposing the devil had in view to counterfeit the holy rites of the church."[48] As in Hurd's case, Percy interprets the Jesuits' ultimate distaste for their native *doppelgängers* as a reaction against the threatening spectacle of excessive affinity. Percy was predisposed to such interpretations, I am suggesting, out of a deep personal familiarity with the paradoxical dynamic that they entail.

These reflections on Percy's China writings will seem of scant significance to his far more influential ballad collection until we recognize that his invention of an English literary tradition in the *Reliques* replicates the simultaneous appropriation and repudiation of Chinese models that had animated his earlier work. Indeed, given the manifest intensity of his engagement with Chinese culture over the very same years that the *Reliques* were taking shape, it is difficult to imagine how this would not be the case. Britain, like China, was the center of a powerful empire that prided itself not only on its military might but also on its storied antiquity, literary laurels, and the refined accomplishments of its elite. Both countries had undergone traumatic political upheavals in the previous century, and both had come back stronger, more confident, and more certain of their own position at the center of the civilized world. The seasoned sinologist Thomas Percy, as he embarked upon the project of reconstructing Britain's literary heritage, could scarcely have avoided such comparisons. And indeed the above discussion would suggest that he was likely motivated in no small degree by a desire to confirm Britain as a worthy rival of the great Eastern empire he had just placed squarely, if ambivalently, in his compatriots' field of vision. In *Bardic Nationalism*, Katie Trumpener argues that "English literature, so called, constitutes itself in the late eighteenth and early nineteenth centuries through the systematic imitation, appropriation, and political neutralization of antiquarian and nationalist literary developments in Scotland, Ireland, and Wales."[49] The sinological contexts of Percy's antiquarian researches suggest that the mimetic structures of English cultural nationalism may have extended well beyond the British Isles.

Apparitional sightings are notoriously difficult to verify, and I cannot prove that Percy's *Reliques* are haunted by the specter of China. I will venture, however, that China serves as a crucial model for certain aspects of Percy's reconstructed literary history of England, and that it simultaneously serves as a convenient antithesis against which English virtues can be all the more clearly delineated. Percy's profound ambivalence towards China, his oscillation between identification and distinction, admiration and disdain, suffuses the later work as well. To the extent that he finds congenial values reflected in Chinese symbols, he attempts to transpose these symbols into his native context. Where he finds himself repulsed by Chinese failings, he derives from his repulsion a clearer definition of the essential English character. Once again, the point I wish to stress is that Percy's constructions of England and China are not just conceptually related, but in a deep sense reciprocally constituting.

Superficial similarities between the two projects abound. As Eun Kyung Min has noted, both began with Percy's serendipitous recovery of neglected old manuscripts. And in both cases, she points out, the incomplete or faulty nature of his source materials encouraged Percy, as editor, to take on the role of a cultural guide or mediator, rendering writings of distant provenance intelligible and providing, through his notes and emendations, a necessary supplement to the original texts.[50] We might add that in both bodies of work Percy also positions himself as an impartial ethnographic observer, ostensibly concerned less with showcasing poetic merit than with exhibiting the cultures of distant times or places. His interest in exhibiting "the customs and opinions of remote ages" in the *Reliques* places their artifacts just a museum case away from the remote "manners and customs of the Chinese" which he had set out to render intelligible in his earlier work.[51] And to the extent that he is concerned with aesthetic judgment, it is notable that the Greeks serve as his standard of comparison in both cases.

The problem of aesthetic judgment in the case of the *Reliques* is a vexing one for Percy. He values the old verses he has collected as literary heirlooms, transmitting the spirit of bardic ancestors through the ages to their descendents among modern-day English readers. He takes the natural pride of a grateful heir in the poetic productions of his forefathers, basking in the reflected glow of their achievements while treating their failings with a good-natured spirit of indulgence; he never assumes the harshly critical tone of the more sinophobic passages in the Chinese works. And yet from the vantage point of a cleric and a cultivated man of taste living in an age that valued a refined sensibility and gentle bearing in its male heroes – *Sir Charles Grandison* had been published in 1753 while the *Vicar of Wakefield* would appear the year after the *Reliques* in 1766 – the literary proclivities and moral outlook of early English balladeers must have appeared not a little problematic. The ballads present a sumptuous orgy of violence. The blood of stabbings, beheadings, and battlefield slaughters soaks their pages. There is no law but that of the strongest and most cunning, and little feeling beyond a limited palette of lust, rage, agony, and despair. For Nick Groom, the entire three-volume collection "welters in gore," its obsession with death and dismemberment and with the spectacle of bodies "eating, drinking, fornicating, singing, and killing" producing a dispiriting sense of "cataclysmic fatalism" and "colossal amorality."[52]

Percy recognizes the ballads' capacity to shock. He presents them apologetically in his dedication to the Countess of Northumberland as the "rude songs of ancient minstrels" and the "barbarous products of unpolished ages." He introduces one poem with the observation, "That our plain and martial ancestors could wield their swords much better than their pens will appear from the following homely rhymes."[53] The adjectives "rude," "unlettered," "uncouth," "coarse," and "simple" appear regularly throughout the volumes with reference to the ballads as well as their authors, their times, and their language. If we are now able to regard such descriptors with equanimity and contemplate the aesthetic merits of a coarse simplicity of style, this is in no small measure owing to the triumph of Percy, Burns, and their sundry romantic heirs in valorizing the unaffected strains of the "popular" voice. For Percy himself, however, to acknowledge the essential "barbarousness" of England's literary heritage surely placed him in something of a quandary. At the time he penned this dedication, Percy had only recently emerged from years of study of a highly advanced, and in many respects attractive civilization famed for regarding other nations as "barbarous" when it deigned to regard them at all. He had bristled on recounting a Chinese official's seeming contempt for Europe's "little barren spot" on a world map and had reacted, as we have seen, by castigating the Chinese as "barbarous" in their own right, at least with regard to their oral and written language. What did it mean, then, for Percy to recognize that his own literary ancestors were, by all appearances, considerably more barbarous than any of their East Asian counterparts, who, whatever their linguistic deficiencies, had evidently not spent the previous thousand years running around bludgeoning each other with clubs and swords? How could he possibly redeem a tradition that seemed, if anything, to vindicate the imagined boasts of the hyper-civilized Chinese?

Percy's reconstruction of an English poetic tradition in the prefaces and commentaries that accompany the ballads of the *Reliques* can be read as a response to the Chinese challenge he had so thoroughly internalized. As in his earlier writings, China evokes reactions that are complex and equivocal, enabling it to serve at once as a model and a foil. Percy's solution to the problem of English barbarousness is to rewrite the brutish physicality of the ballads through the transformative discourses of aesthetics, history, and teleology. In each instance, paradigms of Chineseness from his previous work guide his rhetorical strategies, resulting in a history of English literature that, for all its nativist pretensions, closely follows the contours of an earlier sinological encounter.

Percy's most obvious and most lastingly influential gesture of cultural redemption in the *Reliques* is his casting of stylistic flaws in the ballads as the hallmarks of a meritorious aesthetic sensibility. While the "noble savage" ideal with its implicit critique of "civilization" was a familiar one by the mid-eighteenth century, the Chinese provided Percy with a more familiar example of the dangers posed by an excess of refinement. He had frequently faulted the Chinese for an exaggerated concern with outward appearances. "The Chinese," according to a typical comment in the *Pleasing History*, "are a very affected people, and all affectation leads to absurdity."[54] It would follow, then, that the total absence of affectation might produce a certain kind of virtue. And indeed, Percy's cautious tributes to the ancient bards seem to exalt them precisely for their un-Chineseness in this respect.

While he apologizes for the "great simplicity" of the popular poems of yore, he also suggests the possibility that "pleasing simplicity and artless grace" might be sources of poetic merit. While the old minstrel-ballads might be subject to censure for being "extremely incorrect" and indulging in "the utmost license of meter," their corollary "romantic wildness" also warrants our praise. "The Ballad of Chevy Chase" stands out for its "genuine strokes of nature and artless passion," while another poem Percy calls the "first attempt at pastoral in our language" is superior in its "natural unaffected sentiments" and "simplicity of style."[55]

Percy's success in transforming the pained perception of the rugged, coarse, and uncouth into an appreciation of the natural, artless, and unaffected, his success, in other words, in aestheticizing barbarousness, is enabled by a conceptual framework derived from his Chinese studies which castigates unnatural affectation as an excess of refinement that borders on the absurd. He recognizes the dangers of over-refinement in later English literary contexts as well, but China's example is crucial in pushing affectation to such an extreme – the Chinese, after all, are "the most ceremonious people in the world" and "affect an exterior beyond all other nations" – that its otherwise problematic antithesis appears admirable by comparison.[56] Decades before Wordsworth's epoch-shifting critique of Augustan poetics, the limit case of rule-bound behavior presented by the Confucian literati made it possible to imagine and to celebrate a viable poetics of the primitive.

If Percy's eulogies to bardic rusticity reflect his sinophobic impulses, his latent sinophilia inflects his reverent worship of Anglo-Saxon ancestors. While an eighteenth-century Englishman as obsessed with his own pedigree as Thomas Percy hardly needed the Chinese to teach him about the legitimizing functions of genealogy, it is difficult to imagine that the high regard for antiquity and for "our ancestors" that suffuses the *Reliques* was not animated to some degree by Percy's admiration for the filial piety and traditionalism of the Chinese. As we have seen, Percy recognized the degree to which the stability and stature of Chinese civilization rested upon these values; his own nationalist enterprise could only stand to benefit from assimilating the pious identification with the past that served the Chinese so well. The barbarousness of old English verse might be forgiven, after all, if its authors could be rendered worthy of filial regard.

Lest we miss the analogy between old poetic fragments and martyrs' bones suggested by his title, Percy elaborates it in the first lines of the preface to the *Reliques*. "The reader is here presented with select remains of our ancient English bards and minstrels, an order of men who were once greatly respected by our ancestors, and contributed to soften the roughness of a martial and unlettered people by their songs and by their music." The phrase "select remains," in its potent ambiguity, effects a transubstantiation of bardic flesh into balladic rhyme. Percy's book becomes a reliquary, a sacred shrine consecrated for the worship of "our ancient English bards." The sacralization of these literary ancestors parallels, in its transcendence of the merely physical or historical, the aestheticization of their bawdy, bodily verse through a poetics of artless simplicity. Percy never misses a chance to emphasize the antiquity of his relics or their connection with the present. Judging from the prefatory remarks he provides for the poems, the chief merit of a good many of them is that they are "very antique." The word "ancient" appears three times on the first page of the preface, the word "ours" four; the ancient bards, ancient manuscripts, and ancient poetry Percy assembles for us here are the legacy of our ancestors, our language, our earliest classical poets. We are called upon to identify with the literary remnants of our heritage, to recognize ourselves through a poetic communion with our past.

The English had proven themselves perfectly competent antiquarians before the Chinese came along, but the peculiar combination of the literary, the religious, and the genealogical that characterizes Percy's fascination with his cultural heritage suggests a marked departure from the virtuosic dilettantism of his predecessors. I mentioned above that the longest note in the *Pleasing History* is devoted to Confucius, and that Percy appears to find a kindred spirit in the Chinese sage. The final portion of that note suggests that the legacy of Confucius may have provided a model as well for the legacy he sought to construct for the "classical" authors of the English past:

> Since his death he hath been regarded by the Chinese, if not as one of their deities or Pagods, yet with a degree of reverence, which it is difficult to distinguish from idolatry: for he is not only called *the great master, the illustrious king of letters, the saint,* or *hero adorned with excellent wisdom,* whatever is cited from him being received as oraculous: but in every city is a magnificent hall where his name is inscribed in letters of gold, and where the highest honours are paid to his memory by all the Literati.[57]

Idolatry or not, it is difficult to imagine that Bishop Percy would have been terribly troubled at the thought of a temple erected in his own memory. But it is harder still to imagine that in consecrating his literary pantheon of ancient English worthies, he was not inspired by the extraordinary respect paid by the Chinese to their ancient lettered heroes.

Confucius, after all, was not an isolated case. He represented to European readers the characteristic literati culture of the Chinese, a set of institutions and practices that had for centuries granted tremendous social and political stature to highly educated men of letters. As Percy recognized, the literati earned their rank and privileges through a series of competitive examinations that assessed their mastery of classical texts. A literary education became the key to success, and literary, and specifically poetic skill the most highly valued cultural attainment. In his collection of Chinese poetry, Percy notes that "this pleasing art is nowhere in higher request than in China, where it was the first vehicle of morality, religion, and politics, and has always been regarded with peculiar reverence and esteem."[58] The English, alas, had never developed a Confucian meritocracy, and – as Percy knew well – only rarely accorded accomplished men of letters the respect that they deserved. The ancient English did, however, produce poets, whom Percy, perhaps in part to compensate for the barbarousness of their productions, found fit to portray in as flattering a light as possible. Given his evident approval of the social status accorded literary men in China, it is not surprising to find that his reconstruction of the minstrel tradition bears resemblances to the Chinese model with which he was so enthralled.

Percy's tale of English minstrelsy evokes a long lost Golden Age when poets reigned supreme. As we have seen, Percy describes English bards and minstrels as "an order of men who were once greatly respected by our ancestors." Before they sank into "contempt and neglect" in Elizabeth's reign, poets were held in "rude admiration." The further back we look, in fact, "the greater respect we find paid to the professors of poetry and music among all the Celtic and Gothic nations."[59] In their brightest hour, these literati of the northern forests occupied a social position more redolent of the Confucian China Percy imagined than of the Georgian England in which he lived:

> Our Saxon ancestors, as well as their brethren the ancient Danes, had been accustomed to hold men of this profession in the highest reverence. Their skill was considered as something divine, their persons were deemed sacred, their attendance was solicited by kings, and they were every where loaded with honours and rewards.[60]

According to Percy, the Chinese literati were also revered for their skill, sought after by their rulers, and honored in life and after death. For Percy to assert that his Saxon ancestors possessed such a closely comparable institution is effectively to appropriate a crucial marker of cultural legitimacy from the Chinese model and to splice it, like a fragment of DNA from a superior strain, into the creation myth of English literature.

Crucially, in Percy's account, the Saxon minstrels were honored at court not just for their skill as entertainers, but for their role as historians. The ancient bards recorded in their songs "the victories of their warriors, and the genealogies of their princes." Though they had been embellished over time, even the most "romantic" of the popular tales recounted in the ballads, Percy assures us, have some basis in truth.[61] In imagining the social roles of these storytellers, Percy might well have, of course, been thinking of the Greek tradition embodied in the Phaiakian minstrel Demodokos, who unwittingly brings the unrecognized Odysseus to tears by recounting the warrior's own history in song. But in elaborating this conjunction between literary and historical traditions, the Chinese could never have been far from his thoughts. They were renowned, as Percy had discovered, for their meticulous historical records, covering the rise and fall of dynasties thousands of years into the past; the study and interpretation of this history was one of the chief occupations of the literati class, who, according to Percy, esteemed "history, antiquity, poetry, [and] law" as the subjects most proper for "learned and ingenious men."[62] The relative paucity of the historical record in England leaves the minstrels' champion sounding almost defensive; their narrations "are supposed to have had at bottom so much of truth as to serve for the basis of more regular annals. At least succeeding historians have taken up with the relations of these rude men, and for want of more authentic records, have agreed to allow them the credit of true history."[63] We saw earlier how keen Percy was to demolish Chinese claims to vast antiquity; in his earnest, almost apologetic attempts to come up with worthy English equivalents to the fabled Chinese annals, we can begin to see the reason for his exasperation.

The one notable advantage offered by a deficient history is the possibility of improving upon it. Percy redeemed the barbarousness of ancient English verse by proposing a new, proto-romantic scale of aesthetic value, inspired by a conspicuous form of Chinese excess. He redeemed the creators of this verse from a nameless oblivion by promoting them to a social stature, inspired by the Chinese literati, which reflected gloriously on all succeeding generations of poets. His final gesture of redemption likewise responds to a Chinese model by finding in it the inspiration for a new myth of Englishness. In crisis-riven seventeenth-century Europe, the storied continuity of Chinese civilization over several millennia had evoked admiration and envy. By the nineteenth century, Hegel and Marx viewed the same continuity with considerably more contempt, as a sign of stagnation and inertia that left

China outside of history altogether and the Chinese peculiarly insensible to otherwise irresistible forces of historical change.

Thomas Percy was one of the earliest English writers to anticipate this most enduring of orientalist tropes. On the antiquity of China he is typically ambivalent. On the one hand, in his comment on the usefulness of a strict adherence to etiquette and ritual, he seems to admire its consequence in "the wonderful stability of the Chinese empire" and the fact of the empire's "having subsisted above 4000 years." On the other hand, an excessive regard for the past evokes disdain: "No people have such blind veneration for antiquity as the Chinese."[64] But when, in the course of his polemical indictment of the Chinese language, he discovers the metaphor of historical stasis, he seizes on the opportunity rhetorically to transform the fabled Chinese past from asset to encumbrance. As discussed above, Percy develops the idea of stasis in attempting to account for the historical divergence between the oral and written languages of China and the apparent lack of a well-developed oral tradition. While the literati have devoted their considerable energies to cultivating the written language, the oral language "has been in proportion neglected, and therefore remains in its original state of barbarism and rudeness." But because the difficulty of mastering characters cramps poetic genius, this stagnation ultimately infects the literary canon as well: "The literature of the Chinese is, we see, more likely to remain what it is, than to be improved by new acquisitions."[65]

If the charge that the Chinese have failed in the continuous improvement of the literary arts provides fodder for subsequent orientalist discourse, it also provides a foil for Percy's own assertions of English literary progress. The project of the *Reliques* is framed as an evolutionary fable: our interest in antiquities is prompted by "natural curiosity to survey the progress of life and manners, and to inquire by what gradations barbarity was civilized, grossness refined, and ignorance instructed." The ancient bards, for all the barbarousness of their productions, played a crucial role in this evolution, for it was through their efforts that "the infancy of genius [was] nurtured and advanced . . . [and] the minds of unlettered warriors softened and enlarged." The poems in the collection, he emphasizes in the preface to the first volume, are meant to testify to the gradual maturation of English genius by showing "the gradation of our language" and "the progress of popular opinions." Percy reiterates this purpose in the opening pages of each of the subsequent two volumes. The poems assembled in the second volume "will show the gradual changes of the English language through a succession of five hundred years"; the third confirms the editor's "desire to throw new light on the rise and progress of English poetry."[66] Percy's imposition of a narrative of progress on what might otherwise appear a motley assortment of poetic fragments provides a teleological solution to the problem of ancestral barbarism that is every bit as effective as his aesthetic and historical re-evaluations of his poetic heritage. And it is equally indebted to Percy's early immersion in sinological researches. For just as a poetics of rustic simplicity is unimaginable in the absence of a negative model of over-refinement and a cult of literary ancestor worship inseparable from contemporary understandings of Chinese social practice, so too is a triumphalist vision of centuries of English literary progress unthinkable without a contrary model of literary stagnation. While the Chinese barbarians of antiquity were producing the guttural howls of the eternal primitive, the barbarians of ancient Saxony were nurturing, through their tales of battlefield glory, the seeds of poetic genius that would eventually ripen into the works of Shakespeare, Milton, and Pope.

Arthur Lovejoy famously argues in "The Chinese Origin of a Romanticism" that the Chinese style in gardening exercised a profound influence on aesthetic ideas and fashions throughout the eighteenth century, and that the "conscious revolt against neo-classical standards" that would eventually coalesce in the new aesthetics of romanticism was "commonly recognized as initially due to the influence and example of Chinese art."[67] In this chapter, I have attempted to extend and to complicate Lovejoy's understanding of the power of the Chinese influence and example in the early formation of romantic ideas by illuminating the Chinese origins of one of the foundational works of English literary romanticism. That these origins, in Percy's case, are largely obscured from view testifies to the psychological complexity of the process of "influence," especially – as Harold Bloom memorably argues – when that influence is coupled with the anxiety born of a consciousness of belatedness or inferiority.[68]

Towards the end of the eighteenth century, the Qing dynasty began a long period of economic and political decline. For the subsequent two centuries of Chinese tumult, the ascendant West has enjoyed the luxury of forgetting Percy's Bloomian struggles with his Chinese fathers, the luxury of forgetting that for much of the previous millennium, China, not Europe, had been, by many measures of economic development and cultural achievement, the center of the world. Thomas Percy, in his profound ambivalence towards this realization, created a powerful myth of Englishness that, by at once incorporating and repudiating elements of his Chinese model, triumphed over his own anxiety and cast a nationalist spell of historical amnesia from which we are only now beginning to recover.

Notes

Introduction: monstrous beauty

1 "All of the erudite books and articles [about the history of footbinding], I maintain, are histories of anti-footbinding," writes Dorothy Ko. "They begin with the premise that footbinding is despicable and generally end with the same conclusion." This shared premise and conclusion have served equally well, in their turn, Protestant missionaries, Marxists, feminists, and Chinese nationalists. See Dorothy Ko, *Cinderella's Sisters: A Revisionist History of Footbinding* (Berkeley: University of California Press, 2005), 1–10. A similar argument about the usefulness to Western observers of the spectacle of Chinese pain is made by Timothy Brook, Jérôme Bourgon, and Gregory Blue in *Death by a Thousand Cuts* (Cambridge, MA: Harvard University Press, 2008), 6–8; and by Eric Hayot, *The Hypothetical Mandarin: Sympathy, China, and the Fate of the Modern Human* (Oxford University Press, 2008), 13–26.

2 Charles Lamb, "Old China," *Complete Works of Charles Lamb* (Philadelphia: W. T. Amies, 1879), 480.

3 *Ibid.*, 481.

4 J. M. Blaut, *The Colonizer's Model of the World: Geographical Diffusionism and Eurocentric History* (New York: Guilford Press, 1993), 11–30.

5 Dipesh Chakrabarty, *Provincializing Europe: Postcolonial Thought and Historical Difference* (Princeton University Press, 2000), 27–8.

6 Paul A. Cohen, *Discovering History in China: American Historical Writing on the Recent Chinese Past* (New York: Columbia University Press, 1984), 9, 67–8.

7 See Andre Gunder Frank, *ReOrient: Global Economy in the Asian Age* (Berkeley: University of California Press, 1998); R. Bin Wong, *China Transformed: Historical Change and the Limits of European Experience* (Ithaca, NY: Cornell University Press, 1997); Kenneth Pomeranz, *The Great Divergence: Europe, China, and the Making of the Modern World Economy* (Princeton University Press, 2000).

8 Gerald M. MacLean, *Looking East: English Writing and the Ottoman Empire before 1800* (New York: Palgrave Macmillan, 2007), 20–1, 45.

9 Robert Markley, *The Far East and the English Imagination, 1600–1730* (Cambridge University Press, 2006), 3, 86, 105, 145, 188, 242.

10 I develop this argument in the third chapter of my previous book, *Ideographia: The Chinese Cipher in Early Modern Europe* (Stanford University Press, 2001), 133–92.

11 Lamb, "Old China," 480.

12 *Ibid.*
13 *Ibid.*, 480–1, 488.

1 Eighteenth-century fashion and the aesthetics of the Chinese taste

1 I am thinking, for example, of Elizabeth Bohls, *Women Travel Writers and the Language of Aesthetics, 1716–1818* (Cambridge University Press, 1995); George Dickie, *The Century of Taste: The Philosophical Odyssey of Taste in the Eighteenth Century* (New York: Oxford University Press, 1996); Robert Jones, *Gender and the Formation of Taste in Eighteenth-Century Britain: The Analysis of Beauty* (Cambridge University Press, 1998); and James Walvin, *Fruits of Empire: Exotic Produce and British Taste, 1660–1800* (New York University Press, 1997).
2 For reasons that will become apparent, I use the term chinoiserie here to refer to any object, whether of Chinese or European origin, that would have been recognized as being in the so-called Chinese style by an observer at the time.
3 The best introductions to chinoiserie are Hugh Honour, *Chinoiserie: The Vision of Cathay* (New York: Dutton, 1962); and Dawn Jacobson, *Chinoiserie* (London: Phaidon Press, 1993). The classical backlash against chinoiserie is discussed at length in Beverly Sprague Allen, *Tides in English Taste (1619–1800): A Background for the Study of Literature*, 2 vols. (New York: Pageant Books, 1958), I: 234–56.
4 In addition to the books by Honour and Jacobson cited above, see also Oliver Impey, *Chinoiserie: The Impact of Oriental Styles on Western Art and Decoration* (New York: Charles Scribner's Sons, 1977); and Madeleine Jarry, *Chinoiserie: Chinese Influence on European Decorative Art, 17th and 18th Centuries*, trans. Gail Mangold-Vine (New York: Vendome Press, 1981).
5 See, for example, Maxine Berg, "Manufacturing the Orient: Asian Commodities and European Industry, 1500–1800," in *Prodotti e tecniche d'oltremare nelle economie europee secc. XIII–XVIII*, ed. Simonetta Cavaciocchi (Prato: Istituto internazionale di storia economica F. Datini, 1998), 385–419.
6 Contemporary responses to the Chinese taste in gardening offer a notable exception to this pattern of disdain; see Chapter 2.
7 Useful starting places in the considerable bibliography on European fascination with China in the early modern period include William W. Appleton, *A Cycle of Cathay: The Chinese Vogue in England during the 17th and 18th Centuries* (New York: Columbia University Press, 1951); Raymond Dawson, *The Chinese Chameleon: An Analysis of European Conceptions of Chinese Civilisation* (London: Oxford University Press, 1967); and Basil Guy, *The French Image of China Before and After Voltaire*, Studies on Voltaire and the Eighteenth Century 21 (Geneva: Institut et musée Voltaire, 1963).
8 Western responses to the achievements of Chinese civilization and the cultural transformations these responses entailed in Europe have been the primary focus of my own recent work; see Porter, *Ideographia*.

9 Grant McCracken, *Culture and Consumption: New Approaches to the Symbolic Character of Consumer Goods and Activities* (Bloomington: Indiana University Press, 1988), 31–41.

10 Joseph Warton, *The World* 26 (June 28, 1753); Oliver Goldsmith, *Citizen of the World and The Bee* (London: J. M. Dent, 1934), 4.

11 William Chambers, for example, identifies classical Greek analogues to various features of Chinese temple architecture (*Designs of Chinese Buildings, Furniture, Dresses, Machines and Utensils* [London, 1757], preface). Arthur Murphy seconds Richard Hurd's view that a widely known Yuan Dynasty play, *The Orphan of the House of Chau*, bore comparison with "the beautiful models of antiquity" ("Letter to Voltaire," in Murphy, *The Orphan of China* [London: 1797], vi).

12 See David Porter, "Chinoiserie and the Aesthetics of Illegitimacy," *Studies in Eighteenth-Century Culture* 28 (1999): 33–7.

13 For the history of the English trade with China, see James Bromley Eames, *The English in China* (London: Pitman and Sons, 1909). Essential primary documents on the conditions of trade at Canton are collected in Hosea Ballou Morse, *The Chronicles of the East India Company Trading to China, 1635–1834*, 5 vols. (Taipei: Ch'eng-wen Publishing Company, 1975). A helpful discussion of the rise of protectionist sentiment in England and the place of the English East India Company in the controversies it generated is provided in P. J. Thomas, *Mercantilism and the East India Trade* (London: Frank Cass & Co., 1963).

14 In *English Imagination*, Robert Markley argues, along similar lines, that English views towards China in this period were shaped by a more generalized awareness of its own inadequacy and belatedness on the stage of world trade.

15 I develop this argument at considerable length in the first two chapters of my previous book; see *Ideographia*, 15–132.

16 See, for example, Neil McKendrick, John Brewer, and J. H. Plumb, *The Birth of a Consumer Society: The Commercialization of Eighteenth-Century England* (Bloomington: Indiana University Press, 1982), 11. For a critique of the reliance on Veblen in this and other recent work, see McCracken, *Culture and Consumption*, 3–10.

17 McKendrick, Brewer, and Plumb, *Consumer Society*, 100–39.

18 Herbert Blumer, "Fashion: From Class Differentiation to Collective Selection," *The Sociological Quarterly* 10 (1969): 280.

19 See especially the first chapter of Pierre Bourdieu, *Distinction: A Social Critique of the Judgment of Taste*, trans. Richard Nice (Cambridge, MA: Harvard University Press, 1984).

20 Warton, *The World.*

21 Anthony Ashley Cooper, third Earl of Shaftesbury, "Advice to an Author," *Characteristics of Men, Manners, Opinions, Times, Etc.*, ed. John Robertson, 2 vols. (London, 1900), I: 219.

22 John Brewer, *The Pleasures of the Imagination: English Culture in the Eighteenth Century* (New York: Farrar Straus Giroux, 1997), 110–18.

23 The best-known chinoiserie design books from this period are Thomas Chippendale, *The Gentleman and Cabinet-Maker's Director* (London, 1754); Paul Decker, *Chinese Architecture* (London, 1759); and William Halfpenny, *Rural Architecture in the Chinese Taste* (London, 1755). For a more extended discussion of the relationship between the Gothic and Chinese styles in England, see Chapter 6.

24 See, for example, Impey, *Chinoiserie*, 101–4; and Craig Clunas, *Chinese Export Art and Design* (London: Victoria and Albert Museum, 1987), 44–70. Some contemporary observers were well aware of the inauthenticity of the so-called Chinese style: "not one in a thousand of all the stiles, gates, rails, pales, chairs, temples, chimney-pieces, &c. &c. &c. which are called Chinese, has the least resemblance to any thing that China ever saw; nor would an English church be a less uncommon sight to a travelling mandarin, than an English pagoda" (*The World* 12 [March 22, 1753]: 59).

25 Tomas Kulka, *Kitsch and Art* (University Park: Pennsylvania State University Press, 1996), 25–37.

26 Joseph Addison, *The Spectator* 412 (June 23, 1712).

27 Walter Houghton, "The English Virtuoso in the Seventeenth Century: Part II," *Journal of the History of Ideas* 3 (1942): 193.

28 Joseph Addison, *The Spectator* 18 (March 21, 1711); Brewer, *Pleasures of the Imagination*, 366–70.

29 Immanuel Kant, *Critique of Judgment*, trans. Werner S. Pluhar (Indianapolis: Hackett, 1987), 65.

30 See Elizabeth A. Bohls, "Disinterestedness and the Denial of the Particular: Locke, Smith, and the Subject of Aesthetics," in *Eighteenth-Century Aesthetics and the Reconstruction of Art*, ed. Paul Mattick (Cambridge University Press, 1993), 8, for a useful discussion of this position.

31 In a very useful article, Anna Somers Cocks argues persuasively that "china collecting began as a woman's hobby in the late seventeenth century, and women remained a major force in the market throughout the next century." "The Nonfunctional Use of Ceramics in the English Country House During the Eighteenth Century," in *The Fashioning and Functioning of the British Country House*, ed. Gervase Jackson-Stops (Washington, DC: National Gallery of Art, 1989), 214. For a helpful discussion of the associations between tea and femininity in the seventeenth and eighteenth centuries, see Elizabeth Kowaleski-Wallace, *Consuming Subjects: Women, Shopping, and Business in the Eighteenth Century* (New York: Columbia University Press, 1997), 19–36. Maxine Berg's study of eighteenth-century wills demonstrates that while there was no significant difference in the ownership patterns of decorative goods between men and women, women's wills offer much more detailed presentations of objects, suggesting that they took on for female owners a greater degree of personal significance. Berg includes china and tea-wares among those objects which served women as "personal and expressive goods, conveying identity personality, and fashion." Maxine Berg,

"Women's Consumption and the Industrial Classes of Eighteenth-Century England," *Journal of Social History* 30 (1996): 415–26.

32 Porter, "Chinoiserie."

33 Aubrey J. Toppin, "The China Trade and Some London Chinamen," *Transactions of the English Ceramic Circle* 3 (1934): 44–6. On contemporary responses to female commerce at the New Exchange, where the retail trade in Chinese export goods was concentrated, see James Turner, "News from the New Exchange: Commodity, Erotic Fantasy, and the Female Entrepreneur," in *The Consumption of Culture 1600–1800: Image, Object, Text*, ed. Ann Bermingham and John Brewer (New York: Routledge, 1995), 419–35.

34 Ros Ballaster, *Seductive Forms: Women's Amatory Fiction from 1684 to 1740* (Oxford University Press, 1992), 29; Paula McDowell, *The Women of Grub Street: Press, Politics, and Gender in the London Literary Marketplace, 1678–1730* (New York: Clarendon Press, 1997), 5.

35 Anthony Pollock, *Gender and the Fictions of the Public Sphere, 1690–1755* (New York: Routledge, 2009), 8.

36 Arthur O. Lovejoy, "The Chinese Origin of a Romanticism," in *Essays in the History of Ideas* (Baltimore: Johns Hopkins University Press, 1948), 99–135.

2 Cross-cultural aesthetics in William Chambers' Chinese garden

1 Felicity Nussbaum, ed. *The Global Eighteenth Century* (Baltimore: Johns Hopkins University Press, 2003), 1.

2 See, for example, *ibid.*; Roxann Wheeler, *The Complexion of Race: Categories of Difference in Eighteenth-Century British Culture* (Philadelphia: University of Pennsylvania Press, 2000); and Srinivas Aravamudan, *Tropicopolitans: Colonialism and Agency, 1688–1804* (Durham, NC: Duke University Press, 1999).

3 The degree of Chinese influence on the development of the English landscape garden is a topic that has long interested scholars and remains the subject of lively debate. Important sources include Shou-yi Ch'ên, "The Chinese Garden in Eighteenth-Century England," *T'ien Hsia Monthly* 2 (1936): 321–39; Patrick Conner, "China and the Landscape Garden: Reports, Engravings and Misconceptions," *Art History* 2 (1979): 430–40; Liangyan Ge, "On the Eighteenth-Century English Misreading of the Chinese Garden," *Comparative Civilizations Review* 27 (1992): 106–26; and, most recently, Yu Liu, *Seeds of a Different Eden: Chinese Gardening Ideas and a New English Aesthetic Ideal* (Columbia, SC: University of South Carolina Press, 2008).

4 Haun Saussy, "Impressions de Chine; or, How to Translate from a Non-Existent Original," in *Sinographies: Writing China*, ed. Eric Hayot, Haun Saussy, and Steven Yao (Minneapolis: University of Minnesota Press, 2008), 64.

5 On finding that his *Dissertation on Oriental Gardening* (London, 1772) met with a less favorable response than he had hoped for, Chambers appended "An Explanatory Discourse by Tan Chet-qua" to the second edition of the

Dissertation, published in 1773. Subsequent textual references to the *Dissertation* and the "Explanatory Discourse" will be to these two editions respectively.

6 Horace Walpole, *Anecdotes of Painting in England*, 4 vols. (London, 1765), I: xiii; Walpole to Mason, May 25, 1772, *The Yale Edition of Horace Walpole's Correspondence*, ed. W. S. Lewis (New Haven, CT: Yale University Press, 48 vols. (1937–83), XXVIII: 34; Horace Walpole, *Anecdotes of Painting in England*, ed. Frederick W. Hilles and Philip B. Daghlian, 5 vols. (New Haven, CT: Yale University Press, 1937), V: 185.

7 William Chambers, *Treatise on the Decorative Part of Civil Architecture*, 3rd edn. (London, 1791), 62–3. This is the final edition of the *Treatise* that Chambers prepared. Apart from changing the title to reflect the book's contents more accurately, he revised the preface and some parts of the main text and added a new introduction. Subsequent textual references will be to this edition.

8 William Chambers, preface to *Designs of Chinese Buildings, Furniture, Dresses, Machines and Utensils* (London, 1757).

9 Liu, *Seeds of a Different Eden*, 2, 34, 67, 79, 131–2.

10 This shift in the prevailing responses to Chinese culture in early modern Europe is a central concern of my previous book, *Ideographia*.

11 John Harris, ed., *Sir William Chambers: Knight of the Polar Star* (London: A. Zwemmer, 1970), 33–4; William Chambers, *Plans, Elevations, Sections, and Perspective Views of the Gardens and Buildings at Kew, in Surrey* (London, 1763), 4–6.

12 Chambers to Frederick Chapman, July 28, 1771, British Library Add. MS 41133 f. 78; Chambers to the Earl of Charlemont, June 13, 1772, BL Add. MS 41133 f. 75; Chambers to J. Leake, March 24, 1773, BL Add. MS 41134 f. 19 (all in William Chambers correspondence).

13 Chambers, "Explanatory Discourse," 112.

14 For representative earlier readings of the *Dissertation*, see R. C. Bald, "Sir William Chambers and the Chinese Garden," in *Discovering China: European Interpretations in the Enlightenment*, ed. Julia Ching and Willard G. Oxtoby (University of Rochester Press, 1992); Isabel Chase, "William Mason and Sir William Chambers' *Dissertation on Oriental Gardening*," *Journal of English and Germanic Philology* 35 (1936): 517–29; Eileen Harris, "*Designs of Chinese Buildings* and the *Dissertation on Oriental Gardening*," in Harris (ed.), *Sir William Chambers*; Liu, *Seeds of a Different Eden*; Nikolaus Pevsner, "The Other Chambers," *Architectural Review* 101 (1947): 195–8; and R. B. Reaves, Jr., "Sir William Chambers: A Study of Georgian Taste" (Ph.D. Dissertation, University of Wisconsin, 1971).

15 Chambers, preface to "Explanatory Discourse."

16 Chambers, *Treatise*, iv.

17 Chambers, *Dissertation*, 25–6.

18 In addition to the works cited above, see also Tony C. Brown, "Joseph Addison and the Pleasures of *Sharawadgi*," *ELH* 74 (2007): 171–93.

19 Chambers, *Treatise*, 14–15.

20 *Ibid.*, 7.
21 Chambers, *Dissertation*, 11.
22 Chambers, *Treatise*, 9–10; Chambers, *Dissertation*, 18–19.
23 Eileen Harris, "*Designs*," 154; Thomas Whately, *Observations on Modern Gardening* (London, 1770), 15, 21–2.
24 John Dixon Hunt, *Gardens and the Picturesque: Studies in the History of Landscape Architecture* (London: MIT Press, 1992), Ch. 2.
25 Chambers, *Dissertation*, 43–4.
26 *Ibid.*, 25–7, 38–40.
27 Stephen Greenblatt, *Marvelous Possessions: The Wonder of the New World* (University of Chicago Press, 1991), 14.
28 "Letter of Sir William Chambers to a Gentleman who had objected to certain parts of his *Treatise on Oriental Gardening*," in Harris (ed.), *Sir William Chambers*, 192.
29 See Hunt, *Gardens*, Ch. 3. The Whately quotation appears on p. 76.
30 Chambers, *Dissertation*, 16–17.
31 *Ibid.*, 39.
32 *Ibid.*, 25, 46–9, 73.
33 Greenblatt, *Marvelous Possessions*, 19.
34 Chambers, *Dissertation*, 92–3.
35 Chambers, "Explanatory Discourse," 125, 128, 132–3.
36 Christopher Tunnard, *Gardens in the Modern Landscape* (London: Architectural Press, 1938), 166. See also Bald, "Sir William Chambers," 175.

3 Gendered utopias in transcultural context

1 For Laurie Langbauer, the romance genre served in the eighteenth century as "the chaotic negative space outside the novel that determined the outlines of the novel's form." *Women and Romance: The Consolations of Gender in the English Novel* (Ithaca, NY: Cornell University Press, 1990), 63.
2 Joseph Addison, *The Spectator* 37 (April 12, 1711), London.
3 See Charles Saumarez Smith, *Eighteenth-Century Decoration: Design and the Domestic Interior in England* (London: Weidenfeld and Nicolson, 1993), 24; Cocks, "Nonfunctional Use of Ceramics"; and Joan Wilson, "A Phenomenon of Taste: The China Ware of Queen Mary II," *Apollo* 96 (1972): 116–23.
4 For the history of women's roles in porcelain collecting, see Ann Eatwell, "Private Pleasure, Public Beneficence: Lady Charlotte Schreiber and Ceramic Collecting," in *Women in the Victorian Art World*, ed. Clarissa Campbell Orr (Manchester University Press, 1995),126–7.
5 The most comprehensive treatment of women as collectors of china in the eighteenth century is Cocks, "Nonfunctional Use of Ceramics," 204; see also Hilary Young, *English Porcelain, 1745–95: Its Makers, Design, Marketing and Consumption* (London: V & A Publications, 1999), 185, 192. In general, the

management of household consumption appears to have fallen to the mistress of the household, who supervised the placement of objects in the home and jealously guarded her role as the family consumer. See Amanda Vickery, "Women and the World of Goods: A Lancashire Consumer and her Possessions, 1751–81," in *Consumption and the World of Goods*, ed. John Brewer and Roy Porter (London: Routledge, 1993), 279–82.

6 Clara Reeve, *The Progress of Romance*, 2 vols. (London: 1785), I: 6; Sarah Richards, *Eighteenth-Century Ceramics: Products for a Civilised Society* (Manchester University Press, 1999), 178.

7 Ballaster, *Seductive Forms*, 48. On the gendering of the Chinese taste in contemporary satire, see Porter, *Ideographia*, 181–92.

8 John J. Richetti, *Popular Fiction before Richardson: Narrative Patterns, 1700–1739* (Oxford: Clarendon Press, 1969), 8–9.

9 Langbauer, *Women and Romance*, 92.

10 Young, *English Porcelain*, 10; Richards, *Eighteenth-Century Ceramics*, 177.

11 See Allen, *Tides in English Taste*, I: 234–56; Honour, *Chinoiserie*; and Porter, *Ideographia*.

12 Lynda Nead, *The Female Nude: Art, Obscenity and Sexuality* (London: Routledge, 1992), 1.

13 According to sinologist François Jullien, "not only are there no nudes to be found in the Chinese tradition, but, more radically, everything about the tradition suggests that the nude is simply an *impossibility*." *The Impossible Nude: Chinese Art and Western Aesthetics*, trans. Maev de la Guardia (University of Chicago Press, 2007), vii.

14 Familiar exceptions might include bathing scenes such as depictions of Diana with her nymphs or *Gabrielle d'Estrees and One of her Sisters in the Bath*. The often intense eroticism of these images, however, suggests an exteriorization of the male gaze more than an outright banishment. The possibility of reading early modern images of women together in terms of lesbian desire is explored in Patricia Simons, "Lesbian (In)Visibility in Italian Renaissance Culture: Diana and Other Cases of *donna con donna*," in *Gay and Lesbian Studies in Art History*, ed. Whitney Davis (New York: Harrington Park Press, 1994), 81–122.

15 See *Glimpses into the Hidden Quarters: Paintings of Women from the Middle Kingdom* (Taipei: National Palace Museum, 1988), 97–8; and Robert Lee Thorp and Richard Ellis Vinograd, *Chinese Art and Culture* (New York: Harry N. Abrams, 2001), 211; as well as Ellen Johnston Laing, "Chinese Palace-Style Poetry and the Depiction of *A Palace Beauty*," *The Art Bulletin* 72 (1990): 284.

16 The paintings mentioned here and many others like them are illustrated in *Glimpses into the Hidden Quarters*. James Cahill suggests, in a close reading of several Ming paintings in this genre, that many of these images were likely intended for female consumption: "Passages of Felt Life: A Genre Shift in Ming-Qing Figure Painting (Or: Paintings Done for Women in Ming-Qing China)," unpublished paper.

17 Chaonan Chen and Yiyou Feng, *Old Advertisements and Popular Culture: Posters, Calendars and Cigarettes, 1900–1950* (San Francisco: Long River Press, 2004), 1–4. For a discussion of the social contexts of such images in the early twentieth century, see Tze-lan Song, *The Emerging Lesbian: Female Same-Sex Desire in Modern China* (University of Chicago Press, 2003).

18 Julia Curtis and Stephen Little, *Chinese Porcelains of the Seventeenth Century: Landscapes, Scholars' Motifs and Narratives* (New York: China Institute Gallery, 1995), 10–18. As would also be the case in eighteenth-century England, the rise of newly prosperous merchant classes led to both an increasing emphasis on the role of taste in social differentiation and debates on the social effects of luxury. See Craig Clunas, "The Art of Social Climbing in Sixteenth-Century China," *Burlington Magazine* 133, no. 1059 (1991): 368–75, and *Superfluous Things: Material Culture and Social Status in Early Modern China* (Urbana, IL: University of Illinois Press, 1991).

19 Julia Curtis, "Markets, Motifs, and Seventeenth-Century Porcelain from Jingdezhen," in *The Porcelains of Jingdezhen*, ed. Rosemary Scott, Colloquies on Art and Archaeology in Asia 16 (London: University of London, 1993), 127–9; Craig Clunas, "Human Figures in the Decoration of Ming Lacquer," *Oriental Art* 32 (1986): 185; Robert Batchelor, "Porcelain as a Global Mass Medium: Transcultural Consumption in England and China, 1600–1750," unpublished paper, 51, 8–9 (www.georgiasouthern.edu/~batchelor/caltechpaper.html#_edn).

20 Craig Clunas, "The West Chamber: A Literary Theme in Chinese Porcelain Decoration," *Transactions of the Oriental Ceramic Society* 46 (1981–2): 72–4.

21 Craig Clunas raises the possibility that the proliferation of porcelains featuring human figures in their designs was in part a response to European demand. See "The West Chamber," 80–1. On the transitional ware style, see Richard S. Kilburn, *Transitional Wares and Their Forerunners: An Exhibition Presented by the Oriental Ceramic Society of Hong Kong* (Hong Kong: Oriental Ceramic Society of Hong Kong, 1981); and Stephen Little, *Chinese Ceramics of the Transitional Period, 1620–1683* (New York: China House Gallery, China Institute of America, 1983).

22 Young, *English Porcelain*, 74; "Kangxi Porcelain in the Grand Chinese Porcelain Collecting Tradition," *The Catalogue of Antiques and Fine Art* (autumn 2001): 41. The phrase "Chinese in origin" is, of course, a relative one. Many of the abstract designs used in "Chinese" porcelain through at least the fifteenth century, not to mention the cobalt used to produce the intense coloration of blue and white, were themselves Persian and Near Eastern imports. See John Carswell, *Blue & White: Chinese Porcelain Around the World* (London: British Museum Press, 2007), 83.

23 Important recent work on women's lives in early modern China includes Dorothy Ko, *Teachers of the Inner Chambers: Women and Culture in Seventeenth-Century China* (Stanford University Press, 1994), and *Cinderella's Sisters*; and Susan Mann, *Precious Records: Women in China's Long Eighteenth Century* (Stanford University Press, 1997).

24 Terry Castle, ed., *The Literature of Lesbianism* (New York: Columbia University Press, 2003).

25 Bridget Hill, "A Refuge from Men: The Idea of a Protestant Nunnery," *Past and Present* 117 (1987): 107–24. See also Barbara Schnorrenberg, "A Paradise Like Eve's: Three Eighteenth-Century English Female Utopias," *Women's Studies* 9 (1982): 263–73. For an examination of this theme in a comparative context, see Qian Ma, *Feminist Utopian Discourse in Eighteenth-Century Chinese and English Fiction: A Cross-Cultural Comparison* (London: Ashgate, 2004).

26 Emma Donoghue, *Poems Between Women* (New York: Columbia University Press, 1997), xxvi.

27 Dianne Dugaw and Amanda Powell, "Sapphic Self-Fashioning in the Baroque Era: Women's Petrarchan Parody in English and Spanish," *Studies in Eighteenth-Century Culture* 35 (2006): 127.

28 Harriette Andreadis, *Sappho in Early Modern England: Female Same-Sex Literary Erotics, 1550–1714* (University of Chicago Press, 2001), 56–8.

29 *Ibid.*, 58, 67; Dugaw and Powell, "Sapphic Self-Fashioning," 140.

30 Elizabeth Wahl, *Invisible Relations: Representations of Female Intimacy in the Age of Enlightenment* (Stanford University Press, 1999), 55–9.

31 Emma Donoghue, *Passions Between Women: British Lesbian Culture, 1668–1801* (New York: Harper Collins, 1993), xxvii–xxviii; George Haggerty finds in *Millennium Hall* an intriguing connection between themes of female friendship and maternal affection. See "'Romantic Friendship' and Patriarchal Narrative in Sarah Scott's *Millennium Hall*," *Genders* 13 (1992): 108–22.

32 Elaine Hobby, *Virtue of Necessity: English Women's Writing, 1649–88* (Ann Arbor, MI: University of Michigan Press, 1989), 85–7.

33 Mary Astell, *The First English Feminist: Reflections Upon Marriage and Other Writings*, ed. Bridget Hill (New York: St. Martin's Press, 1986), 1–2, 14; Hill, "Refuge from Men," 115–17; Donoghue, *Poems Between Women*, 128. Felicity Nussbaum calls attention to a contemporary historian, Gregory King, who estimated in 1694 that there were ten men for every thirteen women in London. *The Brink of All We Hate: English Satires on Women, 1660–1750* (Lexington, KY: University Press of Kentucky, 1984), 9. For additional historical background on unmarried women and sapphism in early modern England, see the essays by Amy Froide and Margaret Hunt in *Singlewomen in the European Past, 1250–1800*, ed. Judith Bennett and Amy Froide (Philadelphia: University of Pennsylvania Press, 1999).

34 Andreadis, *Sappho in Early Modern England*, 38. Terry Castle gives special weight to Ovid in prompting the "imaginative rediscovery of homosexuality" in early modern Europe: *The Literature of Lesbianism*, 120–1. See also Valerie Traub, *The Renaissance of Lesbianism in Early Modern England* (Cambridge University Press, 2002), 190.

35 Maren-Sofie Rostvig, *The Happy Man: Studies in the Metamorphoses of a Classical Ideal, 1700–1760* (Oslo University Press, 1958), 7–23.

36 Frank, *ReOrient*, 226–7.

37 These and other meanings and uses of gardens are explored at length in Craig Clunas, *Fruitful Sites: Garden Culture in Ming Dynasty China* (Durham, NC: Duke University Press, 1996). A richly illustrated source with further details on contexts and contents of gardens is Maggie Keswick, *The Chinese Garden* (New York: St Martin's Press, 1986).

38 Rostvig, *The Happy Man*, 15.

39 *Ibid.*, 7–23.

40 Margaret Cavendish, *The Convent of Pleasure*, in *Plays, Never Before Printed* (London, 1668), 3.

41 Cavendish, *Convent of Pleasure*, 12. It is interesting to note that at the time she wrote this play, Cavendish lived in a "Cavalier pleasure palace" whose wall and ceiling panels were decorated with erotic images of pairs of female Virtues sensuously embracing in pastoral settings. See Traub, *Renaissance of Lesbianism*, 160–2.

42 J. David Macey, "Eden Revisited: Re-visions of the Garden in Astell's *Serious Proposal*, Scott's *Millennium Hall*, and Graffigny's *Lettres d'une péruvienne*," *Eighteenth-Century Fiction* 9 (1997): 165–6.

43 Sarah Scott, *A Description of Millennium Hall*, ed. Gary Kelly (Peterborough, ON: Broadview Press, 2001), 21–2, 56–7.

44 Anne Killigrew, "On a Picture Painted by Herself, Representing Two Nymphs of Diana's, One in a Posture to Hunt, the Other Bathing," and "On the Soft and Gentle Motions of Eudora," in Castle, ed., *Literature of Lesbianism*, 178–80.

45 Quoted in Donoghue, *Passions Between Women*, 114–15.

46 Aphra Behn, "To the Fair Clorinda, Who Made Love to Me, Imagin'd More Than Woman," in Castle, ed., *Literature of Lesbianism*, 173.

47 Traub, *Renaissance of Lesbianism*, 175.

48 See, for example, Louis Le Comte, *Memoirs and Observations Made in a Late Journey through the Empire of China* (London, 1697), 124–5; J. B. Du Halde, *The General History of China*, 4 vols. (London, 1736), II: 140.

49 Ko, *Teachers of the Inner Chambers*, 1–3.

50 *Ibid.*, 16.

51 *Ibid.*, 82, 234, 267–8.

52 L. C. P Bertholet, *Dreams of Spring: Erotic Art in China* (North Clarendon, VT: Tuttle, 1997), 177. For a detailed discussion of the literary history and social context of these themes in the Ming–Qing period, see Song, *The Emerging Lesbian*, 2–95.

53 Ko, *Teachers of the Inner Chambers*, 91, 215, 266–74.

54 This notion of resonance might also be understood within the framework of "cycles of salience" that Valerie Traub proposes for thinking about the recurring patterns of behaviors, meanings, and "explanatory meta-logics" that might eventually give shape to "a transnational history of lesbianism over the *longue durée*." See Valerie Traub, "The Present Future of Lesbian Historiography," in *A*

Companion to Lesbian, Gay, Bisexual, Transgender, and Queer Studies, ed. George Haggerty and Molly McGarry (Oxford: Blackwell, 2007), 126–7.

55 McCracken, *Culture and Consumption*, 104–8.

56 Kathryn King, "The Unaccountable Wife and Other Tales of Female Desire in Jane Barker's *A Patch-Work Screen for the Ladies*," *The Eighteenth Century: Theory and Interpretation* 35 (1994): 167.

57 Traub, *Renaissance of Lesbianism*, 1–3, 17–18; Castle, *Literature of Lesbianism*, 25.

58 Traub, *Renaissance of Lesbianism*, 198, 202.

59 *Ibid.*, 199–203. See also Andreadis, *Sappho in Early Modern England*, 4.

60 Castle, ed., *Literature of Lesbianism*, 154, 264.

61 Thorp and Vinograd, *Chinese Art and Culture*, 327. See also Judith Zeitlin, *Historian of the Strange: Pu Songling and the Chinese Classical Tale* (Stanford University Press, 1993), 3–5.

4 William Hogarth and the gendering of Chinese exoticism

1 See Dena Goodman and Kathryn Norberg, eds., *Furnishing the Eighteenth Century: What Furniture Can Tell Us about the European and American Past* (New York: Routledge, 2007).

2 On the history and implications of disinterestedness as a component of the aesthetic attitude, see Jerome Stolnitz, "On the Origin of Aesthetic Disinterestedness," *Journal of Aesthetics and Art Criticism* 20 (1961): 131–43, and Elizabeth A. Bohls, "Disinterestedness and the Denial of the Particular: Locke, Smith, and the Subject of Aesthetics," in *Eighteenth-Century Aesthetics and the Reconstruction of Art*, ed. Paul Mattick (Cambridge University Press, 1993).

3 Edmund Burke, *A Philosophical Enquiry into the Origin of Our Ideas of the Sublime and Beautiful*, ed. James T. Boulton (University of Notre Dame Press, 1968), 115.

4 *Ibid.*

5 Ronald Paulson, introduction to *The Analysis of Beauty*, by William Hogarth, ed. Ronald Paulson (New Haven, CT: Yale University Press, 1997), xxxiii, xxxvii, xlix.

6 *Ibid.*, xi; Wallace Jackson, "Hogarth's *Analysis*: The Fate of a Late Rococo Document," *SEL* (*Studies in English Literature*) 6 (1966): 543–50; William Hogarth, *The Analysis of Beauty*, ed. Joseph Burke (Oxford: Clarendon Press, 1955), xlvi–xlvii.

7 Hogarth, *The Analysis of Beauty*, ed. Burke, li.

8 Hogarth, *The Analysis of Beauty*, ed. Paulson, 59, 34–5, 40. All subsequent citations refer to this edition.

9 *Ibid.*, 18.

10 *Ibid.*, 49.

11 See the chapters on tea in Kowaleski-Wallace, *Consuming Subjects*, 19–72; and Walvin, *Fruits of Empire*, 9–31.

12 Hogarth, *Analysis*, 21.

13 *Ibid.*, 32.

14 Lars Tharp, *Hogarth's China: Hogarth's Paintings and Eighteenth-Century Ceramics* (London: Merrell Hoberton, 1997), 49.

15 Hogarth, *Analysis*, 12.

16 William Hogarth, *Anecdotes*, ed. J. B. Nichols (London, 1833), 37.

17 "Tea: A Poem; or, Ladies into China-Cups: A Metamorphosis" (London, 1729).

18 "The Prize Aenigma," *The Woman's Almanack* (London, 1741), 20; John Gay, "To a Lady on Her Passion for Old China" (London, 1725).

19 Anna Williams, "The Nunnery," *Miscellanies in Prose and Verse* (London, 1766), 107–8.

20 *A Chinese Tale* (London, 1740), 16.

21 This argument is elaborated at more length in Porter, *Ideographia*, 181–92.

22 Bruce P. Lenman, "The English and Dutch East India Companies and the Birth of Consumerism in the Augustan World," *Eighteenth-Century Life* 14, no. 1 (1990): 58.

5 The socio-aesthetics of the Chinese scholar's stone

1 Jonathan Swift, *Gulliver's Travels* (New York: Penguin, 1985), 230–1.

2 W. David Kingery, ed., *Learning from Things: Method and Theory of Material Culture Studies* (Washington, DC: Smithsonian Institution Press, 1996); Mihalyi Csikszentmihalyi and Eugene Rochberg-Halton, *The Meaning of Things: Domestic Symbols and the Self* (Cambridge University Press, 1981); Steven Lubar and W. David Kingery, eds., *History from Things: Essays on Material Culture* (Washington, DC: Smithsonian Institution Press, 1993); Arjun Appadurai, ed., *The Social Life of Things: Commodities in Cultural Perspective* (Cambridge University Press, 1986); Bill Brown, "Thing Theory," *Critical Inquiry* 28, no. 1 (2001): 1–22; Bill Brown, *Material Cultures: Why Some Things Matter* (University of Chicago Press, 1998).

3 See, for example, Alfred Gell, "Newcomers to the World of Goods: Consumption among the Muria Gonds," in *The Social Life of Things*, ed. Appadurai, 110–38; and Eric Arnould and Richard Wilk, "Why Do the Natives Wear Adidas?" in *Advances in Consumer Research* XI, ed. Thomas C. Kinnear (Provo, UT: Association for Consumer Research, 1984), 748–52.

4 Lady Mary Wortley Montagu, *Selected Letters*, ed. Isobel Grundy (New York: Penguin, 1997), 148–9.

5 The best introductions to chinoiserie are Honour, *Chinoiserie: The Vision of Cathay*; and Jacobson, *Chinoiserie*. For a comprehensive overview of this period of British fascination with China, see Appleton, *A Cycle of Cathay*; or Porter, *Ideographia*.

6 On the relationship between rococo and the Chinese taste in England, see Jacobson, *Chinoiserie*, 123–50. The best treatment of the classicist response to the Chinese taste is Allen, *Tides in English Taste*, I: 234–56. On the pleasures of mercantile fantasy, see Louis Landa, "Pope's Belinda, the General Emporie of the World, and the Wondrous Worm," *South Atlantic Quarterly* 70 (1971): 215–35. On the feminization of images of China in chinoiserie, see Porter, *Ideographia*, 181–92.

7 John Hay, *Kernals of Energy, Bones of Earth: The Rock in Chinese Art* (New York: China Institute in America, 1986), 27.

8 The best introductions to rock sculpture and its place in Chinese art and culture are John Hay, "The Rock and Chinese Art," *Orientations* 16, no. 12 (1985): 16–32; and Hay, *Kernals of Energy*.

9 Johannes Nieuhof, *An Embassy from the East-India Company of the United Provinces to the Grand Tartar Cham, Emperor of China*, trans. John Ogilby (London, 1673), 122.

10 The comparison is suggested in Hay, "The Rock and Chinese Art," 18.

11 Clunas, *Fruitful Sites*, 68–103.

12 A representative selection of the essays comprising this conversation can be found in Dabney Townsend, ed., *Eighteenth-Century British Aesthetics* (Amityville: Baywood, 1999).

13 As James Cahill notes, "It is a curious circumstance that no Chinese writer between the ninth and the twentieth centuries attempted any comprehensive history of Chinese painting. This is especially surprising in view of the fact that the Chinese have left a literature on painting far greater in volume and richness, for all periods up to the nineteenth century, than that of any other artistic tradition." James Cahill, *The Distant Mountains: Chinese Painting of the Late Ming Dynasty, 1570–1644* (New York: Weatherhill, 1982), 6.

14 Sir Joshua Reynolds, *Discourses*, ed. Pat Rogers (New York: Penguin, 1992), 102–9.

15 Reynolds, *Discourses*, 102–4.

16 I explore more fully some of the methodological difficulties attendant on cross-cultural comparison between Chinese and Western traditions in David Porter, "China is Not a Foreign Country: The Promises and Perils of Cross-Cultural Comparison," *Michigan Quarterly Review* 47, no. 2 (2008): 169–81.

17 See, for example, Thomas Lawton, *Chinese Figure Painting* (Washington, DC: Smithsonian Institution, 1973), ix.

18 Hay, *Kernals of Energy*, 52.

19 Susan Bush puts it more bluntly: "The concept of beauty does not figure in Chinese aesthetic concerns." Susan Bush and Hsio-yen Shih, *Early Chinese Texts on Painting* (Cambridge, MA: Harvard University Press, 1985), 2.

20 Hay, "The Rock and Chinese Art," 28.

21 Eliot Deutsch, "Comparative Philosophy as Creative Philosophy," *APA Newsletter on Asian and Asian-American Philosophers and Philosophy* 2, no. 1 (2002): 24.
22 Introduction to Du Wan's *Stone Catalogue of Cloudy Forest*, quoted in Hay, *Kernals of Energy*, 38.
23 Hay, *Kernals of Energy*, 24, 38; Richard Rosenblum, *Art of the Natural World: Resonances of Wild Nature in Chinese Sculptural Art*, ed. Valerie Doran (Boston: MFA, 2001), 129.
24 Introduction to Du Wan, *Stone Catalogue*, quoted in Hay, *Kernals of Energy*, 38.
25 Richard Barnhart, "The 'Wild and Heterodox School' of Ming Painting," in *Theories of the Arts in China*, ed. Susan Bush and Christian Murck (Princeton University Press, 1983), 365–71.
26 *Ibid.*, 371, 373.
27 See, for example, Cocks, "Nonfunctional Use of Ceramics," 195–215.
28 See Kowaleski-Wallace, *Consuming Subjects*, 19–36.
29 Patricia Meyer Spacks, *Gossip* (New York: Knopf, 1985), 40, 156; Janet M. Todd, *The Sign of Angellica: Women, Writing, and Fiction, 1660–1800* (New York: Columbia University Press, 1989), 39; Ballaster, *Seductive Forms*, 114–52. The quotation, used by Ballaster, is from Bridget MacCarthy, *Women Writers: Their Contribution to the English Novel 1621–1744* (Cork, 1944), 216. Paula McDowell discusses the real political impact of Manley's gossip in *The Women of Grub Street*, 222.
30 On the relation of gossip and news in Jonson's play, see Don Wayne, "The 'Exchange of Letters': Early Modern Contradictions and Postmodern Conundrums," in *Consumption of Culture*, ed. Bermingham and Brewer, 152–5. On the vogue for scandal-mongering journalism in the 1770s, see John Brewer, "Personal Scandal and Politics in Eighteenth-Century England: Secrecy, Intimacy, and the Interior Self in the Public Sphere," in *Media and Political Culture in the Eighteenth Century*, ed. Marie-Christine Skuncke (Stockholm: Vitterhetsakademien, 2005), 100–1.
31 Spacks, *Gossip*, 13.
32 Richetti, *Popular Fiction before Richardson*, 10.
33 For notable examples, see Hay, *Kernals of Energy*, 40; Keswick, *The Chinese Garden*, 158–62; Le Comte, *Memoirs and Observations*, 166–7; Allen, *Tides in English Taste*, I: 234–56.
34 Spacks, *Gossip*, 11, 32, 60, 151.
35 Christopher Smart, "The Tea-Pot and Scrubbing Brush," *The Poems of the Late Christopher Smart*, 2 vols. (Reading, 1791), II: 12–14.
36 Hay, *Kernals of Energy*, 44.
37 Barbara Benedict, *Curiosity: A Cultural History of Early Modern Inquiry* (University of Chicago Press, 2001), 1–23.
38 Bernard Capp, *When Gossips Meet: Women, Family, and Neighborhood in Early Modern England* (Oxford University Press, 2003), 50.

39 Spacks, *Gossip*, 22–7; Capp, *When Gossips Meet*, 51, 62.
40 Capp, *When Gossips Meet*, 57, 59.
41 Spacks, *Gossip*, 132–47.
42 Hay, *Kernals of Energy*, 42–50.

6 Horace Walpole and the Gothic repudiation of chinoiserie

1 Horace Walpole, Letter to Horace Mann, February 25, 1750, *Walpole's Correspondence*, ed. W. S. Lewis, XIX: 242–3. All further citations to Walpole's letters refer to this edition. The case in question seems to be the trial of Jane Wilson on April 9, 1746; see *Old Bailey Proceedings Online* (http://oldbaileyonline.org), April 1746, trial of Jane Wilson (t17460409–48). The trial transcript corroborates Walpole's account in most details.
2 On Walpole's changing views regarding the authenticity of the Macpherson poems, see letters to Dalrymple, April 14, 1761 (XV: 71–2) and to Montagu, December 8, 1781 (IX: 407). For discussions of the Chatterton affair, see R. W. Ketton-Cremer, *Horace Walpole: A Biography* (Ithaca, NY: Cornell University Press, 1964), 241–52; and Timothy Mowl, *Horace Walpole: The Great Outsider* (London: John Murray, 1996), 224–6.
3 Letter to Lady Ossory, September 6, 1788 (XXXIV: 15).
4 Letters to Mason, February 17, 1777 (XXVIII: 281), and to Bewley, May 23, 1778 (XVI: 131).
5 *The Works of Horatio Walpole, Earl of Orford*, 7 vols. (London, 1798), IV: 368, quoted in Lewis's note to Walpole's letter to Lady Ossory, October 26, 1791 (XXXIV: 128). For a useful cultural history of contemporary forgery including the debates surrounding James Macpherson's and Thomas Chatterton's productions, see Jack Lynch, *Deception and Detection in Eighteenth-Century Britain* (London: Ashgate, 2008).
6 For background on the chinoiserie style, see Honour, *Chinoiserie: The Vision of Cathay*; Impey, *Chinoiserie: The Impact of Oriental Styles*; Jacobson, *Chinoiserie*; and Jarry, *Chinoiserie: Chinese Influence*.
7 On the relationship of chinoiserie to the more scholarly responses to Chinese culture promoted by the Jesuits in this period, see David Porter, "Writing China: Legitimacy and Representation, 1606–1773," *Comparative Literature Studies* 33 (1996): 98–122.
8 See Kenneth Clark, *The Gothic Revival: An Essay in the History of Taste* (New York: Charles Scribner's Sons, 1929), Chs. 1–2; Allen, *Tides in English Taste*, Ch. 14; and Lovejoy, "The First Gothic Revival and the Return to Nature," in *Essays*.
9 Walpole, Letter to Mann, April 27, 1753 (XX: 371–2).
10 *The World* 59 (February 14, 1754).
11 *The World* 109 (January 30, 1755).
12 John Shebbeare, *Letters on the English Nation* (London, 1755), letter 56.
13 *The World* 117 (March 27, 1755).

14 On the declining interest in chinoiserie towards the end of the eighteenth century, see Honour, *Chinoiserie: The Vision of Cathay*, 175–98. For a helpful account of the rise and fall of China in the European imagination over this period, see Appleton, *A Cycle of Cathay*.
15 Letter from Lord Hervey, October 2, 1745 (XL: 18).
16 Letter to Montagu, June 6, 1752 (IX: 134); letter to Conway, November 8, 1752 (XXXVII: 347).
17 Walpole, *Works*, I: 195–204. The book-burning emperor was Shi Huangdi of the Qin dynasty. Walpole would have picked up these details from Du Halde or from one of the many other Chinese histories in circulation during his lifetime.
18 Letter to Mann, August 2, 1750 (XX: 166).
19 Letter to Mann, February 25, 1750 (XX: 127).
20 On the English use of the term, see Lovejoy, *Essays*, 110–22. For an account of its likely Chinese etymology, see Y. Z. Chang, "A Note on Sharawadgi," *Modern Language Notes* 45 (April 1930): 221–4.
21 See letter to Bentley, July 9, 1754 (XXXV: 177) and Lewis' note.
22 Letter to Bentley, August 5, 1752 (XXV: 143).
23 Letter to Bentley, August 4, 1755 (XXXV: 241).
24 Letter to Montagu, September 24, 1762 (X: 43); letter to Strafford, June 13, 1781 (XXXV: 359).
25 For additional discussion of Chambers' writings on Chinese gardening, see Eileen Harris, "*Designs*," and Bald, "Sir William Chambers."
26 Letter to Mason, May 25, 1772 (XXVIII: 34).
27 Walpole, *Anecdotes* (1937), V: 185.
28 Letter to Cole, January 10, 1771 (I: 211); Walpole, *Works*, III: 8.
29 William Mason, *The English Garden* (York, 1783), 90–2 (book IV, ll. 65–109).
30 Chase, "William Mason," 526–7.
31 Walpole, *Works*, III: 32–3.
32 Letter to Chatterton, March 28, 1769 (XVI: 105–6).
33 Walpole, *Works*, III: 483.
34 Letter to Robertson, June 20, 1791 (XV: 211–12). For a detailed discussion of the theme of Chinese cultural stagnation as it developed in the late eighteenth-century British context, see Porter, *Ideographia*, Ch. 4.
35 Letter to Conway, August 29, 1748 (XXXVII: 292).
36 Letter to Lady Ossory, August 11, 1771 (XXXII: 55–6).
37 Walpole, *Works*, II: 533. *The History of the Modern Taste in Gardening* is also reprinted in Isabel Chase's very useful *Horace Walpole: Gardenist* (Princeton University Press, 1943).
38 Letter to Mason, September 6, 1775 (XXVIII: 222).
39 Walpole, *Works*, II: 533–4.
40 William Mason, *Satirical Poems*, ed. Paget Toynbee (Oxford: Clarendon Press, 1926), 44–5.

41 Lovejoy, "Chinese Origin," in *Essays*, 99–135. For a more recent and exhaustive treatment of the topic, see Liu, *Seeds of a Different Eden*.

42 Walpole, *Works*, II: 7–8.

43 William Chambers, *A Dissertation on Oriental Gardening* (Westmead, England: Gregg International Publishers, 1972), v. Subsequent references to Chambers' *Dissertation* in this chapter are from this edition.

44 *Ibid.*, 19.

45 *Ibid.*, 35.

46 Walpole, *Works*, III: 94.

47 Mowl, *Horace Walpole*, 177–89. For an overview of some of the limitations of Mowl's biography, see the review by Pat Rogers in the *Times Literary Supplement*, October 4, 1996, 33.

7 Chinaware and the evolution of a modern domestic ideal

1 Claude Lévi-Strauss, writing on the subject of totems, suggests that animals are not so much "good to eat" as "good to think," meaning that, quite apart from any pragmatic uses to human society, they can serve a useful and even indispensable function in the broader cultural enterprise of meaning-making. See Claude Lévi-Strauss, *Totemism*, trans. R. Needham (Boston: Beacon Press, 1963), 89. For a helpful overview of many directions in which the field of material culture studies has developed this insight along with a useful bibliography, see Victor Buchli's introduction to his *Material Culture Reader* (Oxford: Berg Press, 2002), 1–22.

2 Jules David Prown, "The Truth of Material Culture: History or Fiction?" in *History from Things*, ed. Lubar and Kingery, 5.

3 Robert Finlay, "The Pilgrim Art: The Culture of Porcelain in World History," *Journal of World History* 9 (1998): 143.

4 On their arrival in London, East India Company goods were typically advertised in newspapers and then sold to dealers at quarterly auctions from the company headquarters in Leadenhall Street. See Saumarez Smith, *Eighteenth-Century Decoration*, 48; and Berg, "Manufacturing the Orient," 405.

5 On the role of women in the china trade, see Young, *English Porcelain*, 158–60; Cocks, "The Nonfunctional Use of Ceramics," 205; *Export Art of China and Japan: The China Trade Sale* (London: Christie's, 1997), 7; and Richards, *Eighteenth-Century Ceramics*, 60. Richards points out that urban shop displays were increasingly designed to generate desires for new products, raising the possibility that in some commercial spaces, erotic and consumerist fantasies may have begun to co-mingle in more explicit and promiscuous ways (67). The quotation is from Pasquin's *Palinodia* (1619), quoted in Lawrence Stone, "Inigo Jones and the New Exchange," *Archaeological Journal* 114 (1957): 120.

6 Ben Jonson, *Epicene; or, The Silent Woman*, in *The Alchemist and Other Plays*, ed. Gordon Campbell (Oxford University Press, 1995), 1.3.36–8.

7 Jonson, *Epicene*, 1.4.25–6.

8 Thomas Southerne, *The Maid's Last Prayer* (London, 1693). Mrs. Siam serves tea and holds raffles at her house, in addition to selling merchandise from East India ships. She is suspected by both her husband (2.1) and Gayman (2.2) of other kinds of dealings, perhaps not surprising when at least one client confesses to spending over one thousand a year at her house (2.2).

9 Nicholas Amhurst, *Oculus Britanniæ: An Heroi-Panegyrical Poem on the University of Oxford* (London, 1724), 25.

10 Henry Fielding, *The Mock Doctor; or, the Dumb Lady Cur'd* (Edinburgh, 1753), scene 6.

11 Smart, "The Tea-Pot and Scrubbing Brush," *Poems*, II: 12–13.

12 William Wycherley, *The Country Wife* in *The Signet Classic Book of Restoration Drama*, ed. Ronald Berman (New York: New American Library, 1980), 86. I treat this scene at greater length in *Ideographia*, 182–7.

13 Henry Fielding, *Love in Several Masques* (Dublin, 1728), 61.

14 Elkanah Settle, *The Lady's Triumph* (London, 1718), 46. This was Settle's second theatrical treatment of a China theme. The first, published in 1675, was the heroic tragedy *The Conquest of China by the Tartars.*

15 J. Paul Hunter argues persuasively that contemporary didactic materials "were perceived to involve a crisis at the center of the culture," and that "most moralists did see cultural deterioration as imminent." J. Paul Hunter, *Before Novels: The Cultural Contexts of Eighteenth-Century English Fiction* (New York: Norton, 1990), 242–3. And as Felicity Nussbaum points out, women were typically the culprits, and in contemporary satire were "accused of rebellion against all aspects of patriarchal order and authority." *The Brink of All We Hate*, 19. For recent work on literary women's political agency in the early eighteenth century, see, for example, Kathryn King, *Jane Barker, Exile: A Literary Career 1675–1725* (Oxford: Clarendon Press, 2000); Ballaster, *Seductive Forms*; and McDowell, *The Women of Grub Street.*

16 Thomas D'Urfey, *Pendragon, or, The Carpet Knight his Kalendar* (London, 1698), 66.

17 Alexander Pope, *The Rape of the Lock* (London, 1714), III: 155–9.

18 Such comparisons are commonplace in Western literature from the classical period through the Renaissance as well. As Valerie Traub points out, "breasts are likened to strawberries, cherries, and apples, alabaster, rubies, and pearls." *Renaissance of Lesbianism*, 144. See also Marilyn Yalom, *A History of the Breast* (New York: Ballantine, 1997), 18, 23, 39.

19 See Carswell, *Blue & White*, 112; Joo Ee Khoo, *Kendi: Pouring Vessels in the University of Malaya Collection*, ed. Dawn F. Rooney (Singapore: Oxford University Press, 1991), 3, 24; and Dawn F. Rooney, "Kendi in the Cultural Context of Southeast Asia: A Commentary," *Dawn F. Rooney Cultural Archive* (http://rooneyarchive.net/articles/kendi/kendi_album/kendi.htm). Jules David Prown offers a sustained, "deep structural" reading of a pewter teapot that reveals it to

be "a structural metaphor for the female breast" in "Truth of Material Culture," 6–10.

20 Nancy Armstrong, *Desire and Domestic Fiction: A Political History of the Novel* (Oxford University Press, 1987), 8.

21 For representative critiques of Armstrong's approach, see Leila Silvana May, "The Strong-Arming of Desire: A Reconsideration of Nancy Armstrong's 'Desire and Domestic Fiction,'" *ELH* 68 (2001): 267–85; Patricia Yaeger, "Beyond the Fragments," *Novel: A Forum on Fiction* 23 (1990): 203–8; and Catherine Gallagher, review of *Desire and Domestic Fiction, Victorian Studies* 32 (1989): 412; see also April Alliston, *Virtue's Faults: Correspondences in Eighteenth-Century British and French Women's Fiction* (Stanford University Press, 1996).

22 According to Hilary Young, the consumption of tea in Britain increased six-fold in the middle years of the eighteenth century: *English Porcelain*, 182. Charles Saumarez Smith dates the emergence of a new domestic ideology to roughly the same period, arguing that women in the latter part of the eighteenth century began "to view the household as their own special territory." *Eighteenth-Century Decoration*, 233.

23 Mary Elizabeth Braddon, *Lady Audley's Secret* (1862; repr., New York: Oxford University Press, 1987), 222, quoted in Kowaleski-Wallace, *Consuming Subjects*, 19.

24 Ruth Perry, "Colonizing the Breast: Sexuality and Maternity in Eighteenth-Century England," *Eighteenth-Century Life* 16 (1992): 185–213.

25 Vanessa Maher, "Breast Feeding in Cross-Cultural Perspective," in Vanessa Maher, ed., *The Anthropology of Breast Feeding* (Oxford: Berg Press, 1992), 24–5; Perry, "Colonizing the Breast," 193.

26 Londa Schiebinger, *Nature's Body: Gender in the Making of Modern Science* (New Brunswick, NJ: Rutgers University Press, 2004), 40.

27 Charlotte Brontë, *Villette*, 3 vols. (London, 1853), II: 18–20.

8 Thomas Percy's sinology and the origins of English romanticism

1 Nick Groom, *The Making of Percy's* Reliques (Oxford University Press, 1999), 2; Stuart Curran, *Poetic Form and British Romanticism* (Oxford University Press, 1986), 129; Bertram Davis, *Thomas Percy: A Scholar-Cleric in the Age of Johnson* (Philadelphia: University of Pennsylvania Press, 1989), preface.

2 Eun Min, "Antiquarian Aesthetics and the Serendipitous Reader: Thomas Percy's *Chinese Miscellanies* and *The Reliques of Ancient English Poetry*" (paper presented at the annual meeting of the American Society for Eighteenth-Century Studies, Montreal, QC, March 31, 2006). At the time of going to press, an expanded version of this paper was scheduled to be published as "Thomas Percy's Chinese Miscellanies and the *Reliques of Ancient English Poetry* (1765)" in *Eighteenth-Century Studies* 43 no. 3 (2010).

3 The friendship between Goldsmith and Percy and its impact on the latter's work is discussed in Alda Milner-Barry, "A Note on the Early Literary Relations of Oliver Goldsmith and Thomas Percy," *Review of English Studies* 2, no. 5 (1926): 51–66.

4 Davis, *Thomas Percy*, 47–56. The details of the possibly multiple translations involved in the production of Percy's edition of the book remain somewhat murky: see L. F. Powell, "Hau Kiou Choaan," *Review of English Studies* 2, no. 8 (1926): 452–4; and Ch'en Shou-Yi, "Thomas Percy and his Chinese Studies," *Chinese Social and Political Science Review* 20 (1936–7): 203–16. An engaging account of the subsequent translation history of the novel (whose title is now romanized as *Hao Qiu Zhuan*) can be found in James St. André, "Retranslation as Argument: Canon Formation, Professionalization, and International Rivalry in 19th-Century Sinological Translation," *Cadernos de Tradução* 11, no. 1 (2003): 59–93.

5 Powell, "Hau Kiou Choaan," 448.

6 Davis, *Thomas Percy*, 91.

7 Thomas Percy to William Shenstone, July 19, 1761, in Percy–Shenstone correspondence, British Library AM 2B2221, quoted in Powell, "Hau Kiou Choaan," 449.

8 Thomas Percy, *Hau Kiou Choaan; or, The Pleasing History*, 4 vols. (London, 1761), I: xiv–xv.

9 Percy, *Pleasing History*, I: xv, xvii, xxiv–xxvi.

10 Thomas Percy to William Shenstone, June 20 and July 19, 1761, in Percy–Shenstone correspondence, British Library AM 2B2221.

11 Thomas Percy, *Miscellaneous Pieces Relating to the Chinese*, 2 vols. (London, 1762), preface [2].

12 Daniel Defoe, *The Farther Adventures of Robinson Crusoe* (London: William Clowes and Sons, 1974); Richard Walter and Benjamin Robins, *A Voyage Round the World by George Anson*, ed. Glyndwr Williams (London: Oxford University Press, 1974). See also Porter, *Ideographia*; and Markley, *English Imagination.*

13 Although individual writers tended to take a fairly uniform position, Percy's ambivalence towards China can be seen as characteristic of contemporary English views more generally. As Robert Batchelor argues, "imagining China and Britain was an open-ended and conflict-ridden process rather than a fixed and instituted set of significations." Robert Batchelor, "Imagining the British Nation through China," in *The Global Eighteenth Century*, ed. Nussbaum, 81.

14 Percy, *Pleasing History*, I: 141–2n.

15 *Ibid.*, I: 163n.

16 *Ibid.*, II: 127–8n.

17 *Ibid.*, II: 51–2n.

18 *Ibid.*, IV: 258–9.

19 *Ibid.*, I: 189n, 234n; Percy, "A Collection of Chinese Proverbs and Apothegms," in *Pleasing History*, III: 206.

20 Percy, dedication to *Pleasing History*, I.
21 Percy, *Pleasing History*, III: 15–16n; IV: 157n.
22 *Ibid.*, II: 116n; Percy, "Fragments of Chinese Poetry," in *Pleasing History*, IV: 226n.
23 Percy, *Pleasing History*, II: 66n; "Fragments of Chinese Poetry," 255.
24 Percy, "Chinese Proverbs," 183, 188, 221, 261.
25 *Ibid.*, 186, 199.
26 *Ibid.*, 199–200.
27 *Ibid.*, 194, 199–200, 213.
28 *Ibid.*, 199.
29 Percy, *Pleasing History* I: 8–9n; "Fragments of Chinese Poetry," 214n.
30 Percy, "Chinese Proverbs," 240.
31 Percy, *Pleasing History*, II: 117n; Davis, *Thomas Percy*, 4, 38, 109; Nick Groom, "Thomas Percy," *The Literary Encyclopedia*, March 15, 2003 (http://www.litencyc.com/php/speople.php?rec=true&UID=3532, accessed July 2, 2008).
32 Percy, *Pleasing History*, II: 117–19n; Davis, *Thomas Percy*, 7, 13–14, 142, 168.
33 Percy, *Pleasing History*, I: xii–xiii.
34 Samuel Johnson, *Lives of the English Poets*, ed. L. Archer-Hind, 2 vols. (London, 1925), II: 211.
35 Daniel Defoe, *The Fortunate Mistress* (London, 1724), 206–8; Daniel Defoe, *Robinson Crusoe*, 3rd edn. (London, 1719), 18.
36 Percy, *Pleasing History*, I: 129n; II: 256n; "Fragments of Chinese Poetry," 201n.
37 Percy, *Pleasing History*, I: xix, 100n, 234n; "Chinese Proverbs," 184, 187, 206.
38 Percy, *Pleasing History*, II: 240n.
39 *Ibid.*, II: 91–2n.
40 See Frank, *ReOrient.*
41 Percy, *Miscellaneous Pieces*, I: preface [8–10].
42 *Ibid.*, I: 12–13.
43 Porter, *Ideographia*, 15–77.
44 Percy, *Miscellaneous Pieces*, I: preface [14], 10.
45 *Ibid.*, I: preface [14], 6–8, 23.
46 *Ibid.*, I: 226, 228, 231–2.
47 *Ibid.*, I: 217.
48 Percy, *Pleasing History*, II: 3–4n.
49 Katie Trumpener, *Bardic Nationalism: The Romantic Novel and the British Empire* (Princeton University Press, 1997), xi.
50 Min, "Antiquarian Aesthetics."
51 Thomas Percy, *Reliques of Ancient English Poetry*, 3 vols. (London, 1765), I: vi.
52 Groom, *Percy's* Reliques, 45, 59.
53 Percy, *Reliques*, II: 22.
54 Percy, *Pleasing History*, I: 116n.

55 Percy, *Reliques*, I: ix–x, 1; II: 54; Percy, "An Essay on the Ancient English Minstrels," *Reliques*, I: xxii.
56 Percy, *Pleasing History*, I: 234n; "Chinese Proverbs," 187.
57 Percy, *Pleasing History*, II: 119.
58 Percy, "Fragments of Chinese Poetry," 214.
59 Percy, *Reliques*, I: ix, 57; "English Minstrels," xv, xix.
60 Percy, "English Minstrels," xv.
61 Percy, *Reliques*, III: ii, v.
62 Percy, *Pleasing History*, III: 161.
63 Percy, *Reliques*, III: ii.
64 Percy, *Pleasing History*, I: 142n; "Chinese Proverbs," 206.
65 Percy, *Miscellaneous Pieces*, I: 14.
66 Percy, *Reliques*, I: vii, ix; II: 4; III: ix.
67 Lovejoy, "Chinese Origin," in *Essays*, 102, 134–5.
68 Harold Bloom, *The Anxiety of Influence: A Theory of Poetry*, 2nd edn. (Oxford University Press, 1997).

Bibliography

Adshead, Samuel Adrian M. *Material Culture in Europe and China, 1400–1800: The Rise of Consumerism.* New York: St. Martin's Press, 1997.

Allen, Beverly Sprague. *Tides in English Taste (1619–1800): A Background for the Study of Literature.* 2 vols. New York: Pageant Books, 1958.

Alliston, April. *Virtue's Faults: Correspondences in Eighteenth-Century British and French Women's Fiction.* Stanford University Press, 1996.

Amhurst, Nicholas. *Oculus Britanniæ: An Heroi-Panegyrical Poem on the University of Oxford.* London, 1724.

Andreadis, Harriette. *Sappho in Early Modern England: Female Same-Sex Literary Erotics, 1550–1714.* University of Chicago Press, 2001.

The Annual Register; or, A View of the History, Politics, and Literature, for the Year 1782. London, 1783.

Appadurai, Arjun, ed. *The Social Life of Things: Commodities in Cultural Perspective.* Cambridge University Press, 1986.

Appleton, William W. *A Cycle of Cathay: The Chinese Vogue in England during the 17th and 18th Centuries.* New York: Columbia University Press, 1951.

Aravamudan, Srinivas. *Tropicopolitans: Colonialism and Agency, 1688–1804.* Durham, NC: Duke University Press, 1999.

Armstrong, Nancy. *Desire and Domestic Fiction: A Political History of the Novel.* Oxford University Press, 1987.

Arnould, Eric, and Richard Wilk. "Why Do the Natives Wear Adidas?" In *Advances in Consumer Research* XI, ed. Thomas C. Kinnear. Provo, UT: Association for Consumer Research, 1984.

Astell, Mary. *The First English Feminist: Reflections Upon Marriage and Other Writings.* Ed. Bridget Hill. New York: St. Martin's Press, 1986.

A Serious Proposal to the Ladies. London, 1694.

Bald, R. C. "Sir William Chambers and the Chinese Garden." In *Discovering China: European Interpretations in the Enlightenment*, ed. Julia Ching and Willard G. Oxtoby. University of Rochester Press, 1992.

Ballaster, Ros. *Seductive Forms: Women's Amatory Fiction from 1684 to 1740.* Oxford University Press, 1992.

Barnhart, Richard. "The 'Wild and Heterodox School' of Ming Painting." In *Theories of the Arts in China*, ed. Susan Bush and Christian Murck. Princeton University Press, 1983.

Barthes, Roland. *Mythologies.* New York: Hill and Wang, 1997.

Batchelor, Robert. "Imagining the British Nation through China." In *The Global Eighteenth Century*, ed. Felicity Nussbaum. Baltimore: Johns Hopkins University Press, 2003.

"Porcelain as a Global Mass Medium: Transcultural Consumption in England and China, 1600–1750." Unpublished paper.

Bayley, Stephen. *Taste: The Secret Meaning of Things*. New York: Pantheon Books, 1991.

Beardsley, Monroe C. *Aesthetics from Classical Greece to the Present: A Short History*. New York: Macmillan, 1966.

Behn, Aphra. "To the Fair Clorinda, Who Made Love to Me, Imagin'd More Than Woman." In *The Literature of Lesbianism*, ed. Terry Castle. New York: Columbia University Press, 2003.

Benedict, Barbara. *Curiosity: A Cultural History of Early Modern Inquiry*. University of Chicago Press, 2001.

Bennett, Judith, and Amy Froide, eds. *Singlewomen in the European Past, 1250–1800*. Philadelphia: University of Pennsylvania Press, 1999.

Berg, Maxine. "Manufacturing the Orient: Asian Commodities and European Industry, 1500–1800." In *Prodotti e tecniche d'oltremare nelle economie europee secc. XIII–XVIII*, ed. Simonetta Cavaciocchi. Prato: Istituto internazionale di storia economica F. Datini, 1998.

"Women's Consumption and the Industrial Classes of Eighteenth-Century England." *Journal of Social History* 30 (1996): 415–34.

Bermingham, Ann, and John Brewer, eds. *The Consumption of Culture, 1600–1800: Image, Object, Text*. New York: Routledge, 1995.

Bertholet, L. C. P. *Dreams of Spring: Erotic Art in China*. North Clarendon, VT: Tuttle, 1997.

Blaut, J. M. *The Colonizer's Model of the World: Geographical Diffusionism and Eurocentric History*. New York: Guilford Press, 1993.

Bloom, Harold. *The Anxiety of Influence: A Theory of Poetry*. 2nd edn. Oxford University Press, 1997.

Blumer, Herbert. "Fashion: From Class Differentiation to Collective Selection." *The Sociological Quarterly* 10 (1969): 275–91.

Bohls, Elizabeth A. "Disinterestedness and the Denial of the Particular: Locke, Smith, and the Subject of Aesthetics." In *Eighteenth-Century Aesthetics and the Reconstruction of Art*, ed. Paul Mattick. Cambridge University Press, 1993.

Women Travel Writers and the Language of Aesthetics, 1716–1818. Cambridge University Press, 1995.

Bourdieu, Pierre. *Distinction: A Social Critique of the Judgment of Taste*. Trans. Richard Nice. Cambridge, MA: Harvard University Press, 1984.

Brewer, John. "Personal Scandal and Politics in Eighteenth-Century England: Secrecy, Intimacy, and the Interior Self in the Public Sphere." In *Media and Political Culture in the Eighteenth Century*, ed. Marie-Christine Skuncke. Stockholm: Vitterhetsakademien, 2005.

The Pleasures of the Imagination: English Culture in the Eighteenth Century. New York: Farrar Straus Giroux, 1997.

Brewer, John, and Roy Porter, eds. *Consumption and the World of Goods.* London: Routledge, 1993.

Brontë, Charlotte. *Villette.* 3 vols. London, 1853.

Brook, Timothy. *The Confusions of Pleasure: Commerce and Culture in Ming China.* Berkeley: University of California Press, 1998.

Brook, Timothy, Jérôme Bourgon, and Gregory Blue. *Death by a Thousand Cuts.* Cambridge, MA: Harvard University Press, 2008.

Brown, Bill. *Material Cultures: Why Some Things Matter.* University of Chicago Press, 1998.

"Thing Theory." *Critical Inquiry* 28, no. 1 (2001): 1–22.

Things. University of Chicago Press, 2001.

Brown, Tony C. "Joseph Addison and the Pleasures of *Sharawadgi.*" *ELH* 74 (2007): 171–93.

Buchli, Victor, ed. *Material Culture Reader.* Oxford: Berg Press, 2002.

Burke, Edmund. *A Philosophical Enquiry into the Origin of Our Ideas of the Sublime and Beautiful.* Ed. James T. Boulton. University of Notre Dame Press, 1968.

Bush, Susan, and Hsio-yen Shih. *Early Chinese Texts on Painting.* Cambridge, MA: Harvard University Press, 1985.

Cahill, James. *The Distant Mountains: Chinese Painting of the Late Ming Dynasty, 1570–1644.* New York: Weatherhill, 1982.

"Passages of Felt Life: A Genre Shift in Ming–Qing Figure Painting (Or: Paintings Done for Women in Ming–Qing China)." Unpublished paper.

Campbell, Colin. *The Romantic Ethic and the Spirit of Modern Consumerism.* Oxford: Basil Blackwell, 1987.

Capp, Bernard. *When Gossips Meet: Women, Family, and Neighborhood in Early Modern England.* Oxford University Press, 2003.

Carswell, John. *Blue & White: Chinese Porcelain Around the World.* London: British Museum Press, 2007.

Castle, Terry, ed. *The Literature of Lesbianism.* New York: Columbia University Press, 2003.

Cavendish, Margaret. *The Convent of Pleasure.* In *Plays, Never Before Printed.* London, 1668.

Chakrabarty, Dipesh. *Provincializing Europe: Postcolonial Thought and Historical Difference.* Princeton University Press, 2000.

Chambers, William. *Correspondence.* British Library, London.

Designs of Chinese Buildings, Furniture, Dresses, Machines and Utensils. London, 1757.

A Dissertation on Oriental Gardening. London, 1772.

A Dissertation on Oriental Gardening. Westmead, England: Gregg International Publishers, 1972.

"An Explanatory Discourse by Tan Chet-Qua." In *Dissertation on Oriental Gardening.* 2nd edn. London, 1773.
"Letter to a Gentleman." In *Sir William Chambers: Knight of the Polar Star*, ed. John Harris. London: A. Zwemmer, 1970.
Plans, Elevations, Sections, and Perspective Views of the Gardens and Buildings at Kew, in Surrey. London, 1763.
Treatise on the Decorative Part of Civil Architecture. 3rd edn. London, 1791.
Chang, Y. Z. "A Note on Sharawadgi." *Modern Language Notes* 45 (April 1930): 221–4.
Chase, Isabel. *Horace Walpole: Gardenist.* Princeton University Press, 1943.
"William Mason and Sir William Chambers' *Dissertation on Oriental Gardening.*" *Journal of English and Germanic Philology* 35 (1936): 517–29.
Chen, Chaonan, and Yiyou Feng. *Old Advertisements and Popular Culture: Posters, Calendars and Cigarettes, 1900–1950.* San Francisco: Long River Press, 2004.
Ch'ên, Shou-yi. "The Chinese Garden in Eighteenth-Century England." *T'ien Hsia Monthly* 2 (1936): 321–39.
"Thomas Percy and His Chinese Studies." *Chinese Social and Political Science Review* 20 (1936–7): 203–16.
A Chinese Tale. London, 1740.
Chippendale, Thomas. *The Gentleman and Cabinet-Maker's Director.* London, 1754.
Clark, Kenneth. *The Gothic Revival: An Essay in the History of Taste.* New York: Charles Scribner's Sons, 1929.
Clunas, Craig. *Art in China.* Oxford University Press, 1997.
"The Art of Social Climbing in Sixteenth-Century China." *The Burlington Magazine* 133, no. 1059 (1991): 368–75.
Chinese Export Art and Design. London: Victoria and Albert Museum, 1987.
Fruitful Sites: Garden Culture in Ming Dynasty China. Durham, NC: Duke University Press, 1996.
"Human Figures in the Decoration of Ming Lacquer." *Oriental Art* 32 (1986): 177–88.
Superfluous Things: Material Culture and Social Status in Early Modern China. Urbana, IL: University of Illinois Press, 1991.
"The West Chamber: A Literary Theme in Chinese Porcelain Decoration." *Transactions of the Oriental Ceramic Society* 46 (1981–2): 69–86.
Cocks, Anna Somers. "The Nonfunctional Use of Ceramics in the English Country House During the Eighteenth Century." In *The Fashioning and Functioning of the British Country House*, ed. Gervase Jackson-Stops. Washington, DC: National Gallery of Art, 1989.
Cohen, Paul A. *Discovering History in China: American Historical Writing on the Recent Chinese Past.* New York: Columbia University Press, 1984.
Colley, Linda. *Britons: Forging the Nation, 1707–1837.* New Haven, CT: Yale University Press, 1992.

Conner, Patrick. "China and the Landscape Garden: Reports, Engravings and Misconceptions." *Art History* 2 (1979): 430–40.

Csikszentmihalyi, Mihalyi, and Eugene Rochberg-Halton. *The Meaning of Things: Domestic Symbols and the Self.* Cambridge University Press, 1981.

Curran, Stuart. *Poetic Form and British Romanticism.* Oxford University Press, 1986.

Curtis, Julia. "Markets, Motifs, and Seventeenth-Century Porcelain from Jingdezhen." In *The Porcelains of Jingdezhen*, ed. Rosemary Scott. Colloquies on Art and Archaeology in Asia 16. University of London, 1993.

Curtis, Julia, and Stephen Little. *Chinese Porcelains of the Seventeenth Century: Landscapes, Scholars' Motifs and Narratives.* New York: China Institute Gallery, 1995.

Davis, Bertram. *Thomas Percy: A Scholar-Cleric in the Age of Johnson.* Philadelphia: University of Pennsylvania Press, 1989.

Dawson, Raymond. *The Chinese Chameleon: An Analysis of European Conceptions of Chinese Civilisation.* London: Oxford University Press, 1967.

Decker, Paul. *Chinese Architecture.* London, 1759.

Defoe, Daniel. *The Farther Adventures of Robinson Crusoe.* London: William Clowes and Sons, 1974.

The Fortunate Mistress. London, 1724.

Robinson Crusoe. 3rd edn. London, 1719.

Deutsch, Eliot. "Comparative Philosophy as Creative Philosophy." *APA Newsletter on Asian and Asian-American Philosophers and Philosophy* 2, no. 1 (2002): 23–6.

Dickie, George. *The Century of Taste: The Philosophical Odyssey of Taste in the Eighteenth Century.* New York: Oxford University Press, 1996.

Donoghue, Emma. *Passions Between Women: British Lesbian Culture, 1668–1801.* New York: Harper Collins, 1993.

Poems Between Women. New York: Columbia University Press, 1997.

Douglas, Mary, and Baron Isherwood. *The World of Goods: Towards an Anthropology of Consumption.* London: Routledge, 2003.

Dugaw, Dianne, and Amanda Powell. "Sapphic Self-Fashioning in the Baroque Era: Women's Petrarchan Parody in English and Spanish." *Studies in Eighteenth-Century Culture* 35 (2006): 127–60.

Du Halde, J. B. *The General History of China.* 4 vols. London, 1736.

D'Urfey, Thomas. *Pendragon, or, The Carpet Knight his Kalendar.* London, 1698.

Eames, James Bromley. *The English in China.* London: Pitman and Sons, 1909.

Eatwell, Ann. "Private Pleasure, Public Beneficence: Lady Charlotte Schreiber and Ceramic Collecting." In *Women in the Victorian Art World*, ed. Clarissa Campbell Orr. Manchester University Press, 1995.

Emmerson, Robin. *British Teapots and Tea Drinking.* London: HMSO Books, 1992.

Export Art of China and Japan: The China Trade Sale. London: Christie's, 1997.

Fielding, Henry. *Love in Several Masques.* Dublin, 1728.

The Mock Doctor; or, the Dumb Lady Cur'd. Edinburgh, 1753.

Finlay, Robert. "The Pilgrim Art: The Culture of Porcelain in World History." *Journal of World History* 9 (1998): 141–87.

Fort, Bernadette, and Angela Rosenthal, eds. *The Other Hogarth: Aesthetics of Difference.* Princeton University Press, 2001.

Frank, Andre Gunder. *ReOrient: Global Economy in the Asian Age.* Berkeley: University of California Press, 1998.

Gallagher, Catherine. Review of *Desire and Domestic Fiction: A Political History of the Novel*, by Nancy Armstrong. *Victorian Studies* 32 (1989): 412.

Gay, John. "To a Lady on Her Passion for Old China." London, 1725.

Ge, Liangyan. "On the Eighteenth-Century English Misreading of the Chinese Garden." *Comparative Civilizations Review* 27 (1992): 106–26.

Gell, Alfred. "Newcomers to the World of Goods: Consumption among the Muria Gonds." In *The Social Life of Things: Commodities in Cultural Perspective*, ed. Arjun Appadurai. Cambridge University Press, 1986.

Goldsmith, Oliver. *Citizen of the World and The Bee.* London: J. M. Dent, 1934.

Goodman, Dena, and Kathryn Norberg, eds. *Furnishing the Eighteenth Century: What Furniture Can Tell Us about the European and American Past.* New York: Routledge, 2007.

Greenblatt, Stephen. *Marvelous Possessions: The Wonder of the New World.* University of Chicago Press, 1991.

Groom, Nick. *The Making of Percy's* Reliques. Oxford University Press, 1999.

Guy, Basil. *The French Image of China Before and After Voltaire.* Studies on Voltaire and the Eighteenth Century 21. Geneva: Institut et musée Voltaire, 1963.

Haggerty, George. "'Romantic Friendship' and Patriarchal Narrative in Sarah Scott's *Millennium Hall.*" *Genders* 13 (1992): 108–22.

Halfpenny, William. *Rural Architecture in the Chinese Taste.* London, 1755.

Halfpenny, William, and John Halfpenny. *Chinese and Gothic Architecture Properly Ornamented.* London, 1752.

Harris, Eileen. "*Designs of Chinese Buildings* and the *Dissertation on Oriental Gardening.*" In *Sir William Chambers: Knight of the Polar Star*, ed. John Harris. London: A. Zwemmer, 1970.

Harris, John, ed. *Sir William Chambers: Knight of the Polar Star.* London: A. Zwemmer, 1970.

Hay, John. *Kernals of Energy, Bones of Earth: The Rock in Chinese Art.* New York: China Institute in America, 1986.

"The Rock and Chinese Art." *Orientations* 16, no. 12 (1985): 16–32.

Hayot, Eric. *The Hypothetical Mandarin: Sympathy, China, and the Fate of the Modern Human.* Oxford University Press, 2008.

Hill, Bridget. "A Refuge from Men: The Idea of a Protestant Nunnery." *Past and Present* 117 (1987): 107–30.

Hobby, Elaine. *Virtue of Necessity: English Women's Writing, 1649–88.* Ann Arbor, MI: University of Michigan Press, 1989.

Hogarth, William. *The Analysis of Beauty.* Ed. Joseph Burke. Oxford: Clarendon Press, 1955.

The Analysis of Beauty. Ed. Ronald Paulson. New Haven, CT: Yale University Press, 1997.

Anecdotes. Ed. J. B. Nichols. London, 1833.

Honour, Hugh. *Chinoiserie: The Vision of Cathay.* New York: Dutton, 1962.

Houghton, Walter. "The English Virtuoso in the Seventeenth Century: Part II." *Journal of the History of Ideas* 3 (1942): 190–219.

Hunt, John Dixon. *Gardens and the Picturesque: Studies in the History of Landscape Architecture.* London: MIT Press, 1992.

Hunter, J. Paul. *Before Novels: The Cultural Contexts of Eighteenth-Century English Fiction.* New York: Norton, 1990.

Hurd, Richard. "On Chinese Drama." In *Miscellaneous Pieces Relating to the Chinese,* ed. Thomas Percy. London, 1762.

Impey, Oliver R. *Chinoiserie: The Impact of Oriental Styles on Western Art and Decoration.* New York: Charles Scribner's Sons, 1977.

Jackson, Wallace. "Hogarth's *Analysis*: The Fate of a Late Rococo Document." *SEL* 6 (1966): 543–50.

Jacobson, Dawn. *Chinoiserie.* London: Phaidon Press, 1993.

Jarry, Madeleine. *Chinoiserie: Chinese Influence on European Decorative Art, 17th and 18th Centuries.* Trans. Gail Mangold-Vine. New York: Vendome Press, 1981.

Johnson, Samuel. *Lives of the English Poets.* Ed. L. Archer-Hind. 2 vols. London, 1925.

Jones, Robert. *Gender and the Formation of Taste in Eighteenth-Century Britain: The Analysis of Beauty.* Cambridge University Press, 1998.

Jonson, Ben. *Epicene; or, The Silent Woman.* In *The Alchemist and Other Plays,* ed. Gordon Campbell. Oxford University Press, 1995.

Jourdain, Margaret, and Soame Jenyns. *Chinese Export Art in the Eighteenth Century.* New York: Scribner, 1967.

Jullien, François. *The Impossible Nude: Chinese Art and Western Aesthetics.* Trans. Maev de la Guardia. University of Chicago Press, 2007.

"Kangxi Porcelain in the Grand Chinese Porcelain Collecting Tradition." *The Catalogue of Antiques and Fine Art* (autumn 2001): 37–43.

Kant, Immanuel. *Critique of Judgment.* Trans. Werner S. Pluhar. Indianapolis: Hackett, 1987.

Kerr, Rose. "The Chinese Porcelain at Spring Grove Dairy." *Apollo* 129 (1989): 30–4.

Keswick, Maggie. *The Chinese Garden.* New York: St. Martin's Press, 1986.

Ketton-Cremer, R. W. *Horace Walpole: A Biography.* Ithaca, NY: Cornell University Press, 1964.

Khoo, Joo Ee. *Kendi: Pouring Vessels in the University of Malaya Collection.* Ed. Dawn F. Rooney. Singapore: Oxford University Press, 1991.

Kilburn, Richard S. *Transitional Wares and Their Forerunners: An Exhibition Presented by the Oriental Ceramic Society of Hong Kong.* Hong Kong: Oriental Ceramic Society of Hong Kong, 1981.

Killigrew, Anne. "On a Picture Painted by Herself, Representing Two Nymphs of Diana's, One in a Posture to Hunt, the Other Bathing." In *The Literature of Lesbianism,* ed. Terry Castle. New York: Columbia University Press, 2003.

"On the Soft and Gentle Motions of Eudora." In *The Literature of Lesbianism,* ed. Terry Castle. New York: Columbia University Press, 2003.

King, Kathryn. *Jane Barker, Exile: A Literary Career 1675–1725.* Oxford: Clarendon Press, 2000.

"The Unaccountable Wife and Other Tales of Female Desire in Jane Barker's *A Patch-Work Screen for the Ladies.*" *The Eighteenth Century: Theory and Interpretation* 35 (1994): 155–72.

Kingery, W. David. *Learning from Things: Method and Theory of Material Culture Studies.* Washington, DC: Smithsonian Institution Press, 1996.

Ko, Dorothy. *Cinderella's Sisters: A Revisionist History of Footbinding.* Berkeley: University of California Press, 2005.

Teachers of the Inner Chambers: Women and Culture in Seventeenth-Century China. Stanford University Press, 1994.

Kowaleski-Wallace, Elizabeth. *Consuming Subjects: Women, Shopping, and Business in the Eighteenth Century.* New York: Columbia University Press, 1997.

Kulka, Tomas. *Kitsch and Art.* University Park: Pennsylvania State University Press, 1996.

Laing, Ellen Johnston. "Chinese Palace-Style Poetry and the Depiction of *A Palace Beauty.*" *The Art Bulletin* 72 (1990): 284–95.

Lamb, Charles. "Old China." In *Complete Works of Charles Lamb.* Philadelphia: W. T. Amies, 1879.

Landa, Louis. "Pope's Belinda, the General Emporie of the World, and the Wondrous Worm." *South Atlantic Quarterly* 70 (1971): 215–35.

Langbauer, Laurie. *Women and Romance: The Consolations of Gender in the English Novel.* Ithaca, NY: Cornell University Press, 1990.

Lawton, Thomas. *Chinese Figure Painting.* Washington, DC: Smithsonian Institution, 1973.

Le Comte, Louis. *Memoirs and Observations Made in a Late Journey through the Empire of China.* London, 1697.

Lenman, Bruce P. "The English and Dutch East India Companies and the Birth of Consumerism in the Augustan World." *Eighteenth-Century Life* 14, no. 1 (1990): 47–65.

Lenygon, Francis. *Decoration in England from 1660 to 1770.* London: B. T. Batsford, 1914.

Levine, George Lewis. *Aesthetics and Ideology.* New Brunswick, NJ: Rutgers University Press, 1994.

Lévi-Strauss, Claude. *Totemism.* Trans. R. Needham. Boston: Beacon Press, 1963.

Little, Stephen. *Chinese Ceramics of the Transitional Period, 1620–1683.* New York: China House Gallery, China Institute of America, 1983.

Liu, Yu. *Seeds of a Different Eden: Chinese Gardening Ideas and a New English Aesthetic Ideal.* Columbia, SC: University of South Carolina Press, 2008.

Lovejoy, Arthur O. *Essays in the History of Ideas.* Baltimore: Johns Hopkins University Press, 1948.

Lubar, Steven, and W. David Kingery, eds. *History from Things: Essays on Material Culture.* Washington, DC: Smithsonian Institution Press, 1993.

Lynch, Jack. *Deception and Detection in Eighteenth-Century Britain.* London: Ashgate, 2008.

Ma, Qian. *Feminist Utopian Discourse in Eighteenth-Century Chinese and English Fiction: A Cross-Cultural Comparison.* London: Ashgate, 2004.

MacCarthy, Bridget. *Women Writers: Their Contribution to the English Novel 1621–1744* (Cork, 1944).

Macey, J. David. "Eden Revisited: Re-visions of the Garden in Astell's *Serious Proposal,* Scott's *Millennium Hall,* and Graffigny's *Lettres d'une péruvienne.*" *Eighteenth-Century Fiction* 9 (1997): 161–82.

MacLean, Gerald M. *Looking East: English Writing and the Ottoman Empire before 1800.* New York: Palgrave Macmillan, 2007.

Maher, Vanessa. "Breast Feeding in Cross-Cultural Perspective." In *The Anthropology of Breast Feeding,* ed. Vanessa Maher. Oxford: Berg Press, 1992.

Mann, Susan. *Precious Records: Women in China's Long Eighteenth Century.* Stanford University Press, 1997.

Markley, Robert. *The Far East and the English Imagination, 1600–1730.* Cambridge University Press, 2006.

Mason, William. *The English Garden.* York, 1783.

Satirical Poems. Ed. Paget Toynbee. Oxford: Clarendon Press, 1926.

May, Leila Silvana. "The Strong-Arming of Desire: A Reconsideration of Nancy Armstrong's 'Desire and Domestic Fiction.'" *ELH* 68 (2001): 267–85.

McCracken, Grant. *Culture and Consumption: New Approaches to the Symbolic Character of Consumer Goods and Activities.* Bloomington: Indiana University Press, 1988.

McDowell, Paula. *The Women of Grub Street: Press, Politics, and Gender in the London Literary Marketplace, 1678–1730.* New York: Clarendon Press, 1997.

McKendrick, Neil, John Brewer, and J. H. Plumb. *The Birth of a Consumer Society: The Commercialization of Eighteenth-Century England.* Bloomington: Indiana University Press, 1982.

Miller, Daniel. *Material Cultures: Why Some Things Matter.* London: UCL Press, 1997.

Milner-Barry, Alda. "A Note on the Early Literary Relations of Oliver Goldsmith and Thomas Percy." *Review of English Studies* 2, no. 5 (1926): 51–66.

Min, Eun Kyung. "Antiquarian Aesthetics and the Serendipitous Reader: Thomas Percy's *Chinese Miscellanies and The Reliques of Ancient English Poetry.*" Paper presented at the annual meeting of the American Society for Eighteenth-Century Studies, Montreal, QC, March 31, 2006.

Montagu, Mary Wortley. *Selected Letters.* Ed. Isobel Grundy. New York: Penguin, 1997.

Morse, Hosea Ballou. *The Chronicles of the East India Company Trading to China, 1635–1834.* 5 vols. Taipei: Ch'eng-wen Publishing Company, 1975.

Mowl, Timothy. *Horace Walpole: The Great Outsider.* London: John Murray, 1996.

Murphy, Arthur. "Letter to Voltaire." In *The Orphan of China.* London, 1797.

Naquin, Susan, and Evelyn Sakakida Rawski. *Chinese Society in the Eighteenth Century.* New Haven, CT: Yale University Press, 1987.

Nead, Lynda. *The Female Nude: Art, Obscenity and Sexuality.* London: Routledge, 1992.

Nieuhof, Johannes. *An Embassy from the East-India Company of the United Provinces to the Grand Tartar Cham, Emperor of China.* Trans. John Ogilby. London, 1673.

Nussbaum, Felicity. *The Brink of All We Hate: English Satires on Women, 1660–1750.* Lexington, KY: University Press of Kentucky, 1984.

Nussbaum, Felicity, ed. *The Global Eighteenth Century.* Baltimore: Johns Hopkins University Press, 2003.

O'Connell, Sheila, and British Museum. *The Popular Print in England: 1550–1850.* London: British Museum Press, 1999.

Old Bailey Proceedings Online. http://oldbaileyonline.org.

Percy, Thomas. *Hau Kiou Choaan; or, The Pleasing History.* 4 vols. London, 1761.

Miscellaneous Pieces Relating to the Chinese. 2 vols. London, 1762.

Reliques of Ancient English Poetry. 3 vols. London, 1765.

Percy, Thomas, and William Shenstone. *Percy–Shenstone correspondence.* British Library, London.

Perry, Ruth. "Colonizing the Breast: Sexuality and Maternity in Eighteenth-Century England." *Eighteenth-Century Life* 16 (1992): 185–213.

Pevsner, Nikolaus. "The Other Chambers." *Architectural Review* 101 (1947): 195–8.

Pollock, Anthony. *Gender and the Fictions of the Public Sphere, 1690–1755.* New York: Routledge, 2009.

Pomeranz, Kenneth. *The Great Divergence: Europe, China, and the Making of the Modern World Economy.* Princeton University Press, 2000.

Pope, Alexander. *Epistle to Burlington.* London, 1731.

The Rape of the Lock. London, 1714.

Porter, David. "China is Not a Foreign Country: The Promises and Perils of Cross-Cultural Comparison." *Michigan Quarterly Review* 47, no. 2 (2008): 169–81.

"Chinoiserie and the Aesthetics of Illegitimacy." *Studies in Eighteenth-Century Culture* 28 (1999): 33–7.

Ideographia: The Chinese Cipher in Early Modern Europe. Stanford University Press, 2001.

"Writing China: Legitimacy and Representation, 1606–1773." *Comparative Literature Studies* 33 (1996): 98–122.

Powell, L. F. "Hau Kiou Choaan." *Review of English Studies* 2, no. 8 (1926): 446–55.
"The Prize Aenigma." In *The Woman's Almanack.* London, 1741.
Prown, Jules David. "The Truth of Material Culture: History or Fiction?" In *History from Things: Essays on Material Culture*, ed. Steven Lubar and W. David Kingery. Washington, DC: Smithsonian Institution Press, 1993.
Radway, Janice A. *Reading the Romance: Women, Patriarchy, and Popular Literature.* Chapel Hill, NC: University of North Carolina Press, 1984.
Reaves, R. B., Jr. "Sir William Chambers: A Study of Georgian Taste." Ph.D. Dissertation, University of Wisconsin, 1971.
Reeve, Clara. *The Progress of Romance.* 2 vols. London, 1785.
Reynolds, Joshua. *Discourses.* Ed. Pat Rogers. New York: Penguin, 1992.
Richards, Sarah. *Eighteenth-Century Ceramics: Products for a Civilised Society.* Manchester University Press, 1999.
Richetti, John J. *Popular Fiction before Richardson: Narrative Patterns, 1700–1739.* Oxford: Clarendon Press, 1969.
Rogers, Pat. Review of *Horace Walpole: The Great Outsider*, by Timothy Mowl. The Times Literary Supplement, October 4, 1996.
Rooney, Dawn F. "Kendi in the Cultural Context of Southeast Asia: A Commentary." *Dawn F. Rooney Cultural Archive.* http://rooneyarchive.net/articles/kendi/kendi_album/kendi.htm.
Rosenblum, Richard. *Art of the Natural World: Resonances of Wild Nature in Chinese Sculptural Art.* Ed. Valerie Doran. Boston: MFA, 2001.
Rostvig, Maren-Sofie. *The Happy Man: Studies in the Metamorphoses of a Classical Ideal, 1700–1760.* Oslo University Press, 1958.
Saumarez Smith, Charles. *Eighteenth-Century Decoration: Design and the Domestic Interior in England.* London: Weidenfeld and Nicolson, 1993.
Saussy, Haun. "Impressions de Chine; or, How to Translate from a Non-Existent Original." In *Sinographies: Writing China*, ed. Eric Hayot, Haun Saussy, and Steven Yao. Minneapolis: University of Minnesota Press, 2008.
Scarry, Elaine. *On Beauty and Being Just.* Princeton University Press, 1999.
Schiebinger, Londa. *Nature's Body: Gender in the Making of Modern Science.* New Brunswick, NJ: Rutgers University Press, 2004.
Schnorrenberg, Barbara. "A Paradise Like Eve's: Three Eighteenth-Century English Female Utopias." *Women's Studies* 9 (1982): 263–73.
Scott, Sarah. *A Description of Millennium Hall.* Ed. Gary Kelly. Peterborough, ON: Broadview Press, 2001.
Settle, Elkanah. *The Conquest of China by the Tartars.* London, 1675.
The Lady's Triumph. London, 1718.
Shaftesbury, Earl of (Anthony Ashley Cooper). *Characteristics of Men, Manners, Opinions, Times, Etc.* Ed. John Robertson. 2 vols. London, 1900.
Shebbeare, John. *Letters on the English Nation.* London, 1755.
Shi Nü Hua Zhi Mei [Glimpses into the Hidden Quarters: Paintings of Women from the Middle Kingdom]. Taipei: National Palace Museum, 1988.

Shou-Yi, Ch'en. "Thomas Percy and his Chinese Studies." *Chinese Social and Political Science Review* 20 (1936–7): 203–16.

Simons, Patricia. "Lesbian (In)Visibility in Italian Renaissance Culture: Diana and Other Cases of *donna con donna*." In *Gay and Lesbian Studies in Art History*, ed. Whitney Davis. New York: Harrington Park Press, 1994.

Smart, Christopher. *The Poems of the Late Christopher Smart.* Reading, 1791.

Snodin, Michael, and Maurice Howard. *Ornament: A Social History since 1450.* New Haven, CT: Yale University Press, 1996.

Snodin, Michael, and John Styles. *Design & the Decorative Arts: Britain, 1500–1900.* London: Victoria and Albert Museum, 2001.

Song, Tze-lan. *The Emerging Lesbian: Female Same-Sex Desire in Modern China.* University of Chicago Press, 2003.

Southerne, Thomas. *The Maid's Last Prayer.* London, 1693.

Spacks, Patricia Meyer. *Gossip.* New York: Knopf, 1985.

Spectator, The. London, 1711–14.

St. André, James. "Retranslation as Argument: Canon Formation, Professionalization, and International Rivalry in 19th-Century Sinological Translation." *Cadernos de Tradução* 11, no. 1 (2003): 59–93.

Stewart, Susan. *On Longing: Narratives of the Miniature, the Gigantic, the Souvenir, the Collection.* Durham, NC: Duke University Press, 1993.

Stolnitz, Jerome. "On the Origin of Aesthetic Disinterestedness." *Journal of Aesthetics and Art Criticism* 20 (1961): 131–43.

Stone, Lawrence. "Inigo Jones and the New Exchange." *Archaeological Journal* 114 (1957): 106–21.

Swift, Jonathan. *Gulliver's Travels.* New York: Penguin, 1985.

"Tea: A Poem; or, Ladies into China-Cups: A Metamorphosis." London, 1729.

Temple, William. *Upon the Gardens of Epicurus.* 1692.

Tharp, Lars. *Hogarth's China: Hogarth's Paintings and Eighteenth-Century Ceramics.* London: Merrell Hoberton, 1997.

Thomas, P. J. *Mercantilism and the East India Trade.* London: Frank Cass & Co., 1963.

Thorp, Robert Lee, and Richard Ellis Vinograd. *Chinese Art and Culture.* New York: Harry N. Abrams, 2001.

Todd, Dennis. *Imagining Monsters: Miscreations of the Self in Eighteenth-Century England.* University of Chicago Press, 1995.

Todd, Janet M. *The Sign of Angellica: Women, Writing, and Fiction, 1660–1800.* New York: Columbia University Press, 1989.

Toppin, Aubrey J. "The China Trade and Some London Chinamen." *Transactions of the English Ceramic Circle* 3 (1934): 44–6.

Townsend, Dabney, ed. *Eighteenth-Century British Aesthetics.* Amityville: Baywood, 1999.

Traub, Valerie. "The Present Future of Lesbian Historiography." In *A Companion to Lesbian, Gay, Bisexual, Transgender, and Queer Studies*, ed. George Haggerty and Molly McGarry. Oxford: Blackwell, 2007.

The Renaissance of Lesbianism in Early Modern England. Cambridge University Press, 2002.

Trumpener, Katie. *Bardic Nationalism: The Romantic Novel and the British Empire.* Princeton University Press, 1997.

Tunnard, Christopher. *Gardens in the Modern Landscape.* London: Architectural Press, 1938.

Turner, James. "News from the New Exchange: Commodity, Erotic Fantasy, and the Female Entrepreneur." In *The Consumption of Culture, 1600–1800: Image, Object, Text*, ed. Ann Bermingham and John Brewer. New York: Routledge, 1995.

Veblen, Thorstein, and C. Wright Mills. *The Theory of the Leisure Class: An Economic Study of Institutions.* New York: New American Library, 1953.

Vickery, Amanda. "Women and the World of Goods: A Lancashire Consumer and her Possessions, 1751–81." In *Consumption and the World of Goods*, ed. John Brewer and Roy Porter. London: Routledge, 1993.

Wahl, Elizabeth. *Invisible Relations: Representations of Female Intimacy in the Age of Enlightenment.* Stanford University Press, 1999.

Walpole, Horace. *Anecdotes of Painting in England.* 4 vols. London, 1765.

Anecdotes of Painting in England. Ed. Frederick W. Hilles and Philip B. Daghlian. 5 vols. New Haven, CT: Yale University Press, 1937.

The Works of Horatio Walpole, Earl of Orford. 7 vols. London, 1798.

The Yale Edition of Horace Walpole's Correspondence. Ed. W. S. Lewis. 48 vols. New Haven, CT: Yale University Press, 1937–83.

Walter, Richard, and Benjamin Robins. *A Voyage Round the World by George Anson.* Ed. Glyndwr Williams. London: Oxford University Press, 1974.

Walvin, James. *Fruits of Empire: Exotic Produce and British Taste, 1660–1800.* New York University Press, 1997.

Warner, William Beatty. *Licensing Entertainment: The Elevation of Novel Reading in Britain, 1684–1750.* Berkeley: University of California Press, 1998.

Wayne, Don. "The 'Exchange of Letters': Early Modern Contradictions and Postmodern Conundrums." In *The Consumption of Culture, 1600–1800: Image, Object, Text*, ed. Ann Bermingham and John Brewer. New York: Routledge, 1995.

Whately, Thomas. *Observations on Modern Gardening.* London, 1770.

Wheeler, Roxann. *The Complexion of Race: Categories of Difference in Eighteenth-Century British Culture.* Philadelphia: University of Pennsylvania Press, 2000.

Williams, Anna. *Miscellanies in Prose and Verse.* London, 1766.

Wilson, Joan. "A Phenomenon of Taste: The China Ware of Queen Mary II." *Apollo* 96 (1972): 116–23.

Wong, R. Bin. *China Transformed: Historical Change and the Limits of European Experience.* Ithaca, NY: Cornell University Press, 1997.

World, The. London, 1753–6.

Wycherley, William. *The Country Wife.* In *The Signet Classic Book of Restoration Drama*, ed. Ronald Berman. New York: New American Library, 1980.

Yaeger, Patricia. "Beyond the Fragments." *Novel: A Forum on Fiction* 23 (1990): 203–8.

Yalom, Marilyn. *A History of the Breast.* New York: Ballantine, 1997.

Young, Hilary. *English Porcelain, 1745–95: Its Makers, Design, Marketing and Consumption.* London: Victoria and Albert Publications, 1999.

Zeitlin, Judith. *Historian of the Strange: Pu Songling and the Chinese Classical Tale.* Stanford University Press, 1993.

Index

17019733R00135

Printed in Great Britain
by Amazon